And They Sung a New Song

And They Sung a New Song

Revelation 5:9 KJV

CLYDE BACCHUS
CHRISTABEL BACCHUS

RESOURCE *Publications* • Eugene, Oregon

AND THEY SUNG A NEW SONG
Revelation 5:9

Copyright © 2022 Clyde Bacchus and Christabel Bacchus. All rights reserved. Except for brief quotations in critical publications or reviews, no part of this book may be reproduced in any manner without prior written permission from the publisher. Write: Permissions, Wipf and Stock Publishers, 199 W. 8th Ave., Suite 3, Eugene, OR 97401.

Resource Publications
An Imprint of Wipf and Stock Publishers
199 W. 8th Ave., Suite 3
Eugene, OR 97401

www.wipfandstock.com

PAPERBACK ISBN: 978-1-6667-4788-1
HARDCOVER ISBN: 978-1-6667-4789-8
EBOOK ISBN: 978-1-6667-4790-4

12/08/22

Scripture quotations from the Authorized (King James) Version. Rights in the Authorized Version in the United Kingdom are vested in the Crown. Reproduced by permission of the Crown's patentee, Cambridge University Press

For our children, grandchildren and future generations

Contents

Introduction		ix
1	A Divided Church	1
2	To the Jew First	5
3	The Canaries	25
4	The New World Order	34
5	How European Countries applied the Papal Bulls: Portugal	48
6	How European Countries applied the Papal Bulls: Spain	55
7	Anglo World Culture and Christianity	71
8	Barbados, the West Indies and Anglo-America	92
9	The Role of the Church in the Anglo New-World	108
10	New-World Culture in Great Britain	131
11	From These Very Shores	146
12	Judgment Must Begin At The House Of God	158
13	What Shall We Do?	172
Appendix: Romanus Pontifex		183
Bibliography		191

Introduction

Rev 5:9 "And they *sung* a new song," is recorded in the King James Version of the Bible. In the New King James version and other versions of the Bible the words are: "And they *sang* a new song." In Ps 96:1 "*O sing unto the LORD a new song! Sing unto the LORD, all the earth.*" Again, in Ps144:9 "*I will sing a new song unto thee, O God: upon a psaltery and an instrument of ten strings will I sing praises unto thee.*"The same form of speech is found in Isa 42:10, "*Sing unto the LORD a new song, and his praise from the end of the earth, ye that go down to the sea, and all that is therein; the isles, and the inhabitants thereof.*" But what is the "new song"? This "new song" foretells the coming of our Saviour, Jesus Christ. John 3:16-17, "*For God so loved the world, that he gave his only begotten Son, that whosoever believeth in him should not perish, but have everlasting life.*"

John 3:17 *For God sent not his Son into the world to condemn the world; but that the world through him might be saved.*"

AT THE CROSS WHEN Jesus died, the veil that separated mankind into two groups, Jews and Gentiles was torn from the top down. Jews are the children, the offspring, the descendants of the children of Abraham, Isaac, and Jacob. By the death and resurrection of Jesus, God gave all of mankind equal access to Himself through His only begotten Son Jesus Christ.

Titus 2:5-6 "*For there is one God, and one mediator between God and men, the man Christ Jesus; Who gave himself a ransom for all, to be testified in due time.*"

What is the source of this division of mankind into two groups; Jews and Gentiles, when all of mankind came out of the loins of one man and one woman: Adam and Eve, the mother of all living? This happened after the Flood. when Noah's children, Shem, and Ham, and Japheth, multiplied. At that time, they all spoke the same language and travelled and lived together. Eventually they decided to settle in one place of their choice and to build a city, with a tower that would reach up to heaven, make a name for themselves and keep themselves from scattering all over the earth.

> Gen 11: 4–9 *And they said, Go to, let us build us a city and a tower, whose top may reach unto heaven; and let us make us a name, lest we be scattered abroad upon the face of the whole earth. And the LORD came down to see the city and the tower, which the children of men builded. And the LORD said, Behold, the people is one, and they have all one language; and this they begin to do: and now nothing will be restrained from them, which they have imagined to do. Go to, let us go down, and there confound their language, that they may not understand one another's speech. So the LORD scattered them abroad from thence upon the face of all the earth: and they left off to build the city. Therefore is the name of it called Babel; because the LORD did there confound the language of all the earth: and from thence did the LORD scatter them abroad upon the face of all the earth.*

The families of Noah's children: Shem, Ham and Japheth dispersed across the earth and settled in the lands as described below:

> Gen 10:21 "*Unto Shem also, the father of all the children of Eber, the brother of Japheth the elder, even to him were children born.*"Gen 10:30 "*And their dwelling was from Mesha, as thou goest unto Sephar a mount of the east.*" Gen 10:31 "*These are the sons of Shem, after their families, after their tongues, in their lands, after their nations.*"

However, there is a thought-provoking verse in the bible that describes the consequence of one group of people from Shem's line, whose history independently confirms the scattering of people "abroad upon the face of the earth." The verse Gen 10:30 "*And their dwelling was from Mesha, as thou goest unto Sephar a mount of the east.*"

> "*There is an interesting footnote to the story of Babel. Among the people scattered at Babel were a group who climbed over the mountains to the east and eventually settled when they reached the sea. They became the great nation of China. Chinese culture goes right back to that day. They left the area of Babel before the Cuneiform alphabet replaced the picture language of ancient Egypt. All languages were pictorial right up to the time of Babel. The language they took to China they put down in picture form. The amazing thing is that it is possible to reconstruct the story of*

INTRODUCTION

> *Genesis 1 to 11 by looking at the symbols which the Chinese use to describe different words.*
>
> *The Chinese word for 'create', for example, is made up of the pictures for mud, life and someone walking. Their word for the 'devil' is a secret person in the garden. Their word for 'tempter' is made up of the word for 'devil' plus two trees and the picture for cover. Their word for "boat" is made up of container, mouth and eight, so a boat in the Chinese language is a vessel for eight people, as was the Noah's ark."*[1]

The children who were the descendants of Japheth seemed to have left Babel and travelled to the north and west, which bears witness to the places named Magog, Ashkenaz and Tarshish. They also became seafaring peoples that spread out to various lands, each identified by its own language, clan, and national identity.

> Gen 10:1-5 *Now these are the generations of the sons of Noah, Shem, Ham, and Japheth: and unto them were sons born after the flood. The sons of Japheth; Gomer, and Magog, and Madai, and Javan, and Tubal, and Meshech, and Tiras. And the sons of Gomer; Ashkenaz, and Riphath, and Togarmah. And the sons of Javan; Elishah, and Tarshish, Kittim, and Dodanim. By these were the isles of the Gentiles divided in their lands; every one after his tongue, after their families, in their nations."*

Of the descendants of Ham some remained in Canaan and others travelled southwards, to the Middle East, and Africa where God later confirmed to Abram that He would build His nation there in Egypt.

All these peoples carried essentially the same Babylonian culture and pagan religion with them, so that Babylon is called in the New Testament *"the mother of harlots and abomination (that is idolatries) of the earth* (Rev 17:5) At the same time, they also carried a knowledge of the true God and His promises, especially remembering the divine judgment of the great Flood in their traditions. Each retained a knowledge of God and could see evidence of Him in both creation and their own natures (John 1:19, Rom 1:20, Rom 2:13-15). These people therefore rebelled against God.

> Gen 1: 27-28 *"So God created man in his own image, in the image of God created he them: male and female created he them. And God blessed them, and God said unto them Be*

---

1. Pawson, Unlocking the Bible 74-75

fruitful and multiply and replenish the earth and subdue it and have dominion over the fish of the sea, and over the fowl of the air and over every living thing that moveth upon the earth."

Ten generations after the Flood, God chose a man from the tribe of Shem, Abram to be the source by whom all families of the earth would be blessed. Abram would have two sons; the child of God's promise was Isaac who would be chosen to be the father of Esau and Jacob. Hence, the children of Abraham, Isaac and Jacob would become the ancestors of the twelve tribes: the children of Israel. God, Himself was their Leader, their King. In the wilderness, He led them by the pillar of fire in the night and by the cloud during the day. When they entered the Promised Land, being led by Joshua, He welcomed them and established His leadership in a new way as The Lord of Hosts. The children of Israel conquered the land which was occupied by the Canaanites and many other idol-worshipping tribes. The Lord then appointed judges to rule over His people. This system worked well until the days of Samuel. The children of Israel envied other nations which were ruled by a king and forsook their judge, Samuel. Samuel inquired of the Lord who informed him that they were not rejecting him, but it was God whom they rejected. God gave them what they wanted in the person of Saul. 1

Saul became their king but disobeyed the Lord and God took away his crown and placed it on the head of David, a man after God's own heart. David ruled the twelve tribes of Israel, and his chief city was at Jerusalem, the city of David. David, before his death appointed his son, Solomon, king and gave him the task of building His temple. Solomon sought the Lord for wisdom to lead his people, Israel. God gave him wisdom above all people of the earth and wealth and honour. But Solomon married women who worshipped other gods which later became a snare to him. Solomon made slaves of the indigenous peoples that they had not conquered. Yet he built shrines to other gods.1 Kings 9:20-22: Solomon makes the indigenous people second class citizens:

> *"And all the people were left of the Amorites, Hittites, Perizzites, Hivites and the Jebusites who were not of the children of Israel, that is their descendants who were left in the land after them, whom the children of Israel had not been able to destroy completely—from these Solomon raised forced labour as it is to this day. But of the children of Israel, Solomon made no forced labourers because they were men of war and his servants: his officers, his captains, commanders of his chariots and his cavalry."*

As prophesied by Ahijah (1 Kings 11:31-35}, the house of Israel was divided into two kingdoms. This division which took place after the death of Solomon and during the reign of his son, Rehoboam, came about as the people revolted against heavy taxes levied by Solomon and Rehoboam. The ten northern tribes became known as Israel and the remnant, two tribes became Judah (and Benjamin).

> Rom 1:16–19 *"For I am not ashamed of the gospel of Christ: for it is the power of God unto salvation to every one that believeth; to the Jew first, and also to the Greek.*
>
> *For therein is the righteousness of God revealed from faith to faith: as it is written, For the wrath of God is revealed from heaven against all ungodliness and unrighteousness of men, who hold the truth in unrighteousness; Because that which may be known of God is manifest in them; for God hath shewed it unto them.*

In the New Testament, Paul, from the tribe of Benjamin, in his letter to the Gentile church in Rome—the book of Romans clearly described the substance of the gospel of Jesus Christ: *"The power of God unto salvation to everyone that believeth to the Jew first and also to the Greek."* In other words, the gospel of Jesus Christ applies to all mankind, as it says in Rev 5:9–10

> *"And they sung a new song saying. Thou art worthy to take the book, and to open the seals thereof: for thou wast slain and hast redeemed us to God by thy blood out of every kindred and tongue and people and nation And has made us unto our God kings and priests and we shall reign on the earth."*

This book will explore the history of division within the church and the need for an acknowledgement by God's people, of the sins of the fathers and the need for us to repent for the ways in which we have repeated them.

1

A Divided Church

"Every kingdom divided against itself is brought to desolation, and every city or house divided against itself will not stand."

MATT 12:25 KJV

HAVE YOU EVER WONDERED why there are churches divided along the lines of 'race' (people groups), social class, and disability? In this book we are focusing on one aspect of these divisions which is 'race'. Why does it seem that some of the 'black' churches are flourishing at a time when the number of people in the UK professing to be Christian has declined dramatically over the last few decades? Since the 17th century Britain has sent out evangelists with the word of God, all over the world, first to the New World and then to the 'uttermost parts.' That word has returned to the UK having been brought back by immigrants from the former colonies. One of the first waves of immigration brought people to Britain from the West Indies in the 1950s. The word "Windrush" is now a familiar name, as it was the first ship to land in England with people from the West Indies, en masse who were British citizens, and whose ancestors the English had enslaved in the 1600s.

When the West Indians arrived in Britain, they were confronted with the unexpected rejection of the British society, including the churches. They went to the churches of their denominations in the West Indies where they functioned in various positions of participation and administration: as deacons, lay preachers, and celebrants in Anglican, Catholic, Methodist churches and in the Pentecostal churches as pastors and evangelists. On visiting the churches of their denominations, the British vicars and pastors asked them to go somewhere else, not to '*our*' churches. They did not want to worship God with black people. This was the common response that West Indians experienced in many of the denominations. Many fell away from life in Christ because they looked to man for salvation and acceptance: man, and not Christ. Others, however, did not reject God or the Bible so they established other venues to worship Him in the sanctuary of holiness, peace, joy, and love. Jesus Christ is Lord.

Many West Indians were utterly disillusioned to discover that Britain was rejecting them on the basis of their race. They had been taught that Britain was the 'mother country'; the country that evangelised the world with the Union Jack flag and the King James Bible and with British jurisprudence as the fairest in the world. However, the experience showed that the work that the British missionaries did in the Colonies and the Empire, seemed to have not been shared with the population and apparently forgotten by the church institutions in Britain. Instead of sharing with the population in Britain the relationship which the West Indians had with the church and with British society, the church was silent and even complicit with the prevailing racism in society in the 1950s and 1960s.

Sadly, the rejection experienced by the first-generation of migrants from the West Indies by British society, has continued, to some extent within the church. Clifford Hill records how church attendance by West Indians plummeted from around 70% (while in Jamaica) to 4% (while living in London). The whole migrant population were dubbed as second-class citizens. He comments:

> "*The loss of their faith in God, together with the loss of their faith in being British, had both psychological and sociological effects. It destroyed two of the pillars of personal stability that had been with them from childhood, and which had been major influences in personal character formation as well as in social identity*"[1]

Ironically, Aubrey Rose, a Jewish lawyer was instrumental in advising West Indian Christians on the establishment of an inter-church Assembly as he reflects:

> "*Many of the West Indians came from an Anglican background. A series of churches and Christians came to me and asked me to form them into an Inter-church Assembly of the New Testament Church of God. Bishop Brown was involved. The New Assembly of*

---

1. Hill, Free at Last? 236

churches (12) I was asked to be the President. I said, "you cannot have a Jew as the Head of your church you must have a Christian!" For some years I became Patron and Bishop Ramsey joined me. This Assembly had what they call a Rescue Unit there and a Community Unit and this became the most effective part of the whole set up."[2]

Half a century later, we see the fruit of this separation: There is presently an ethnically divided church in Britain: the White church; Black-led churches; Black and Ethnic Majority churches. This may be unpalatable for some, who might argue that there are many 'black' people in their congregations, but why do we refer to 'black majority churches', or 'African-led churches' and so on? The growth of the so called 'Black church' in Britain is a misnomer. The names of the churches represent the focus of their worship: New Testament Church of God, Kingsway Christian Centre, Ruach, Jesus' House, Redeemed Christian Church of God to name a few. A report by the Evangelical Alliance, published in 2015, made the following observations regarding the growth of 'Black churches' in London:

> *"As Great Britain has become increasingly multi-cultural, we are seeing a picture emerging where nearly half of churchgoers in inner London (48 per cent) are of 'black' African heritage, 28 per cent in London as a whole, compared with 13 per cent of the capital's population. That means nearly one in five (19 per cent) of 'black' African heritage Londoners goes to church each week. Two-thirds attend Pentecostal churches, though the black community is represented in every denomination. The same is not necessarily the same for the white community.*
>
> *Growth is strongest in the parts of London that already have large churches or have significant African and/or Caribbean populations. Southwark, Lambeth, and Newham saw at least a 25 per cent growth of new churches. church attendance in these boroughs also grew over the same period, with Southwark and Lambeth seeing a 50 per cent growth and Newham growing by a third. These findings were supported in an article entitled: Black and ethnic minority."*[3]

There is, however, a situation where many second and third generation West Indian heritage people, (men in particular), the descendants of committed Believers, no longer read what they consider to be the 'white man's Bible' and are searching for an identity based on their ethnicity rather

---

2. Rose, Brief Encounters of a Legal Kind, 129
3. Evangelical Alliance, Christians lead London church growth (July 2015)

than in Christ. It is important to examine the source of the belief (even in the church) that one race of people is superior to another. The irony of the development of a so called 'Black church' is that it only serves to highlight the fact that black people have been rejected within the 'White church'. In this book we will address two questions: 'how has this division come about within the Body of Christ? And 'Why were the Jewish community (who continue to suffer from antisemitism which in effect is racism against Jews) so supportive of black people when they first arrived in the UK in the mid-twentieth century?'

2

To the Jew First

The Development of Roman Christianity: Pentecost—AD 325—1302

IN THIS CHAPTER WE will explore how the divisions that are prevalent within British society also permeate the church. We ask the question "How did the belief of racial hierarchy with special reference to Europeans and other non-European people groups become so prevalent as a Christian doctrine? To find the answer we turn to the Bible for the truth and to see how Christians deviated from that truth.

Christianity was born in AD 33 in the town of Jerusalem on the day of Pentecost, when three thousand Jews were saved. This was the fulfilment of the declaration that God made to Abraham:

> Gen 12:1–3 *Now the LORD had said unto Abram, Get thee out of thy country, and from thy kindred, and from thy father's house, unto a land that I will shew thee:*
>
> *And I will make of thee a great nation, and I will bless thee, and make thy name great; and thou shalt be a blessing: And I will bless them that bless thee and curse him that curseth thee: and in thee shall all families of the earth be blessed.*

Thus, began the story that led to the growth of the Children of Israel and from which tribe, Judah, came the Messiah, Jesus of Nazareth. He was further prophesied in Isa 7:14.

> *Therefore, the Lord Himself will give you a sign: Behold, the virgin shall conceive and bear a Son, and shall call His name Immanuel.*

Jesus' birth and purpose were further prophesied in Luke 1:30-33 when the angel Gabriel visited Mary to announce that she, a virgin, would bear a son:

> *Then the angel said to her, "Do not be afraid, Mary, for you have found favour with God. And behold, you will conceive in your womb and bring forth a Son and shall call His name Jesus. He will be great and will be called the Son of the Highest; and the Lord God will give Him the throne of His father David. And He will reign over the house of Jacob forever, and of His kingdom there will be no end.*

Jesus was born in Bethlehem in Judea and after He was baptised by John the Baptist, began His earthly ministry. After three short years He was crucified, He died, and was buried. On the third day God raised Him from the dead and He now sits at the right hand of the Father, interceding for us. Before He ascended into heaven, He promised His disciples that He would send the Holy Spirit, who would be with them forever. This happened on the day of Pentecost which has significance in both Judaism and Christianity although for different reasons. For the Jews it is known as Shavout which is a major Jewish festival which takes place fifty days after the second day of Passover. Shavout was also sometimes referred to as Pentecost, a Greek word meaning fifty and is a celebration of the first fruits of the year's harvest. In a sense that is what Pentecost is to Christians. Those believers in Jerusalem on that momentous day were the "first fruits" of the great harvest that was just beginning. On the day of Pentecost, the Holy Spirit came upon the disciples who were gathered in Jerusalem and in Acts 2:1-11 we read that the disciple Peter, preached to those gathered and established the first church of Jesus Christ:

> Acts 2:1 *And when the day of Pentecost was fully come, they were all with one accord in one place.* 2 *And suddenly there came a sound from heaven as of a rushing mighty wind, and it filled all the house where they were sitting.*
>
> 3 *And there appeared unto them cloven tongues like as of fire, and it sat upon each of them.*
>
> 4 *And they were all filled with the Holy Ghost, and began to speak with other tongues, as the Spirit gave them utterance.*
>
> 5 *And there were dwelling at Jerusalem Jews, devout men, out of every nation under heaven.*

> 6 *Now when this was noised abroad, the multitude came together, and were confounded, because that every man heard them speak in his own language.*
>
> 7 *And they were all amazed and marvelled, saying one to another, Behold, are not all these which speak Galileans?*
>
> 8 *And how hear we every man in our own tongue, wherein we were born?*
>
> 9 *Parthians, and Medes, and Elamites, and the dwellers in Mesopotamia, and in Judaea, and Cappadocia, in Pontus, and Asia,*
>
> 10 *Phrygia, and Pamphylia, in Egypt, and in the parts of Libya about Cyrene, and strangers of Rome, Jews and proselytes,* 11 *Cretes and Arabians, we do hear them speak in our tongues the wonderful works of God.*

Note the various people groups that comprised the Roman Empire at that time. They were Jews and those converted to Judaism who had come to celebrate the feast of Pentecost.

Peter addressed all these people in Jerusalem and reminded them in Acts 2:16 of the words of the prophet Joel, "*But this is that which was spoken by the prophet Joel:*"

> Joel 2:28–32 *And it shall come to pass afterward, that I will pour out my spirit upon all flesh; and your sons and your daughters shall prophesy, your old men shall dream dreams, your young men shall see visions: And also upon the servants and upon the handmaids in those days will I pour out my spirit. And I will shew wonders in the heavens and in the earth, blood, and fire, and pillars of smoke. The sun shall be turned into darkness, and the moon into blood, before the great and the terrible day of the LORD come. And it shall come to pass, that whosoever shall call on the name of the LORD shall be delivered: for in mount Zion and in Jerusalem shall be deliverance, as the LORD hath said, and in the remnant whom the LORD shall call.*

Peter, having quoted from the words of the prophet Joel (whom they all knew), went on to describe in Acts 2:32–47 that they were witnessing the fulfilment of that prophecy:

> Acts 2: 32 *This Jesus hath God raised up, whereof we all are witnesses.* 33 *Therefore being by the right hand of God exalted and having received of the Father the promise of the Holy Ghost, he hath shed forth this, which ye now see and hear.* 34 *For David is not ascended into the heavens: but he saith himself, The LORD said unto my Lord, Sit thou on my right hand,* 35 *Until I make*

thy foes thy footstool. 36 Therefore let all the house of Israel know assuredly, that God hath made that same Jesus, whom ye have crucified, both Lord and Christ. 37 Now when they heard this, they were pricked in their heart, and said unto Peter and to the rest of the apostles, Men and brethren, what shall we do? 38 Then Peter said unto them, Repent, and be baptized every one of you in the name of Jesus Christ for the remission of sins, and ye shall receive the gift of the Holy Ghost. 39 For the promise is unto you, and to your children, and to all that are afar off, even as many as the Lord our God shall call. 40 And with many other words did he testify and exhort, saying, Save yourselves from this untoward generation. 41 Then they that gladly received his word were baptized: and the same day there were added unto them about three thousand souls. 42 And they continued stedfastly in the apostles' doctrine and fellowship, and in breaking of bread, and in prayers.

43 And fear came upon every soul: and many wonders and signs were done by the apostles.

44 And all that believed were together and had all things common.

45 And sold their possessions and goods, and parted them to all men, as every man had need.

46 And they, continuing daily with one accord in the temple, and breaking bread from house to house, did eat their meat with gladness and singleness of heart,

47 Praising God and having favour with all the people. And the Lord added to the church daily such as should be saved.

Pontius Pilate was the representative of the Emperor of the Roman Empire at that time. The countries of the world (Roman Empire) from which Jewish people and Jewish proselytes came, (who were also mentioned in Acts 2, at Pentecost), covered Rome, Asia Minor, Asia –Parthians from the river Tigris to the borders of India; Judea (land between the Euphrates and the Tigris rivers;) Arabia and Africa. Thousands of them already lived in Rome and on the island of Crete. After Pentecost, many of them returned to their towns and villages, filled with the Holy Spirit and enthusiastic about making disciples as Jesus had instructed. These believers became yet another group of disobedient colonials; Jews; two types of Jews, those fighting for independence and the others; wonderful citizens but refusing to worship the gods of the Roman Empire. The numbers of this latter group seemed to be increasing by quantum leaps; they were soon to be found within the whole Roman Empire.

With the Romans persecuting the rebellious Jews and any other Jew for that matter; and the Scribes and Pharisees persecuting the Jesus Jews (with the full support of the state) the people of the Way (Christians) had to scatter. They scattered to every part of the Roman Empire. Believers were to be found everywhere; in Samaria, Corinth, Ephesus, Galatia, Corinth (Turkey) and every part of the Mediterranean, including Rome!

In the same book of Acts 8: 26–39 (when Saul was persecuting Christians), we read the report of the Holy Spirit instructing Phillip to leave Samaria and go into the desert to meet with an Ethiopian eunuch. He was an important official in charge of the treasury of the Queen of Ethiopia, on his way back from Jerusalem. When Philip joined him in his chariot, he was studying the part of the bible which said, *"He was led as a sheep to the slaughter and like a lamb dumb before his shearer, so opened he not his own mouth."* After a short exchange of greetings and questions about the passage, Phillip explained the passage. Having understood and believed in that Jesus, the Ethiopian, (a sub-Saharan African) accepted Jesus Christ as Savior. Phillip immediately baptised him. This Negro, (this African) went away rejoicing.

Acts 9 leads on to an account of the conversion of Saul of Tarsus who was a leader of the Jews but born in Turkey. Saul studied in Jerusalem under a highly regarded Rabbi called Gamaliel and was a member of the Pharisees, the most conservative sect of the Jewish religion. He did everything to oppose the Lord's disciples. He was even present at the execution of Stephen, the first martyr. He sought and obtained commissions from the leading Pharisees to leave Jerusalem and travel one hundred and thirty-six miles to Damascus with armed guards to pursue some more of the followers of Jesus (who, at that time was called The Way). It was on that trip when a very bright light struck him, and Saul fell off his horse. Those with him heard voices but saw no one. Acts 9:4–18 reads:

> Acts 9: 4 *And he fell to the earth, and heard a voice saying unto him, Saul, Saul, why persecutest thou me?*
>
> 5 *And he said, Who art thou, Lord? And the Lord said, I am Jesus whom thou persecutest: it is hard for thee to kick against the pricks.*
>
> 6 *And he trembling and astonished said, Lord, what wilt thou have me to do? And the Lord said unto him, Arise, and go into the city, and it shall be told thee what thou must do.*
>
> 7 *And the men which journeyed with him stood speechless, hearing a voice, but seeing no man.*
>
> 8 *And Saul arose from the earth; and when his eyes were opened, he saw no man: but they led him by the hand, and brought him into Damascus.*
>
> 9 *And he was three days without sight, and neither did eat nor drink.*

> 10 *And there was a certain disciple at Damascus, named Ananias; and to him said the Lord in a vision, Ananias. And he said, Behold, I am here, Lord.*
>
> 11 *And the Lord said unto him, Arise, and go into the street which is called Straight, and enquire in the house of Judas for one called Saul, of Tarsus: for, behold, he prayeth,* 12 *And hath seen in a vision a man named Ananias coming in, and putting his hand on him, that he might receive his sight.*
>
> 13 *Then Ananias answered, Lord, I have heard by many of this man, how much evil he hath done to thy saints at Jerusalem:*
>
> 14 *And here he hath authority from the chief priests to bind all that call on thy name.*
>
> 15 *But the Lord said unto him, Go thy way: for he is a chosen vessel unto me, to bear my name before the Gentiles, and kings, and the children of Israel:*16 *For I will shew him how great things he must suffer for my name›s sake.*
>
> 17 *And Ananias went his way, and entered into the house; and putting his hands on him said, Brother Saul, the Lord, even Jesus, that appeared unto thee in the way as thou camest, hath sent me, that thou mightest receive thy sight, and be filled with the Holy Ghost.*
>
> 18 *And immediately there fell from his eyes as it had been scales: and he received sight forthwith, and arose, and was baptized.*

Saul did not know who the Lord was because he said, "Who art thou Lord"? He was a senior member of the faith: but he did not know Jesus. Those who do not know Jesus, will use their power and authority to try and imprison, torture, and even kill people who know Jesus. The reason for treating them in that manner, is not because of anything criminal that they do, but because they worship Jesus and their persecutors do not; they worship the god of this world.

This practice of persecuting Christians in many areas of the world exists to this day! Indeed, Jesus warned his followers (us) in Luke 21:10–19, that they would face persecution:

> Luke 21:10 *Then said he unto them, Nation shall rise against nation, and kingdom against kingdom:*
>
> 11 *And great earthquakes shall be in divers places, and famines, and pestilences; and fearful sights and great signs shall there be from heaven.*
>
> 12 *But before all these, they shall lay their hands on you, and persecute you, delivering you up to the synagogues, and into prisons, being brought before kings and rulers for my name's sake.*

> 13 *And it shall turn to you for a testimony.*
> 14 *Settle it therefore in your hearts, not to meditate before what ye shall answer:*
> 15 *For I will give you a mouth and wisdom, which all your adversaries shall not be able to gainsay nor resist.*
> 16 *And ye shall be betrayed both by parents, and brethren, and kinsfolks, and friends; and some of you shall they cause to be put to death.*
> 17 *And ye shall be hated of all men for my name's sake.*
> 18 *But there shall not an hair of your head perish.*
> 19 *In your patience possess ye your souls.*

After his conversion, Saul (who was renamed Paul) first taught about Jesus Christ in the synagogues. As a result, he was persecuted by the Jews who also wanted to kill him, (Acts 9:23–31)

He quickly disappeared into Arabia for a period of three years. However, after that sojourn, he went to Jerusalem to join the apostles, but they were afraid of him, except for Barnabas who had heard of Paul's conversion and his teaching in Damascus. Barnabas introduced Saul to the apostles, and they welcomed him. Saul debated with some Greek-speaking Jews with whom he encountered the same murderous response as in Damascus. The apostles, fearing for his life, took him to Caesarea and sent him home back to Tarsus.

> Acts 9:26–30 GNB
>
> *Saul went to Jerusalem and tried to join the disciples. But they would not believe that he was a disciple, and they were all afraid of him.*
>
> *Then Barnabas came to his help and took him to the apostles. He explained to them how Saul had seen the Lord on the road and that the Lord had spoken to him. He also told them how boldly Saul had preached in the name of Jesus in Damascus.*
>
> *And so Saul stayed with them and went all over Jerusalem, preaching boldly in the name of the Lord.*
>
> *He also talked and disputed with the Greek-speaking Jews, but they tried to kill him.*
>
> *When the believers found out about this, they took Saul to Caesarea and sent him away to Tarsus.*[1]

It was sometime later that the apostles in Jerusalem heard that some of the believers who were scattered after the murder of Stephen, were preaching the word of God to those as far as Phenice, and Cyprus, and Antioch,

---

1. Good News Bible (GNB)

but only to the Jews. However, those believers from Cyprus and Cyrene who went to Antioch preached the good news of the Lord Jesus to the Gentiles. Many believed and turned to the Lord. Hence the apostles in Jerusalem sent Barnabas to assist with the work there. After some time, there in Antioch, and seeing that many were turning to the Lord, Barnabas went to seek out Paul who by this time was in Tarsus for about ten years. When he found Paul, he brought him back to Antioch. In the church at Antioch there were certain prophets and teachers; Simeon that was called Niger (a black man) and Lucius another man from Cyrene, (Libya) Africa, and Manaen, who grew up with Herod. One day as they were ministering to the Lord in fasting and praying, the Holy Spirit instructed them to separate unto Himself Barnabas and Paul for the work they had to do. After they had fasted and prayed some more, they laid hands on them, and they sent them on their way. They left their base in Antioch and proceeded to evangelise the northeastern part of the Mediterranean world, planting, and revisiting churches on the way. Paul's ministry ended in Rome after a period of about thirty-three years, AD 63–6.

Another specific move of the Holy Spirit to reach the Gentiles is recorded in the book of Acts 10. The Holy Spirit instructed Peter to go to the house of Cornelius, a Roman centurion, and teach him about Jesus. Peter had major challenges in obeying the Lord on this mission. His opposition was so great that while he recognised the Holy Spirit as Lord, he flatly refused to go. This he did three times. He finally relented just when the messengers from Cornelius called on him. As a result, Peter, with a few of his brethren, left his house in Joppa and travelled with Cornelius' servants to his home. He was warmly greeted, but Peter explained his misgivings based on the law, as per Deut 7:2, which instructed Jews about their relationship with Gentiles. God had shown him that he must not consider anyone ritually unclean or defiled. Peter enquired about the circumstances that led to his invitation. Cornelius told him how he had been fasting some time ago and a man stood before him in bright clothing, confirming that his prayers were heard, and his alms were received. The man instructed him to send his servants to Joppa to a man named Peter who would speak to him. At this reply, Peter opened his mouth and spoke Acts 10:28–43:

> Acts 10:28 *And he said unto them, Ye know how that it is an unlawful thing for a man that is a Jew to keep company, or come unto one of another nation; but God hath shewed me that I should not call any man common or unclean. 29 Therefore came I unto you without gainsaying, as soon as I was sent for: I ask therefore for what intent ye have sent for me? 30 And Cornelius said, Four*

days ago I was fasting until this hour; and at the ninth hour I prayed in my house, and, behold, a man stood before me in bright clothing,

31 And said, Cornelius, thy prayer is heard, and thine alms are had in remembrance in the sight of God. 32 Send therefore to Joppa, and call hither Simon, whose surname is Peter; he is lodged in the house of one Simon a tanner by the sea side: who, when he cometh, shall speak unto thee.

33 Immediately therefore I sent to thee; and thou hast well done that thou art come. Now therefore are we all here present before God, to hear all things that are commanded thee of God.

Gentiles Hear the Good News 34 Then Peter opened his mouth, and said, Of a truth I perceive that God is no respecter of persons: 35 But in every nation he that feareth him, and worketh righteousness, is accepted with him. 36 The word which God sent unto the children of Israel, preaching peace by Jesus Christ: (he is Lord of all:) 37 That word, I say, ye know, which was published throughout all Judaea, and began from Galilee, after the baptism which John preached;

38 How God anointed Jesus of Nazareth with the Holy Ghost and with power: who went about doing good, and healing all that were oppressed of the devil; for God was with him.

39 And we are witnesses of all things which he did both in the land of the Jews, and in Jerusalem; whom they slew and hanged on a tree: 40 Him God raised up the third day, and shewed him openly;

41 Not to all the people, but unto witnesses chosen before of God, even to us, who did eat and drink with him after he rose from the dead. 42 And he commanded us to preach unto the people, and to testify that it is he which was ordained of God to be the Judge of quick and dead.

43 To him give all the prophets witness, that through his name whosoever believeth in him shall receive remission of sins.

Peter preached that Jesus is the only way to the Father. While he spoke to these Gentiles, (Romans) the Holy Spirit fell on all of those who heard the word and believed. They all began to speak in tongues and magnified God, just as the believing Jews had experienced for themselves at Pentecost. Peter immediately baptized them.

The apostles and brothers in Christ in Jerusalem, heard that the Gentiles had received the word of God. The circumcised Jewish believers who still followed the Law challenged Peter in going to the Gentiles and eating with them. In response Peter gave them a detailed account about the amazing conversion of the Gentiles. When they heard it, Acts 11:18-20 tells us that they ceased their criticism and praised God saying that "God has also granted to the Gentiles repentance to life."

> *When they heard these things, they held their peace, and glorified God, saying, Then hath God also to the Gentiles granted repentance unto life.*
>
> *Now they which were scattered abroad upon the persecution that arose about Stephen travelled as far as Phenice, and Cyprus, and Antioch, preaching the word to none but unto the Jews only.*
>
> *And some of them were men of Cyprus and Cyrene, which, when they were come to Antioch, spake unto the Grecians, preaching the Lord Jesus.*

This meeting in which Peter submitted to an assembly of apostles and believers is understood to be the first Council of Believers ever recorded. The authority that they wielded is recognised in their response to Peter's detailed report: *"Then God has also granted the Gentiles, repentance unto life."* The Jewish believers spread to other parts of the Roman Empire, preaching only to the Jews as reported in Acts 11. It was not generally known that Gentiles could become Christians. The church of Jesus Christ was being filled with more Gentiles as they heard the Word and believed.

Greek thinking and Roman colonial administration impacted on the belief system of the early Christians. Early in his letter to the Romans, Paul stated quite categorically, in part:

> Rom 1:14-18 *I am debtor both to the Greeks, and to the Barbarians; both to the wise, and to the unwise.*
>
> *15 So, as much as in me is, I am ready to preach the gospel to you that are at Rome also. 16 For I am not ashamed of the gospel of Christ: for it is the power of God unto salvation to everyone that believeth; to the Jew first, and also to the Greek. 17 For therein is the righteousness of God revealed from faith to faith: as it is written, The just shall live by faith.*
>
> *18 For the wrath of God is revealed from heaven against all ungodliness and unrighteousness of men, who hold the truth in unrighteousness;*

Paul would speak to all the people groups in the regions as far west as Rome. The Jews had some belief issues to confront as this new Christian religion, which included all books of the Old Testament now included a relationship with God that was not based on the observance of the Law but on being 'born again'. Their issue was basically whether the Messiah came in the person of Jesus or whether the Messiah was yet to come. Paul was most instrumental in clarifying these anomalies for both the Hebrews, the Grecians, and the Romans and those who lived in other Asian cities, Ephesus, Galatia, Antioch (mainland). In the letter to the Romans, Paul laid out very clearly how the believer should live, forsaking lifestyles and beliefs which were contrary to God's definition of worship of one God: sexuality, social relations, and responsibilities to God and to government.

In the book of Romans, chapters 9–11, Paul was inspired to detail the significance of the Jews, the children of Abraham, Isaac and Jacob to the Gentiles. He explained that their belief in the same Jewish Jesus as Savior could as it were, provoke the Jews to jealousy and turn unto the Lord.[2]

> *Rom 11:11 I say then, Have they stumbled that they should fall? God forbid but rather through their fall salvation is come unto the Gentiles, for to provoke them to jealousy.*

To the Jews, belief that Jesus is the way, the truth and the life and the only way to Father God, was a stumbling block and to the Romans it was foolishness. These two heritages would prove to be the source of di-vision among Christians. Those of the Hebraic heritage were ambivalent about the obedience to the Law: to circumcise or not to circumcise, that was the question. To eat what the Gentiles ate or retain the dietary laws was yet another major issue for them. Paul addressed these two issues with clarity. In Gal 2:11–21 he publicly chastised Peter, who was already influencing James, Barnabas, and other disciples into obeying Hebraic laws (when among the Jews), and concerning circumcision:

> Gal 2:11 *But when Peter was come to Antioch, I withstood him to the face, because he was to be blamed. 12 For before that certain came from James, he did eat with the Gentiles: but when they were come, he withdrew and separated himself, fearing them which were of the circumcision.*
>
> *13 And the other Jews dissembled likewise with him; insomuch that Barnabas also was carried away with their dissimulation. 14 But when I saw that they walked not uprightly according to the truth of the gospel, I said unto Peter before them all, If thou, being a Jew, livest after the manner of Gentiles, and not as do the Jews, why compellest thou the Gentiles to live as do the Jews? 15 We who are Jews by nature, and not sinners of the Gentiles, 16 Knowing that a man is not justified by the works of the law, but by the faith of Jesus Christ, even we have believed in Jesus Christ, that we might be justified by the faith of Christ, and not by the works of the law: for by the works of the law shall no flesh be justified. 17 But if,*

---

2. Pawson, Unlocking the Bible 1023

> *while we seek to be justified by Christ, we ourselves also are found sinners, is therefore Christ the minister of sin? God forbid. 18 For if I build again the things which I destroyed, I make myself a transgressor. 19 For I through the law am dead to the law, that I might live unto God. 20 I am crucified with Christ: nevertheless I live; yet not I, but Christ liveth in me: and the life which I now live in the flesh I live by the faith of the Son of God, who loved me, and gave himself for me. 21 I do not frustrate the grace of God: for if righteousness come by the law, then Christ is dead in vain.*

Paul went on to describe proper Christian propriety: If a pagan invited you to his feast go, eat, and enjoy the event. If, however, you saw them offer the foods to idols, then refrain from eating, if not, just bless the food and eat it. On another occasion he noted that the Bereans did not take anything for granted which was preached as doctrine about Jesus: they searched the scriptures to obtain God's word on the matter. The substance of Jesus was never in doubt. He identified himself as 'the Son of man'. This definition is referenced in Dan 7:13–14.

> *I saw in the night visions, and, behold, one like the Son of man came with the clouds of heaven, and came to the Ancient of days, and they brought him near before him.*
> *And there was given him dominion, and glory, and a kingdom, that all people, nations, and languages, should serve him: his dominion is an everlasting dominion, which shall not pass away, and his kingdom that which shall not be destroyed.*

During the first three hundred years Biblical (Kingdom) Christianity spread quickly within the Roman Empire, reaching Britannia (England) it's most western out-post in AD 47. Jews and Gentiles from various regions of the Roman Empire were embracing this Christian religion.

Over the following two hundred years, the Roman Empire continued to persecute the Jews, because they refused to worship any other god. They persecuted the Gentile Christians because they refused to worship any other god, believing in the saving grace of Jesus. They suffered death rather than submit to any form of idol worship. Polycarp, Bishop of Smyrna a disciple of Apostle John, was one of the early martyrs.

Greco/Roman thinking crept into the church which became more Roman in its practice. Assemblies originally had many bishops who were really elders drawn from within the body and who performed the role of overseer over many other assemblies. Under the Roman culture, the significance of bishop was modified; the numbers were reduced, and the role became more of an administrator with power and authority to administer discipline.

Other practices which had their roots in the feelings or wisdom of man, assumed more validity as they attracted more followers who did not have the Jewish heritage or even those Jews who chose to adopt the Greco/Roman culture as their terms of reference in their worship. In his book, David Pawson describes four areas in which the world came into the churches: *"regional bishops; a 'magic' view of the sacraments, established religion: and nominal membership."*[3]

Finally, the wisdom of man assumed such great importance that the wisdom of God as described in the Old Testament and the writings of the apostles (who were all Jews) were seriously challenged. The very substance of Jesus Christ became the major issue. Who or what then was Jesus? Was He God, was He like God, was He created?

The resolution of these various issues and more came to a head for the Gentiles in AD 325.

To address this issue, some background information is necessary. In his book *"How the Church Lost The Way and How it Can Find it Again"* Steve Maltz (pages 44–47) writes that in AD 312 Constantine, a Roman Emperor, while preparing for another battle is reputed to have seen a vision of a cross, which said 'conquer'. Constantine interpreted it to mean that his army must go into battle under the sign of the cross. This he did and they were victorious. *'The result was that Christianity, the religion of the cross, was to become the state religion of the Roman Empire.'*[4]

In AD 325 Emperor Constantine chaired the Council of Nicaea that produced the Nicaean Creed, which included the truth of the personhood of Jesus Christ as taught by the apostles.

The other issue settled at that Council meeting, however, was the timing of Easter. The Council decided *'to strip away all connection between this festival (Easter) and the Jewish festival of Passover, where it owes its origins.'*[5]

Subsequent Councils consolidated the direction of the Roman church: The Council of Antioch AD 345 threatened excommunication for any Christian celebrating Passover with the Jews.

The Council of Laodicea in AD 365 extended this threat to all Jewish festivals as well as the Saturday Sabbath.[6]

Baptism was deemed as the most significant definition and proof of membership in the Roman expression of Christianity. This baptism however was not based on it being an outward sign and seal of the spiritual washing

---

3. Pawson, Where has the Body been for 2000 years? 44–51
4. Maltz, How the church Lost the Way, 46
5. Maltz, How the church Lost the Way, 47
6. Maltz, How the church Lost the Way, 48

away of sins and a resurrection of the new man in Christ but on totally different criteria i.e. a Christian was deemed to be one who was baptised in the Roman church. A Christian was one who was 'christened' (baptised as a baby or later) and 'confirmed' later, usually as a young adult. Christianity had become an institution.

The Roman church adopted Greek philosophers' ideas of spiritual things being good and physical things being bad, and it became institutionalised in the separation of the clergy from the laity, which among other things distanced the Roman church from its Hebraic origins.

The state church of the Roman Empire was, it seems, defining itself based on its historical Greek philosophical roots with its Greco/Roman gods on the one hand and on the other, the Christian teachings of the apostles. Its march through the centuries is briefly presented as follows:

The period between the fourth century and the eleventh century (The Dark Ages) was marked by the diminishing of the Roman Empire and the subsequent consolidation of Roman Christianity, as the religion of the countries, extending across three continents: Europe, Asia, and Africa (north along the Mediterranean Sea)

Roman Christianity was challenged by other expressions of Orthodox Christianity; those of Greece, Asia Minor, Syria, and Egypt. They also fought amongst themselves, and the split was finally completed by the year 1054.

However, Christianity's major competition came from a new religion/faith—Islam that was also birthed in the Middle East. These two major religions; Roman Christianity and Islam competed for the lands off the Mediterranean; west, east, north, and south.

This religion, Islam developed by Mohamed in AD 613 (and who died in 632), spread with such rapidity that by AD 642, Islam had conquered as far north as Syria, much of Mesopotamia and all of Egypt. Within about one hundred years, Islam (the Ottomans) added Greece, Bulgaria, Serbia, Bosnia, Albania, Romania, and Hungary to their empire.

By AD 711, seventy-four years after the death of Mohamed) the Muslims crossed the straits of Gibraltar and began the conquest of Spain. Jews (who had been by this time abused in the Roman Empire for six hundred years) welcomed them as liberators. During this period of the Muslim establishment as a conquering religion, they would attack only the wealthy and not the common people. They did not rape the women, in direct contrast to the Roman Catholic Christians yet in some cases the Jews welcomed them as the lesser of two evils—Roman Christianity and Islam. Islam replaced Roman Christianity by force, in Western Europe, in France up to the gates of Lyons, into Eastern Europe as far as Vienna.

In his book "Where has the Body been for 2,000 years?," David Pawson writes:

> "Despite the overt domination of Roman Christianity over the nations, there was always a remnant whose belief, was based on the Word of God, the Bible and their relationship with Jesus and the Holy Spirit. These groups were persecuted and even the records of their persecution destroyed. Groups like the Bogomils in Bulgaria, Paulicians in Armenia and Thracia and Asia Minor and Catharians met in the Balkans.[7]

Christianity was present in Roman Britain under Emperor Claudius in AD43, ten years after the death of Jesus. The gospel rode swiftly on the back of the conquering Romans and within years had penetrated Britain for the first time. We have evidence that the Christian church grew and prospered in Britain until the beginning of the fifth century. Around AD 200, the first Carthaginian theologian, Tertullian included Britain in a list of places reached by Christianity in his work "*Adversus Judaeous.*" The Greek theologian Origen also wrote that Christianity had reached Britain. This first phase lasted until the end of the Roman imperial administration in the early fifth century, when the Roman soldiers left the country after Rome fell—the end of the Empire.

With the departure of the Romans, the Angles, Saxons and Jutes from Germany and Denmark invaded England and finally conquered most of Southern and Eastern England by the end of sixth century. However, there was a remnant in northern England and Scotland that retained and practiced New Testament Christianity as taught by Saint Columba an Irish Abbot and missionary. He died in 597.

The Romans returned in 596, this time, under the authority of Pope Gregory, who sent a mission of about forty men. The confrontation between New Testament Christianity and Papal Christianity ensued. Papal Christianity won and England became a Roman Catholic country in 660.

By the beginning of the eleventh century, the leadership by the Pope over kings and queens and rulers over nations had been established.

Pope St. Gregory VII (born Hildebrand in 1020) became Pope in 1073 until his death in 1085, is the Pope who established the sacred authority over the church and secular authority over the state. "*From then and for the next five hundred years the Pope is the most influential figure, and the Papacy is the power that controls the Western world. The church is now the empire again. . ..*" "*This put the physical force of armies at the church disposal . . ..*

---

7. Pawson, Where has the Body been for 2000 years? 63

he began to use force to establish the kingdom of Christ."[8] The first mission of the church was to reclaim Jerusalem from the Saracens (Muslims). They had conquered this holy city during their other conquests in the Levant (632–661) and restored the rule of Christ in that city. Peter the Hermit in 1095, led the first Crusade and in 1099 conquered the Saracens and took back Jerusalem, and the Holy Land and freed the Eastern Christians. In victory, the Crusaders pillaged the city, raped the women, slaughtered the Saracens, and established the 'rule of Christ'.

> *"Now is that Christian? Of course not. They were misled and thousands of people thought that this was what the church was meant to be, an earthly empire, establishing itself by force. The basic failure is that it was thought that you established the kingdom of Christ by force."*[9]

Crusaders came largely from Europe (east, west, north and south, including the Mediterranean) from among the following nations, people groups, principalities, fiefdoms and countries: Portugal, Spain, Andora, Britannia, France, Monaco, Luxembourg, Belgium, Netherlands, Germany, Switzerland, Liechtenstein, Italy, San Martino, Vatican City, Malta, Austria, Czech Republic, Slovakia, Croatia, Bosnia—Herzegovina, Hungary, Yugoslavia, Albania, Greece, FYR Macedonia, Romania, Bulgaria, Turkey, Armenia, Cyprus.

Armenia and Turkey however, had a peculiar political/ religious persona, oscillating between Christianity and Islam, a practice which continues to this day.

The Remnant: However, during the period 1000 to 1500 in European countries there were many groups whose belief in biblical Christianity brought them in direct conflict with Roman Christianity. The Beghards from the Netherlands; the Waldenses, from the Waldensian Valley in northern Italy; the Albigensian from Southern France and in Germany, the Brethren of the Common Life in Germany; these groups all based their beliefs on the bible and rejected the teachings of the Roman Catholic church. They were all persecuted to death.

After seven Crusades, the Saracens finally defeated the Crusaders in 1270.

The Roman church based on its successes of marshalling nations to its cause since the Crusades in the 11–13th Centuries, and the Pope being the spiritual father of these nations, became the empowerment of all authority.

---

8. Pawson, Where has the Body been for 2000 years? 66
9. Pawson, Where has the Body been for 2000 years? 67–68

Papal Bulls would become the instrument by which nations would conduct their foreign policy and how people would be perceived and consequently treated.

The following is an edited chronology of some Papal Bulls and Catholic Christianity practices that were implemented over the centuries, and which formed the basis of Western and New-World societies and relationships with non-Europeans. The Bulls divided mankind as a group into four religious' categories: Portugal (Roman Catholics), Saracens and pagans whatsoever, and 'other enemies of Christ'.

Replacement Theology?

On November 18, 1302, Pope Boniface V111 issued a Papal Bull called Unam Sanctam (The One) which declared that there is no salvation outside the church (Extra Ecclesiam nulla salus) and that the church must remain united. The consequence of that Papal Bull upon the Europeans (former peoples under the Roman Empire) consolidated the basis for the belief that shifted 'salvation' from Jesus to an institution, called 'the church'. The church then became the instrument by which people would obtain salvation. Jesus himself said that He is the way the truth and the life; no man comes to the Father, but by Him. He is the only way to salvation as the following Biblical text from John 14 states:

> *John 14:6 Jesus saith unto him, I am the way, the truth, and the life: no man cometh unto the Father, but by me.*

The bible is replete with texts which state that God alone is the source of salvation.

> *Ps 68:20 He that is our God is the God of salvation; and unto GOD the Lord belong the issues from death.*
>
> *Ps 70:4 Let all those that seek thee rejoice and be glad in thee: and let such as love thy salvation say continually, Let God be magnified.*
>
> *Isa12:2 Behold, God is my salvation; I will trust, and not be afraid: for the LORD JEHOVAH is my strength and my song; he also is become my salvation.*
>
> *Isa 49:6 And he said, It is a light thing that thou shouldest be my servant to raise up the tribes of Jacob, and to restore the preserved of Israel: I will also give thee for a light to the Gentiles, that thou mayest be my salvation unto the end of the earth.*
>
> *Jonah 2:9 But I will sacrifice unto thee with the voice of thanksgiving; I will pay that that I have vowed. Salvation is of the LORD.*

> *Mic 7:7 Therefore I will look unto the LORD; I will wait for the God of my salvation: my God will hear me.*
>
> *Rom 1:16 For I am not ashamed of the gospel of Christ: for it is the power of God unto salvation to everyone that believeth; to the Jew first, and also to the Greek.*
>
> *Rom 10:10 For with the heart man believeth unto righteousness; and with the mouth confession is made unto salvation.*
>
> *Rev 12:10 And I heard a loud voice saying in heaven, Now is come salvation, and strength, and the kingdom of our God, and the power of his Christ: for the accuser of our brethren is cast down, which accused them before our God day and night.*
>
> *Rev 19:1 And after these things I heard a great voice of much people in heaven, saying, Alleluia; Salvation, and glory, and honour, and power, unto the Lord our God.*

Salvation is of the Lord!

Opposition to this Papal Bull first came from England. Sustained opposition to the doctrine of Rome concerning the church came from England in the person and writings of John Wycliffe 1329-1384. He was the first to produce a complete translation of the Bible into the English language, making the word of God available to the masses (who could not read Latin, the language of the Bible and which was only accessible to the clergy at that time).

Wycliffe had come to regard the scriptures as the only reliable guide to the truth about God and maintained that all Christians should rely on the Bible rather than the unreliable and frequently self-serving teachings of Popes and clerics. He said that there was no scriptural justification for the papacy's existence and attacked the riches and power that Popes and the church had acquired. His disapproved of imposed clerical celibacy, pilgrimages, the selling of indulgences and praying to saints. He thought that England should be ruled by its monarchs and the lay administration with no interference from the papacy and the church. In his 'On Civil Dominion' of 1376 he said: "*England belongs to no Pope. The Pope is but a man, subject to sin, but Christ is the Lord of Lords, and this kingdom is to be held directly and solely of Christ alone*".[10]

Wycliffe soon had a following of supporters called the Lollards. They commonly believed also and most notably that as human beings we are all brothers.

Jan Hus (1369-1415) a Czech Roman Catholic priest followed the teaching of John Wycliffe. Sometime around 1402, priest and scholar he denounced what he judged as the corruption of the church and the Papacy,

---

10. Cavendish, historytoday.com volume-65-issue-5-may-2015

and he promoted the reformist ideas of English theologian John Wycliffe. His preaching was widely heeded in Bohemia, and provoked suppression by the church, which had declared Wycliffe a heretic.

In 1414, Sigismund of Hungary convened the Council of Constance to end the Schism and resolve other religious controversies. Hus went to the Council, under a safe-conduct from Sigismund, but was imprisoned, tried, and executed on 6 July 1415.

Responding with horror to the execution of Hus, the people of Bohemia moved even more rapidly away from Papal teachings, provoking Rome to pronounce a crusade against them (1 March 1420): Pope Martin V: issued a Papal Bull called 'Omnium Plasmatoris Domini' authorizing the killing of all supporters of reformers like Hus and Wycliffe. The Hussite Wars, also called the Bohemian Wars or the Hussite Revolution, were fought between the Hussites and various European monarchs who sought to enforce the authority of the Roman Catholic church on them.

The Hussites defeated five crusades proclaimed against them by the Pope (1420, 1421, 1422, 1427 and in 1431), and intervened in the wars of neighboring countries.

However, between 1433 and 1436, the movement was split, and the Hussite movement came to an end. The Wars ended in 1434 with a peace agreement. The Hussites agreed to submit to the authority of the King of Bohemia and the Church and were allowed to practice their rites. The moderate party thus obtained the upper hand and wanted to find a compromise between the council and the Hussites. It formulated its demands in a document which was accepted by the Church of Rome in a slightly modified form, and which is known as "the compacts." The compacts, mainly founded on the articles of Prague, declare that:

1. The Holy Sacrament is to be given freely in both kinds to all Christians in Bohemia and Moravia, and to those elsewhere who adhere to the faith of these two countries.
2. All mortal sins shall be punished and extirpated by those whose office it is so to do.
3. The word of God is to be freely and truthfully preached by the priests of the Lord, and by worthy deacons.
4. The priests in the time of the law of grace shall claim no ownership of worldly possessions.

On 5 July 1436, the compacts were formally accepted and signed in Moravia, by King Sigismund, on behalf of the Hussite delegates, and by the representatives of the Roman Catholic Church.

The Czech sheep had gone astray. The church was re-united; Roman Christianity remained the dominant religion and belief system of the Europeans.

By the end of the fifteenth century the lands in the known western world were divided up by the two major religions: Roman Christianity and Islam. Judaism was confined to the Jews, many of whom lived in the Roman Christian countries either as (Conversos) converts to Roman Christianity or in ghettoes on the outskirts of its cities. They were persecuted and abused. Kingdom Christians were scattered among the countries in the Roman Empire; Muslims had conquered North Africa and most of the Iberian Peninsula since the eighth century. Portugal drove the Muslims out in 1255 and developed their naval resources while expanding their trade southward to north Africa and the Atlantic. Spain, yet to complete its full reconquest from the Muslims, also developed its naval resources and explored the seas westwards from the coasts of Africa.

The future would be based on maritime exploration and domination of a new world; south and west of Europe and anywhere that was previously unknown to them. The known world was not enough for these two major religions!

In this chapter we have looked at how Rome replaced the Hebraic roots of Christianity. At that time, the Jews were controlled by the Romans. The followers of Christ were martyred, originally by the Jews and later by the Romans, yet for believers, there is always a remnant! Later, the Romans, gained an empire that embraced the whole of Europe, and through Emperor Constantine, made Christianity a state religion, based on military might. This formed the template that would dominate the world, in competition with the Nation of Islam, Saracens (Muslims).

3

The Canaries

Prototype for the 'New World'

*15th Century: Establishment & Specifications
of New-World Culture*

As early as 1415, Portugal, (a Catholic country) invaded another continent, Africa. They gained control of Ceuta in North Africa, a commercially important city trading in gold, ivory, and slaves. The other Iberian Catholic maritime country, Castile (Spain) was also engaged in sailing south expanding its influence and trade in spices and slaves in the Canary Islands, off the west coast of Africa. The Canaries comprise 7 islands located about 100 kilometers (62 miles) west of Morocco. The main islands are (from largest to smallest) Tenerife, Fuerteventura, Gran Canaria, Lanzarote, La Palma, La Gomera and El Herero. There are also six smaller islets.

The Canary Islands were apparently known to the Carthaginians of Cadiz. The Roman writer Pliny the Elder (AD 23–79) called them "the Fortunate Islands." Genoese navigator Lancelotto Malocello is credited with the re-discovery of the Canary Islands in 1312. In 1339, Majorcan Angelino Dulcert drew the first map of the Canaries, labeling one of the islands "Lanzarote."

In the fourteenth century the people of the islands (Guanches) suffered from kidnappings and were forced into slavery by the Genoese, the Portuguese and the Spanish *razzias* (slavers). The Guanches found themselves the centre of attention to the leading maritime Catholic countries of the time: the Spanish and the Portuguese. They were part of a new venture in trading.

The process of complete conquest of these non-Europeans took almost one hundred years, from the tentative exploits of a Norman explorer (Jean Bethencourt) in 1402 to that of the military commander Fernández de Lugo in 1496.

This pattern of conquest and colonization initiated the methodology for the development of the New World; the Age of Discovery; defining the culture of the world to this day.

The first phase of the conquest would be achieved by the crown of a country engaging a non-national (foreign) entrepreneur to confirm a proposal for lands hitherto un-claimed by European powers. This venture would be immediately monitored by priests who would be seeking new souls and provide religious legitimacy for the enterprise. Jean de Bethencourt, the Norman mercenary and Gadifer de la Salle between 1402 and 1405 satisfied these criteria and subdued the islands of Lanzarote, El Hierro and Fuerteventura on behalf of the King of Spain.

On May 1, 1402, Jean de Bethencourt who possessed textile factories and dye works set sail on a ship with some eighty men from La Rochelle on the west coast of France for the Canaries which were known to be a rich source of dyes for fabrics. The expedition reached Cadiz and docked there for some time while he (and other supporters) negotiated with the king for the opportunity to settle in Lanzarote and establish his textile business based on the natural dyes extracted from the Orchilla and Cochineal moss and insect. With influential support, he successfully negotiated a contract in which he would conquer the Canaries in exchange to becoming a vassal of the Spanish King.

Procedures for conquest: Research, tales, history, and promise of great wealth!

On landing in Lanzarote on 27th February 1404, Bethencourt and his men were welcomed by the islanders who offered gifts and treated them as friends. In the previous years, Lanzarote had suffered scores of piratical raids and the inhabitants saw in Bethencourt a great chance of protection. One of the islanders who was quite clearly the local king pleaded with Bethencourt to protect them from the plunderers. In return, the king promised friendship and his submission to Bethencourt and the King of Spain 'as friend, not as subject.'

Bethencourt was delighted with the peaceful reception and the avoidance of bloodshed. The Normans established themselves on the south of the island of Lanzarote where they constructed a fortress detailed one of his colleagues as its commander and founded the Bishopric of Rubicon.

The friendly welcome by natives was taken as license to conquer and establish military control by:

- Building a fort and appointing the island's military commander

    Having put in place both physical (the fort) and institutional arrangements; the church, Bethencourt decided to set sail on a reconnaissance trip to the nearby island of Fuerteventura. That trip proved to be a disaster. Bethencourt immediately returned to Lanzarote only to discover that many of his men had already mutinied there. The only thing to be done was to return to Spain and replenish stocks and men as soon as possible. He appointed his second-in-command, Gadifer de la Salle, governor of Lanzarote, in his absence.

- If there is mutiny, restore order with state support

    Institutional accolades granted to the leader and provision of heavily armed and well-manned naval support from the Crown to subdue a mutiny.

    On his return to Spain, Bethencourt received a hero's welcome. King Henry bestowed the government of the islands to Bethencourt, gave him the right to his own coinage, one fifth [Gen 47:23] of the exports and furnished him with 20,000 maravedis to pay for a second expedition. A heavily armed and well-manned ship was immediately dispatched to Lanzarote to help Gadifer.

- Rewards—Fame, fortune and a new contract and re-investment from the Crown in exchange for royal rewards (financial and colonial)

While Bethencourt was in Spain a power struggle had broken out on Lanzarote between his officers, Berthin and Gadifer. Guanche leaders were drawn into the conflict and scores of Spaniards and islanders died in what was to become a bloodbath in the first few months of Bethencourt's absence. Treason and treachery were rife among both the conquistadores and the Canarians.

It was only with the return of Bethencourt that peace was restored to the troubled island. To quell any further uprising, Bethencourt captured the local king of Lanzarote, Guardarfia, and ten of his followers. And on

February 27, 1404, according to Bethencourt's chroniclers, the people of Lanzarote surrendered.

The Franciscan priest, Le Verrier baptised Guadarfia as Luis, (his name was changed to a European 'slave' name as with Moses and Daniel in the Bible) and soon after, all the islanders followed suit and were initiated into the Catholic faith. The island of Lanzarote, the first of the Canary Islands, had now come under the direct control of Spain with Bethencourt as governor.

Non-Europeans suffered more than Europeans and lost literally everything.

El Hierro: In 1405 the scattered natives submitted to the Spanish under Jean de Béthencourt. In return for control over the island, Béthencourt promised to respect the liberty of the natives, but his son eventually broke his promise, selling many of the *bimbaches* into slavery. It was one of the first islands to be re-populated with Norman and Castilian immigrants/settlers.

Fuerteventura: Bethencourt's next move was to be the conquest of Fuerteventura.

It was not until 1405 that Fuerteventura was finally conquered, largely due to the influence of the two priestesses, who persuaded Ayoze and Guize, the two kings, to surrender and accept baptism. Conquests Completed: Lanzarote: 1404, El Hierro: 1405, Fuerteventura:1405

Upon examining the conquest of these islands and their people, one observes the application of a pattern that would be applied in future. These actions would be repeated in many of the future colonial exploits, and the method of addressing them would have their origins/precedents replicated in this short period of time; 1402–1405.

Charismatic adventurers willing to seek out and discover new things- products, places, and people, for financial gain and recognition, on behalf of any flag that would respond to the challenge. They would seek to acquire gold, lands, trade, and slaves (in the name of religious beliefs) and would employ the following methodology to conquer new lands.

1. Research: Prior knowledge, or speculation, or travellers' tales, other nations trading successes: anything that would yield a profit that originated beyond the established geographical boundaries!
2. Adventurers seeking to provide a new product that was scarce but was increasing in demand.
3. Sponsors: financial and institutional with connections to flags of support.
4. Religion: Institutional presence of religious personnel for conversion and submission.

5. The Crown would take ownership of the land and the people that they are going to conquer.
6. Encourage European immigration/occupation to secure the territory to establish ownership.
7. Agriculture: Development of produce for export and trade.

Rebranding of the land:

- The creation of the island's capital Betancuria, situated in a fertile inland valley, and less prone to pirate attacks that on its vulnerable coastline.
    - ▶ Import new skilled craftsmen to transform the country: masons, carpenters, metal workers, etc.
- Religion of the European implemented; the island's first church, the Santa Maria de Betancuria 1418, where the islanders' spiritual needs were catered for. A tithe of 10% of all merchandise and agricultural produce was payable to the church and
- 20% to the ruler of the island. (Referencing Gen 47:26 And Joseph made it a law over the land of Egypt unto this day, *that* Pharaoh should have the fifth *part;* except the land of the priests only, *which* became not Pharaoh's.)
- Re-naming the islands and the towns to reflect European ownership and religion.

Bethencourt remained on the islands until 1412 when he returned permanently to his lands in Normandy, leaving Maciot de Bethencourt in charge of his possessions. The Bethencourt era ended in 1418, (the year Portugal invaded and conquered Ceuta in North Africa). From then on the King of Castile assumed greater control. Between 1418 and 1445 dominion over the islands changed hands on several occasions. However, the ownership of the lands had been the subject of dispute between the Kingdom of Castile (Spain) and Portugal, the two Catholic nations. This situation persisted for decades till in 1434 the Portuguese, after a failed mission against the natives in Gran Canaria, plundered the Castilian missions on Lanzarote and Fuerteventura. The Castilian Bishop lodged a complaint, which was supported by the Archbishop of Seville, to the Pope informing him of the pillaging carried out by the Portuguese pirates.

At this point it is important to look at the Roman Catholic Popes of this period in history. From the election of Pope Martin V of the Council of Constance in 1417 to the Reformation in the sixteenth century western

Christianity was largely free from schism. There were many important divisions over the direction of the religion, but these were resolved through the then-settled procedures of the Papal conclave.

The popes of this period reflected the College of Cardinals that elected them. The College was dominated by cardinal nephews (relatives of the popes that elevated them), crown-cardinals (representatives of the Catholic monarchies of Europe), and members of the powerful Italian families. The wealthy popes and cardinals from families such as the Borgias and Medicis increasingly supported Renaissance art and architecture.

During this period, the papacy took an increasingly active role in European wars and diplomacy. Popes were more frequently called upon to arbitrate disputes between competing colonial powers than to resolve complicated theological disputes. To the extent that this period is relevant to modern Catholic dogma, it is in Papal supremacy. None of these popes have been canonised as a saint, or even regarded as Blessed or Venerable.

This second period (1478–1496) of the Spanish conquest of the Canaries was different from the first in several ways: This aspect, too was an extension of the precedent for the Age of Discovery!

- The Catholic monarchs commanded and armed their invading forces.
- Funding for the enterprise was the responsibility of the Crown and of individuals interested in the economic exploitation of the island's resources.
- The islands involved, Gran Canaria, La Palma and Tenerife had larger populations and offered the best economic rewards.
- The Guanches of the three islands, but particularly those of Gran Canaria and Tenerife, offered a clear and prolonged resistance to the conquest.

Conquest of Gran Canaria (1478–1487)

Spain maintained its belligerent posture and control of the other islands, for another forty-five years before they could begin the completion of the conquest of the people of the four remaining islands that comprise the Canaries. La Gomera, conquered in 1450 however, was a negotiated component of the first stage conquest.

Guayarmina Semidán, considered to be queen of Gran Canaria, surrendered at Ansite Fortress.

- Tenerife (in 1494–1496) Germ warfare. Despite the Spanish military and technological advantage over the primitive Guanches, it was not until the Spanish were able to gain a foothold on the coast of the island

and introduced their own animals and germs that they were able to gain victory. With the defeat of Tenerife in 1496, the Canaries Archipelago was integrated into the Kingdom of Castile. The *Conquista realenga* (Royal Conquest) took place between 1478 and 1496.

Conquests Completed: The Canaries are Spanish.

- Lanzarote: 1404, El Hierro & Fuerteventura:1405.
- Grand Canary: 1483, La Gomera 1488, La Palma—1492–1493, Tenerife: 1494–1496

This open competition: Catholic naval nations; Portugal and Spain against the islanders of the Canaries continued for years. What was the competition—more lands, trade, and non-European slaves; or was it more trade, non-European slaves, and lands? A decision on the priority resulted in the same outcome- slavery and misery for the islanders and outlets for economic expansion and European occupation. This was tempered by the consequential increase in the spreading of Catholic Christianity to heathens and infidels, many of whom later embraced Roman Christianity.

In summary, the procedures identified above can be codified as a practice, a manual or precedents for the conquest and control/colonisation of non-European lands and people:

Precedents:

1. Adventurer's desire for fame & fortune:
    - ▶ Engage with sympathetic influential religious personnel (monks);
    - ▶ Kidnap and baptise natives.
    - ▶ Use them as trophies (for the Crown).
    - ▶ Bring back new plant life (setting new trends to follow and exploit).
2. Consider friendly natives' welcome as a boost for easy conquest (never with grace and equity).
3. Restore rebellion among Europeans according to European-only rules.
4. Secure contracts and (if necessary) re-investment from the Crown.
5. Natives only to be punished for any social disturbances (despite Europeans' participation and involvement).
6. New identity imposed on natives
    - ▶ New foreign owner (Crown)
    - ▶ New laws

- New religion
- New names.

7. Europeans are encouraged and invited to settle and occupy their new countries and make fortunes, with no or little regard for the indigenous peoples.
8. European disturbances among themselves were to be addressed according to 'Europeans-only' rules.
9. Fame and Fortune adventurers given termed contracts with fabulously rich rewards: no questions asked.
10. Make Covenants (equitable contracts) with the natives; with no intention of keeping them:
    - Break Covenants
    - Ambush native leaders on their way to planned meetings
    - Sell natives as slaves (when victory is established)
    - Integrate some natives into the European society (as second-class citizens or worse)
    - Germ warfare: Introduce when the military cannot succeed in battle (within the given time and budget).

This system of governance was developed in which the crown and the church worked in unison; the crown being the agency by which the church would become joint heirs to the lands and peoples across the globe, beginning in the Canaries and including the countries yet to be acquired. After almost one hundred years of conflict, the Spanish finally conquered the Canaries. de Lugo consolidated it by building another fort (Santa Cruz) in the capital of Tenerife. The *conquistador's* capital remains Tenerife's capital to this day. For the people of the island, Federico de Lugo's victory meant enslavement and extermination through disease and overwork. In his book[1] "Anarchists Library Precedent for the New World," John Connor, the author, writes:

> "Ultimately seven sugar mills were established on the island, and we have no reason to doubt the brutalities meted out against plantation workers so graphically described in Voltaire's Candide weren't also meted out to the remnant Guanches 200 years earlier. The survival option was in many ways worse than this, the adoption of Christian religion and the mask of Leviathan. Those that

---

1. Connor, Anarchists Library Precedent for the New World,

were not slaves opted to be slave drivers, traders in wine and human misery on the African main land. Bar a few local idiosyncrasies, they lost their faith, their language, their spirit of brotherhood and independence was reduced to the acquisitive individualism of their conquerors ('I owe fealty to the king alone and he is far away'), and ultimately, they all but lost to history as a distinct culture: There were originally 100,000 Guanches. By 1530, they were reduced to a diseased, apathetic handful; by 1600, there remained only some mixed-blood [sic] Hispano-Guanches, and soon even this remnant vanished. Today all that survives of them are some mummified nobles hidden in caves and a half-dozen sentences written in their otherwise lost language.".

The template for the implementation of the New World Order for ownership, religion, people, and economy was developed and completed in the Canaries. Indeed, the Canary Islands was the launch pad for Columbus' first trip across the Atlantic Ocean and modern colonisation initiating what is also known as the Age of Discovery.

4

The New World Order

Fifty nine years of Papal Global Leadership (1434–1493)

IN THE LAST CHAPTER we read how the two Roman Catholic countries (Portugal and Spain) competed for land and trade in the Canaries. Pope Eugene IV, having been invited into the fray, began to bring order in 1434, and took the initiative to divide the whole world between the Portuguese and the Spanish. Eugene was also concerned for the welfare of the people of the lands that the two nations would conquer in the laws he passed concerning them. This was the beginning of Papal world order which lasted until 1493. The Pope at once responded to this 'New-World' request from Portugal and Spain to mediate between them. In his concern for the baptized islanders, he passed two Papal Bulls: *Regimini Gregis* on 29 September 1434, and *Creator Omnium*, on 17 December 1434, forbidding any further raids on the Canaries and ordered the immediate manumission of all Christian converts enslaved during the attack. The penalty for enslaving newly converted Christians, was to stand until the captive was restored to their liberty and possessions.[1] J. Gordon Melton (American Religious Scholar, Baylor University) says that the Bull neglected to provide similar protection to those resisting conversion. It is noteworthy that Pope Eugene did not mention the name of either nation although both Portugal and Spain were engaged in the enslaving of these non-Europeans. He also and specifically attributed

---

1. Melton, Faiths Across Time, 975

personal responsibility for the committing of these sins: "*to rebuke each sinner about his sin.*"

Despite the issuance of these Bulls, Portuguese soldiers continued to raid the Canary Islands during 1435. Resistance to Papal authority by Catholic nations, would be a recurring feature. Nevertheless, the Pope persisted in his role as head of the church and the person to whom nations would submit for their spiritual leadership and doctrine. Pope Eugene issued a further edict (Sicut Dudum 1435) that prohibited wars being waged against the islands and affirming the ban on enslavement.

The text of Sicut Dudum reads as follows:

> SS Eugenius IV Sicut Dudum, January 13, 1435,
>
> *Eugene, Bishop, Servant of the Servants of God, To our venerable brothers, peace, and apostolic benediction, etcetera.*
>
> *Not long ago, we learned from our brother Ferdinand, bishop at Rubicon and representative of the faithful who are residents of the Canary Islands, and from messengers sent by them to the Apostolic See, and from other trustworthy informers, the following facts: in the said islands—some called Lanzarote—and other nearby islands, the inhabitants, imitating the natural law alone, and not having known previously any sect of apostates or heretics, have a short time since been led into the Orthodox Catholic Faith with the aid of God's mercy. Nevertheless, with the passage of time, it has happened that in some of the said islands, because of a lack of suitable governors and defenders to direct those who live there to a proper observance of the Faith in things spiritual and temporal, and to protect valiantly their property and goods, some Christians (we speak of this with sorrow), with fictitious reasoning and seizing and opportunity, have approached said islands by ship, and with armed forces taken captive and even carried off to lands overseas very many persons of both sexes, taking advantage of their simplicity. 2. Some of these already baptized people were; others were even at times tricked and deceived by the promise of Baptism, having been made a promise of safety that was not kept. They have deprived the natives of the property, or turned it to their own use, and have subjected some of the inhabitants of said islands to perpetual slavery, sold them to other persons, and committed other various illicit and evil deeds against them, because of which very many of those remaining on said islands, and condemning such slavery, have remained involved in their former errors, having drawn back their intention to receive Baptism, thus offending the majesty of God, putting their souls in danger, and causing no little harm to the Christian religion3. Therefore, We, to whom it*

pertains, especially in respect to the aforesaid Matters, to rebuke each sinner about his sin, and not wishing to pass by dissimulating, and desiring—as is expected from the pastoral office we hold—as far as possible, to provide salutarily, with a holy and fatherly concern, for the sufferings of the inhabitants, beseech the Lord, and exhort, through the sprinkling of the Blood of Jesus Christ shed for their sins, one and all, temporal princes, lords, captains, armed men, barons, soldiers, nobles, communities, and all others of every kind among the Christian faithful of whatever state, grade, or condition, that they themselves desist from the aforementioned deeds, cause those subject to them to desist from them, and restrain them rigorously. 4. And no less do We order and command all and each of the faithful of each sex, within the space of fifteen days of the publication of these letters in the place where they live, that they restore to their earlier liberty all and each person of either sex who were once residents of said Canary Islands, and made captives since the time of their capture, and who have been made subject to slavery. These people are to be totally and perpetually free, and are to be let go without the exaction or reception of money. If this is not done when the fifteen days have passed, they incur the sentence of excommunication by the act itself, from which they cannot be absolved, except at the point of death, even by the Holy See, or by any Spanish bishop, or by the aforementioned Ferdinand, unless they have first given freedom to these captive persons and restored their goods. We will that like sentence of excommunication be incurred by one and all who attempt to capture, sell, or subject to slavery, baptized residents of the Canary Islands, or those who are freely seeking Baptism, from which excommunication cannot be absolved except as was stated above. 5. Those who humbly and efficaciously obey these, our exhortations and commands deserve, in addition to our favor, and that of the Apostolic See, and the blessings which follow there from, but are to be possessors of eternal happiness and to be placed at the right hand of God, etcetera SS Eugenius IV Sicut Dudum January 13, 1435, Given at Florence, January 13, in the Year of Our Lord, 1435[2]

Uneasy lies the head that wears the crown: The two combatting Catholic Christian nations, Portugal, and Spain, took their individual claims to the Pope. This time, Portugal appealed to the Pope, saying that he responded to the claims that Seville made and had not considered their position concerning Africa in his Bull. The Pope listened to their claim and made some adjustments to his earlier Bull. This resulted in the issuance of further

---

2. www. papalencyclicals

Bulls, supplying the means of satisfying the other side—Portugal. This contest between these two Catholic nations would persist until a 'fair' solution could be reached and agreed on the specific issues of trade, land ownership and slavery.

Pope Eugene tempered "Sicut Dudum" with another Bull (15 September 1436), this time allowing the Portuguese to conquer any unconverted parts of the Canary Islands.

Not totally satisfied with the Pope's position on slavery, Portugal persisted in its quest for increased trade and a legitimization of its slave trade, this time its trade in Africans. In 1441 following the arrival of the first African slaves in Lisbon during 1441 Prince Henry asked Pope Eugene to designate Portugal's raids along the West African coast as a 'crusade'. Such a consequence would be the legitimization of enslavement for captives taken during the 'crusade'. On 19 December 1442 Eugene replied by issuing another Papal Bull "*Illius qui*" in which he granted full remission of sins to those who took part in any expeditions against the Saracens (Islam), a competing religious belief.

Armed with these supporting Bulls, Prince Henry the Navigator of Portugal established a trading post (factory) on the island of Arguin off the West Coast of Africa in 1445. On it they acquired gum Arabic and slaves for Portugal. They brought in copperware, cloth, tools, wine, and horses and later included arms and ammunition. In exchange, they received gold from the mines of Akan, Guinea, and ivory. The expanding market opportunities in Europe and the Mediterranean resulted in increased trade across the Sahara. At that time there was a small market for African slaves as domestic workers in Europe and as workers on the sugar plantations of the Mediterranean and later Madeira. However, the Portuguese found they could make considerable amounts of gold by transporting slaves from one trading post to another, along the Atlantic coast of Africa. Muslim merchants had a high demand for slaves, which were used as porters on the trans-Saharan routes and for sale in the Islamic Empire. By 1448 Portugal had completed the construction of the first Slave Castle in Arguin, Northwest Africa and from 1455, eight hundred slaves were shipped from Arguin to Portugal every year.

While the Portuguese were engaged in trade with the Muslim merchants, Crusaders were engaged in a war with the Muslims of the Ottoman Empire for Constantinople. In late spring of 1452 Byzantine Emperor Constantine XI wrote to Pope Nicholas V for help against the impending siege by Ottoman Sultan Mehmed II.

Pope Nicholas V issued the Papal Bull "*Dum Diversas*" (18 June 1452) authorizing King Alfonso V of Portugal to "*attack, conquer, and subjugate Saracens, pagans and other enemies of Christ wherever they may be found.*"[3]

The geographical area of the concession given in the Bull is not explicit, but historian Richard Raiswell believes that it clearly referred to the recently discovered lands along the coast of West Africa. Portuguese ventures were intended to compete with the Muslim trans-Sahara caravans, which held a monopoly on West African gold and ivory. The Portuguese claimed territorial rights along the African coast by virtue of having invested time and treasure in discovering it. At the same time the Castilian claim for trading in Africa was based on their being the heirs of their Visigoth ancestors. The Visigoth Kingdom or Kingdom of the Visigoths was a kingdom that occupied what is now southwestern France and the Iberian Peninsula from the 5th to the 8th centuries. In 1454 a fleet of caravels from Seville and Cadiz traded along the African coast and upon their return, were intercepted by a Portuguese squadron. Enrique IV of Castile (Spain) threatened war. Afonso V of Portugal appealed to the Pope for moral support of Portugal's right to a monopoly of trade in lands it discovered. In response to that appeal, Pope Nicholas V prepared yet another Bull: "*Romanus Pontifex*," issued on January 8, 1455, endorsing Portuguese possession of the African town, Ceuta (which they already held since 1415), and the exclusive rights to trade, navigation, and fishing in the discovered lands, and reaffirmed the previous Papal Bull '*Dum Diversas*'. It granted permission to Afonso and his heirs to "*. . . make purchases and sales of any things and goods, and victuals whatsoever, as it may seem fit, with any Saracens and infidels in said regions; . . . provided they be not iron instruments, wood used for construction, cordage, ships, and any kinds of armour.*"[4] This Bull Romanus Pontifex was the first time that the papacy had identified a named people group: "*Guineamen and other negroes*" for this special treatment. The only other people group that received special discriminatory attention by the papacy as it led all other European nations, was the Jews! The Jews, however, have had an exceptionally long and controlled relationship with the Europeans, dating back to biblical times. By the fifteenth century, Jews were finally confronted with the Inquisition and given the choice—expulsion or conversion. At various times, Jews had played key roles in various sectors of the society in finance, medicine, intellectual and academic activities, but they were never treated as slaves.

---

3. Dum Diversas. www.papalencyclicals.com
4. Dum Diversas. www.papalencyclicals.com

Romanus Pontifex conferred exclusive trading rights to the Portuguese between Morocco and the Indies with the rights to conquer and convert the inhabitants. A significant concession given by Pope Nicholas in a brief which was issued to King Alfonso in 1454, extended the rights granted to existing territories to all those that might be taken in the future.[5]

It has been argued that collectively the two Bulls issued by Nicholas gave the Portuguese the rights to acquire slaves along the African coast by force or trade. The concessions given in them were confirmed by Bulls issued by Pope Callixtus III (*Inter Caetera quae* in 1456), Sixtus IV, (*Aeterni regis* in 1481), [and renewed even as late as 1514 by Leo X], and they became the models for subsequent Bulls issued by Pope Alexander VI: *Eximiae devotionis* (3 May 1493), Inter Caetera, (4 May 1493) and *Dudum Siquidem* (23 September 1493), in which he conferred similar rights to Spain relating to the newly discovered lands in the Americas.

In summary:

- Diversas 1452 "In 1452, Nicholas V issued the Papal Bull '*Dum Diversas*', granting the King of Portugal the right to reduce any "*Saracens, pagans and any other unbelievers*" to hereditary slavery. "*Dum Diversas*" legitimised the colonial slave trade that begun around this time with the expeditions by Henry the Navigator to find a sea route to India, financed with African slaves. This approval of slavery was reaffirmed and extended in his "*Romanus Pontifex*" of 1455."[6]

- "*Romanus Pontifex*" 8 January 1455: The Bull issued by Nicholas reaffirmed "*Dum Diversas*" and sanctioned the purchase of black slaves from "the infidel."

- The Papal Bull "*Aeterni Regis*" 21 June 1481 issued by Pope Sixtus IV confirmed the substance of the Treaty of Alcáçovas, between Spain and Portugal of 1479, reiterating that treaty's confirmation of Castile in its possession of the Canary Islands and its granting to Portugal all further territorial acquisitions made by Christian powers in Africa and eastward to the Indies.

As a consequence of the formation of the New World Order, these four Papal Bulls have been identified as the instruments that inscribed the establishment of a New World Culture.

---

5. Pope Nicholas V, Wikipedia
6. US Supreme Court, Johnson v M'Intosh 1823, Doctrine of Discovery

"**Culture:** *The integrated pattern of human knowledge, belief, and behavior that depends upon the capacity for learning and transmitting knowledge to succeeding generations.*"[7]

"Romanus Pontifex," January 8, 1455, specifies people groups and defines the nature of the relationship between Europeans and others. There are two people groups: Europeans (Portuguese currently and Spanish) and infidels and pagans. However, there was a caveat concerning the Indians whom they expected did worship the name of Christ. As such the Pope anticipated that they would therefore be amenable to an alliance with them in the war *against the Saracens* and . . . to subdue certain other gentile or pagan peoples:

> "*Moreover, since, some time ago, it had come to the knowledge of the said infante that never, or at least not within the memory of men, had it been customary to sail on this ocean sea toward the southern and eastern shores, and that it was so unknown to us westerners that we had no certain knowledge of the peoples of those parts, believing that he would best perform his duty to God in this matter, if by his effort and industry that sea might become navigable as far as to the* Indians *who are said to worship the name of Christ, and that thus he might be able to enter into relation with them, and to incite them to aid the Christians against the Saracens and other such enemies of the faith, and might also be able forthwith to subdue certain gentile or pagan peoples, living between, who are entirely free from infection by the sect of the most impious Mahomet, and to preach and cause to be preached to them the unknown but most sacred name of Christ, strengthened, however, always by the royal authority, he has not ceased for twenty-five years past to send almost yearly an army of the peoples of the said kingdoms with the greatest labor, danger, and expense, in very swift ships called caravels, to explore the sea and coast lands toward the south and the Antarctic pole. And so it came to pass that when a number of ships of this kind had explored and taken possession of very many harbors, islands, and seas, they at length came to the province of Guinea, and having taken possession of some islands and harbors and the sea adjacent to that province, sailing farther they came to the mouth of a certain great river commonly supposed to be the Nile, and war was waged for some years against the peoples of those parts in the name of the said King Alfonso and of the infante, and in it very many islands in that neighborhood were subdued and peacefully possessed, as they are still possessed together with the adjacent sea. Thence also*

---

7. Merriam Webster Dictionary

many Guineamen and other negroes, taken by force, and some by barter of unprohibited articles, or by other lawful contract of purchase, have been sent to the said kingdoms. A large number of these have been converted to the Catholic faith, and it is hoped, by the help of divine mercy, that if such progress be continued with them, either those peoples will be converted to the faith or at least the souls of many of them will be gained for Christ."[8]

1. Saracens (followers of Mahomet; Muslims): The Roman Catholic church had by this time initiated many crusades against the Muslims and at the time of writing this Bull (1452), were involved in a war in Constantinople) Portugal had already achieved its Reconquista (1249); Castile (Spain) would not regain their country until 1492.

   "We have lately heard, not without great joy and gratification, how our beloved son, the noble personage Henry, infante of Portugal, uncle of our most dear son in Christ, the illustrious Alfonso, king of the kingdoms of Portugal and Algarve, treading in the footsteps of John, of famous memory, king of the said kingdoms, his father, and greatly inflamed with zeal for the salvation of souls and with fervor of faith, as a Catholic and true soldier of Christ, the Creator of all things, and a most active and courageous defender and intrepid champion of the faith in Him, has aspired from his early youth with his utmost might to cause the most glorious name of the said Creator to be published, extolled, and revered throughout the whole world, even in the most remote and undiscovered places, and also to bring into the bosom of his faith the perfidious enemies of him and of the life-giving Cross by which we have been redeemed, namely the Saracens and all other infidels whatsoever, [and how] after the city of Ceuta, situated in Africa, had been subdued by the said King John to his dominion, and after many wars had been waged, sometimes in person, by the said infante, although in the name of the said King John, against the enemies and infidels aforesaid."

2. Guineamen and negroes: They would be treated as heathens. Their lands would be invaded and taken for a possession by Papal decree and King Alfonso and the Portuguese nation would be their true lords. The Guinea men and negroes' possessions would be taken, and they would be traded purchased or bartered. The Pope decreed such laws that disinherited the Guineamen and negroes (sub-Saharan Africans) from everything they owned and declared themselves "true lords over

---

8. Romanus Pontifex, www.papalencyclicals.net

them." He also recognised that at the time of their capture, they were not slaves and that it would be imperative that he reduce them to perpetual slavery.

The Pope continued to declare in part—

> "We [therefore] weighing all and singular the premises with due meditation, and noting that since we had formerly by other letters of ours granted among other things free and ample faculty to the aforesaid King Alfonso—to invade, search out, capture, vanquish, and subdue all Saracens and pagans whatsoever, and other enemies of Christ wheresoever placed, and the kingdoms, dukedoms, principalities, dominions, possessions, and all movable and immovable goods whatsoever held and possessed by them and to reduce their persons to perpetual slavery, and to apply and appropriate to himself and his successors the kingdoms, dukedoms, counties, principalities, dominions, possessions, and goods, and to convert them to his and their use and profit."[9]

3. Methodology for maintaining Guineamen and other negroes in perpetual slavery:

> Exclusive rights of lordship: over all nations and or individuals and
>
> Forbidden: teaching of constructive or technical skills to the negroes (infidels) by Europeans. That knowledge could be construed as dangerous to the safety of the Europeans.

> . . .lest strangers induced by covetousness should sail to those parts, and desiring to usurp to themselves the perfection, fruit, and praise of this work, or at least to hinder it, should therefore, either for the sake of gain or through malice, carry or transmit iron, arms, wood used for construction, and other things and goods prohibited to be carried to infidels or should teach those infidels the art of navigation, whereby they would become more powerful and obstinate enemies to the king and infante, and the prosecution of this enterprise would either be hindered, or would perhaps entirely fail, not without great offense to God and great reproach to all Christianity, to prevent this and to conserve their right and possession, [the said king and infante] under certain most severe penalties then expressed, have prohibited and in general have ordained that none, unless with their sailors and ships and on payment of a certain tribute and with an express license previously obtained from the said king or infant."

With regard to the term 'Perpetual Slavery', the Papal Bull states:

---

9. Romanus Pontifex, www.papalencyclicals.net

> "We [therefore] weighing all and singular the premises with due meditation, and noting that since we had formerly by other letters of ours granted among other things free and ample faculty to the aforesaid King Alfonso—to invade, search out, capture, vanquish, and subdue all Saracens and pagans whatsoever, and other enemies of Christ wheresoever placed, and the kingdoms, dukedoms, principalities, dominions, possessions, and all movable and immovable goods whatsoever held and possessed by them and to reduce their persons to perpetual slavery..."

Regarding 'Perpetual Ownership' (Slavery; Colonialism—uncertain future, restricted elevation, profit, and progress) the Bull continues:

> ..."and to apply and appropriate to himself and his successors the kingdoms, dukedoms, counties, principalities, dominions, possessions, and goods, and to convert them to his and their use and profit—by having secured the said faculty, the said King Alfonso, or, by his authority, the aforesaid infante, justly and lawfully has acquired and possessed, and doth possess, these islands, lands, harbors, and seas, and they do of right belong and pertain to the said King Alfonso and his successors, nor without special license from King Alfonso and his successors themselves has any other even of the faithful of Christ been entitled hitherto, nor is he by any means now entitled lawfully to meddle therewith—in order that King Alfonso himself and his successors and the infant might be able the more zealously to pursue and may pursue this most pious and noble work, and most worthy of perpetual remembrance (which, since the salvation of souls, increase of the faith, and overthrow of its enemies may be procured thereby, we regard as a work wherein the glory of God, and faith in Him, and His commonwealth, the Universal church, are concerned)"[10]

Guineamen and other negroes were for the expressed purpose of conversion for profit. All their property, belongings and even themselves were decreed as being '*of right belonged and pertain to King Alfonso and his successors*'.

In these Papal Bulls, the decrees relating to the domination by Europeans over non-Europeans (including those yet to be 'discovered') in their explorations seem to be:

Conversion to the Roman Catholic Religion of the Europeans; that Europeans would be 'perpetually lords over Guineamen and other negroes. Europeans would have the lawful right of total unequivocal conquest (of the

---

10. Romanus Pontifex, www.papalencyclicals.net

property and dominions of the Guineamen and negroes.) There would also be limited opportunity for changing their status quo.

The understanding of salvation was based on an understanding of what it meant to be a '*Catholic*' and '*true soldier of* Christ'. This understanding seems to be at variance with a biblical definition of '*soldier of Christ*' as found in 2Tim 2:1–6.

> *1 Thou therefore, my son, be strong in the grace that is in Christ Jesus. 2 And the things that thou hast heard of me among many witnesses, the same commit thou to faithful men, who shall be able to teach others also. 3 Thou therefore endure hardness, as a good soldier of Jesus Christ.*
>
> *4 No man that warreth entangleth himself with the affairs of this life; that he may please him who hath chosen him to be a soldier. 5 And if a man also strive for masteries, yet is he not crowned, except he strive lawfully. 6 The husbandman that laboureth must be first partaker of the fruits.*

Within the context of Romanus Pontifex, the Roman Catholic Church was the source of salvation (and not faith in Jesus Christ alone). A penalty for disobeying the laws of the Papal Bull would be excommunication, which is the harshest penalty. The Pope instituted the full force of the agencies of the law (Notary Public), the church (the seal of episcopal or any superior ecclesiastical court.) Being excommunicated from the Roman Catholic Church meant that there was no hiding place; if he were not apprehended on earth, the Papal Bull states that:

> . . ."*he will incur the wrath of Almighty God and of the blessed apostles Peter and Paul.*"
>
> "*And we decree that whosoever shall infringe these orders [shall incur the following penalties], besides the punishments pronounced by law against those who carry arms and other prohibited things to any of the Saracens, which we wish them to incur by so doing; if they be single persons, they shall incur the sentence of excommunication; if a community or corporation of a city, castle, village, or place, that city, castle, village, or place shall be thereby subject to the interdict; and we decree further that transgressors, collectively or individually, shall not be absolved from the sentence of excommunication, nor be able to obtain the relaxation of this interdict, by apostolic or any others In authority, unless they shall first have made due satisfaction for their transgressions to Alfonso himself and his successors and to the infante, or shall have amicably agreed with them thereupon.*

> *Therefore let no one infringe or with rash boldness contravene this our declaration, constitution, gift, grant, appropriation, decree, supplication, exhortation, injunction, inhibition, mandate, and will. But if anyone should presume to do so, be it known to him that he will incur the wrath of Almighty God and of the blessed apostles Peter and Paul. Given at Rome, at Saint Peter's, on the eighth day of January, in the year of the incarnation of our Lord one thousand our hundred and fifty-four, and in the eighth year of our pontificate. On 8 January 1455 both Portugal and Castile (Spain) ratified this Bull Romanus Pontifex."*[11]

In Spain, sixty years earlier, there was an outbreak of anti-Semitism where hundreds of Jews were killed, and a synagogue destroyed. Jews in the large cities of Cordoba, Valencia and Barcelona were not spared, instead they were offered conversion to the Roman Catholic faith. Consequently, there was mass conversion of thousands of surviving Jews who felt it safer to remain in their new religion. Thus, after 1391, a new socio-religious group appeared: the *Conversos* or *New Christians*. With the increasing success of the Spanish Reconquista programme, the followers of the other competing 'world religions', at the time, were offered the same opportunity of conversion to the Roman Catholic religion. Many Muslims accepted the offer of conversion. Those who accepted were called *Moriscos*.

However, in the fifteenth century the increasingly confident Spaniards felt that they could not trust the Jewish Conversos nor the Islamic Moriscos, so in 1478, King Ferdinand II of Aragon and Queen Isabella of Castile established the Spanish Inquisition. The Inquisition would be staffed by clergy and orders of the church and was intended to primarily identify heretics among those who converted from Judaism and Islam to Catholicism. This was the first initiative of the state taking control of a religious function. All earlier inquisitions were implemented completely under the authority of the Holy See. Following a petition from the Spanish crowns, Pope Sixtus IV issued a Bull in 1478 to set up a Holy Office of the Inquisition in Castile. The Papal Bull gave the sovereigns full powers to name inquisitors, but the papacy kept the right to formally appoint the royal nominees. The Pope also granted the Catholic Kings the right of patronage over the ecclesiastical establishment in Granada and the Canary Islands, which meant the control of the state in religious affairs. It was the system whereby the state controlled major appointments of church officials and the management of church revenues, thereby providing the subsidies for missionary activities in the newly conquered and discovered territories.

---

11. Romanus Pontifex, www.papalencyclicals.net

The Treaty of Alcacovas in 1479 settled the disputes between Castile and Portugal over the control of the Atlantic, in which Castilian control of the Canary Islands was recognized but which also confirmed Portuguese possession of the Azores, Madeira, the Cape Verde islands, off the coast of Guinea and gave them rights to lands discovered and yet to be discovered. This treaty was ratified by the Papal Bull "*Aeterni Regis*" in 1481, issued by Pope Sixtus IV'.

Spain smelt success in their Reconquista against the Saracens and having sorted out its issues with Portugal turned their attention to the 'enemies within'. Ferdinand and Isabella ordered the expulsion from Spain of all Jews and Muslims. People who converted to Catholicism were not subject to expulsion, but between 1480 and 1492 hundreds of those who had converted, the Conversos and Moriscos, were accused of secretly practicing their original religion and arrested, imprisoned, interrogated under torture, and in some cases burned to death, in both Castile and Aragon.

In 1492 the monarchs issued a decree of expulsion of Jews, known formally as the Alhambra Decree which gave Jews in Spain four months to either convert to Catholicism or leave Spain. Tens of thousands of Jews emigrated to other lands such as Portugal, North Africa, the Low Countries, Italy and even the Ottoman Empire.

The 'enemies within'; having been expelled, Spain then turned its attention to its overseas expansion in competition with Portugal. This required Papal intervention, acting as the World Trade Organiser, that the two nations respected. The negotiations took all year to be completed. During that year, to obtain some lasting agreement, the Pope issued three Papal Bulls commonly called the Bulls of Donation delivered in May 1493 which purported to grant overseas territories to Portugal and the Catholic Monarchs of Spain. The two countries rejected the Bulls.

The fourth Bull "*Dudum Siquidem*" (23 September 1493), increased the rights of Spain to the prejudice of Portugal. The specific mention of India caused consternation in Portugal, which sought further clarity. The Pope refused to reconsider his position. As a result, King John II of Portugal negotiated directly with Ferdinand and Isabella, accepting the Bull, "*Inter Caetera,*" *May 1493* as the starting point. This resulted in an agreement to move the boundary line established in "*Inter Caetera*" 270 leagues further to the west, given effect as the 1494 Treaty of Tordesillas. This Treaty between Spain and Portugal divided the newly discovered lands outside Europe between the Portuguese Empire and the Crown of Castile, along a meridian 370 leagues west of the Cape Verde islands, off the west coast of Africa. This line of demarcation was about halfway between the Cape Verde islands (already Portuguese) and the islands entered by Christopher Columbus on his first voyage (claimed for Castile and León), named in the treaty as Cipangu and Antilia (Cuba and Hispaniola).

The lands to the east would belong to Portugal and the lands to the west to Castile. The treaty was signed by Spain, 2 July 1494, and by Portugal, 5 September 1494. The treaty effectively countered the Bulls of Alexander VI but was subsequently sanctioned by Pope Julius II by means of the Bull: *Ea Quae pro bono pacis of 24 January 1506*.

Even though the treaty was negotiated without consulting the Pope, a few sources call the resulting line the "Papal Line of Demarcation." The other side of the world was divided a few decades later by the Treaty of Zaragoza signed on 22 April 1529, which specified the anti-meridian to the line of demarcation specified in the Treaty of Tordesillas. Originals of both treaties are kept at the General Archive of the Indies in Spain and at the Torre do Tombo National Archive in Portugal in 1577, the final treaty! This treaty would be observed well by Spain and Portugal, despite considerable ignorance as to the geography of the New World. It gave Spain a free hand in the Pacific Ocean, hence the Philippines was named after King Philip of Spain in the east. Portugal gained access to South America in the New World by the relocated line of demarcation passing through its North-western tip, which later became Brazil the only Portuguese speaking nation in the New World. Originally, these arrangements were respected by most other European powers, but as the Protestant Reformation (1517–1648) progressed, that respect ended when they posed a religious and political challenge to the Roman Catholic church. The states of Northern Europe came to consider the Papal Bulls relating to non-European countries of the New World as a private arrangement between Spain and Portugal.

1493: Thus, ended the actual direct leadership role of the papacy in the development of the new-world and the beginning of the scramble of the 'Age of Discovery'

5

How European Countries applied the Papal Bulls: Portugal

PORTUGAL'S HISTORY OF EXPLORATION of Africa began in 1415 when they captured Ceuta in North Africa. In 1445, Prince Henry the Navigator of Portugal established a trading post (factory) on the island of Arguin off the West Coast of Africa. On it they acquired gum Arabic and slaves for Portugal. They brought in copperware, cloth, tools, wine, and horses and later included arms and ammunition. In exchange, they received gold from the mines of Akan, Guinea, and ivory.

The expanding market opportunities in Europe and the Mediterranean resulted in increased trade across the Sahara. At that time there was a small market for African slaves as domestic workers in Europe and as workers on the sugar plantations of the Mediterranean and later Madeira. However, the Portuguese found they could make considerable amounts of gold by transporting slaves from one trading post to another, along the Atlantic coast of Africa. In 1441 they continued that practice as slave traders. Slaves exported from Africa during this initial period of the Portuguese slave trade primarily came from Mauritania, and later the Upper Guinea coast. Scholars estimate that as many as 156,000 slaves were exported from 1441 to 1521 to Iberia and the Atlantic islands of the African coast. Muslim merchants had a high demand for slaves, which were used as porters on the trans-Saharan routes and for sale in the Islamic Empire. By 1448 Portugal had completed the construction of the first Slave Castle in Arguin and from 1455, eight hundred slaves were shipped from Arguin to Portugal every year.

The Portuguese seem to have been the first Europeans to have developed an active relationship with Sub-Saharan Africa. When the Portuguese first sailed down the Atlantic coast to coastal Africa, they were interested in gold. Trade in Sub-Saharan Africa was controlled by Muslims, who controlled Trans-Saharan trade routes for salt, kola, textiles, fish, and grain and engaged in the Arab slave trade. From the time of their arrival on the shores of Serra da Leoa (later called Sierra Leone) in 1460, and until their gradual decline as leaders in world exploration in the sixteenth century, the Portuguese had an ambiguous relationship with their African trading partners:

> *"Disembarking at cities that were equally large, complex, and as technologically advanced as Lisbon at the time, the Portuguese actually experienced far less culture shock than we might expect. In fact, they encountered urban centres in West Africa comparable to those back in Europe, governed by elaborate dynasties, organised around apprenticeship-based artistic guilds, and with agricultural systems capable of feeding their large populaces. Many African cities were even deemed to be larger, more hygienic, and better organized than those of Europe. Additionally, the Portuguese shared many beliefs about magic, the supernatural, and the treatment of illness with the African societies they encountered. Protective amulets in both cultures were considered medicinally valuable, and sickness in general was attributed to witchcraft."*[1]

On the international front, Portugal appears to have been the most adventurous country in the western world. The Roman Catholic Church was there supporting them in their expansionist efforts, maintaining their spiritual coverage and interceding with other countries on their behalf.

However, by 1453 the religio/political battle between Roman Christianity and Islam was not over. Using European artillery and expertise, disciplined Muslim forces of the Ottoman Turks break through Constantinople's walls. This fall of Constantinople in 1453, marked the end of the centre of Eastern Orthodox Christianity and the heart of what remained of the Roman Empire. The Muslims won that war in Constantinople.

The Ottoman Turks continued their march across Europe (north, west, and east) into Athens, superimposing their religion in the most sacred place of western civilisation. In 1456 they overran Athens and began a stay which lasted 200 years. The Turks expanded into Bosnia, Egypt and Herzegovina and joined it administratively with Bosnia.

The shift of religio/political power and trade moved from the Mediterranean with armies of foot soldiers and cavalry to the application of naval

---

1. Ross, The Portuguese in Africa,

power with armies of pioneers backed up by the military, in the west and the globe. Trade with the Far East was restricted by the Muslim control of the Middle East. Europeans thus turned their attention to Africa on the west coast. This move reaped a harvest of gold, spices, and a lucrative African slave trade with the Muslims. The initial successes of discovery and exploration of the new regions in the south and trade by the Portuguese on the African west coast were met with great pleasure by the Pope at that time.

In view of the competition between Spain and Portugal concerning Africa, the Pope was asked to mediate between the two countries, to determine how the two countries would divide the world. The Treaty of Alcáçovas (also known as Treaty or Peace of Alcáçovas-Toledo) was signed on 4 September 1479 between the Catholic Monarchs of Castile and Aragon on one side and Alfonso V and his son, Prince John of Portugal, on the other side. It put an end to the War of the Castilian Succession, which ended with a victory of the Catholic Monarchs on land and a Portuguese victory on the sea. In other words, Portugal was given Africa and the East with exclusive rights and Spain the west. The four peace treaties signed at Alcáçovas reflected that outcome: Isabella was recognized as Queen of Castile while Portugal reached hegemony in the Atlantic Ocean. The treaty intended to regulate:

- The renunciation of Afonso V and Catholic Monarchs to the Castilian throne and Portuguese throne, respectively
- The division of the Atlantic Ocean and overseas territories into two zones of influence
- The contract of marriage between Isabella, the eldest daughter of the Catholic Monarchs, with Afonso, heir of Prince John. This was known as Tercerias de Moura, and included the payment to Portugal of a war compensation by the Catholic Monarchs in the form of marriage dowry.
- The pardon of the Castilian supporters of Juana

This treaty, ratified later by the Papal Bull Aereni Regis in 1481, essentially gave the Portuguese free rein to continue their exploration along the African coast while guaranteeing Castilian sovereignty in the Canaries. It also prohibited Castilians from sailing to the Portuguese possessions without Portuguese license. The Treaty of Alcáçovas, establishing Castilian and Portuguese spheres of control in the Atlantic, settled a period of open hostility, but it also laid the basis for future claims and conflict. In 1482, the Portuguese erected Elmina Castle and factory in Ghana. It was the first trading post built in the Gulf of Guinea and the oldest European building in in existence in sub- Saharan Africa.

As the Portuguese explored the coastlines of Africa, they left behind a series of padroes stone crosses inscribed with the Portuguese coat of arms marking their claims, and built forts and trading posts. From these bases, the Portuguese engaged profitably in the slave and gold trades. Portugal enjoyed a virtual monopoly of the Atlantic slave trade for over a century, exporting around 800 slaves annually. Most were brought to the Portuguese capital Lisbon, where it is estimated Africans came to constitute 10 percent of the population. The Tordesillas Treaty, 1494, meridian divided the world between Portugal and Castille (Spain and later, the Moluccas antemeridian set at the Treaty of Zaragoza 1529.

The travel led by Vasco da Gama to Calicut was the starting point for deployment of the Portuguese along the east coast of Africa and in the Indian Ocean. The first contact occurred on 20 May 1498. After some conflict, Vasco da Gama got an ambiguous letter for trade with the Zamorin of Calicut, leaving there some men to establish a trading post. Since then, exploration lost its private nature, to be replaced by King Manuel 1 in 1500 by the exclusive authority of the Portuguese Crown. Shortly after, they established in Lisbon the Casa da India which was a state-run commercial organization during the Age of Discovery. It regulated international trade and the Portuguese Empire's territories, colonies, and factories across Asia and Africa. Central to the Casa da Índia›s objectives was the establishment and protection of a Portuguese total control of the seas in the Atlantic Ocean, Indian Ocean, Arabian sea, and the Indies. (Precedent 1,4, 6)

The aim of Portugal in the Indian Ocean was to ensure the monopoly of the spice trade. Taking advantage of the rivalries that pitted Hindus against Muslims, the Portuguese established several forts and trading posts between 1500–1510. In East Africa, small Islamic states along the coast of Mozambique, Kilwa, Brava, Sofala and Mombasa were destroyed, or became either subjects or allies of Portugal. Pero da Covilha had reached Ethiopia, traveling secretly overland, as early as 1490; a diplomatic mission reached the ruler of that nation on October 19, 1520.

In 1500 the second fleet to India who came to discover Brazil explored the East African coast, where Diogo Dias discovered the island that he named St. Lawrence, later known as Madagascar. This fleet, commanded by Pedro Alvares Cabral, arrived at Calicut in September, where the first trade agreement in India was signed. For a short time, a Portuguese factory was installed there, but was attacked by Muslims on December 16 and several Portuguese, including the scribe Pero Vaz de Caminha, died. After bombarding Calicut as a retaliation, Cabral went to rival Kochi.

Profiting from the rivalry between the Maharaja of Kochi and the Zamorin of Calicut, the Portuguese were well received and seen as allies, getting a permit to build a fort (Fort Manuel) and a trading post that were the first European settlement in India. There in 1503 they built the St. Francis church.

Between 1502–1509 the Portuguese gained control of East Africa, building forts in Tanzania and Kenya and on the western side of the Indian Ocean. These included islands in the Indian Ocean, for example Madagascar, Mauritius, and smaller islands.

In 1509, the Portuguese won the sea Battle of Diu against the combined forces of the Ottoman Sultan Beyazid II, Sultan of Gujarat, Mamluk, Sultan on Cairo, Samoothiri Raja of Kozhikode, Venetian Republic, and Ragusan Republic (Dubrovnik). The Portuguese victory was critical for its strategy of control of the Indian Sea: Turks and Egyptians withdrew their navies from India, leaving the seas to the Portuguese, setting its trade dominance for almost a century, and greatly assisting the growth of the Portuguese Empire. It also marked the beginning of the European colonial dominance in Asia. A second Battle of Diu in 1538 finally ended Ottoman ambitions in India and confirmed Portuguese hegemony in the Indian Ocean.

Coveted for being the best port in the region, Goa became the seat of the Portuguese government in 1510, with the conquest triggering compliance of neighbor kingdoms: Gujarat and Calicut sent embassies, offering alliances and grants to fortify. In that year in Goa the first Portuguese mint in India was established, the Portuguese taking the opportunity to announce this achievement.

The trade made the shift from Europe to the Americas as a primary destination for slaves around 1518. Prior to this time, slaves had to pass through Portugal to be taxed before making their way to the Americas.

Although the Portuguese first visited Brazil in 1500, they did not establish a settlement there until 1532. The colonization effort proved to be a difficult undertaking on such a vast continent, and indigenous slave labor was quickly turned to for agricultural workforce needs. Aggressive mission networks of the Portuguese Jesuits were the driving force behind this recruitment, and they successfully mobilized an indigenous labor force to live in colonial villages to work the land. These indigenous enslaving expeditions were known as *bandeiras*.

African slavery became more common in Brazil during the mid-sixteenth century, though the enslavement of Indigenous people continued into the seventeenth and even the eighteenth century in the backlands of Brazil. Indigenous slaves remained much cheaper during this time than their African counterparts, though they did suffer horrendous death rates from European diseases. Although the average African slave lived to be only twenty-three years old due to appalling conditions, this was still about four years longer than Indigenous slaves,(which contributed to the high price of African slaves). Even though prices for indigenous slaves were cheaper, there was never a focus on maintaining slave families. Because enslaved peoples were always so available, either through conquest or buying them through the market, the economic incentive to keep families together never manifested itself.

During the Atlantic slave trade era, Brazil imported more African slaves than any other country. An estimated 4.9 million slaves from Africa came to Brazil during the period 1501–1866. Until the early 1850s, most enslaved Africans who arrived on Brazilian shores were forced to embark at West Central African ports, especially in Luana (present-day Angola). Today, except for Nigeria, the largest population of people of African descent is in Brazil.

Slave labor was the driving force behind the growth of the sugar economy in Brazil, and sugar was the primary export of the colony from 1600–1650.

This letter written by a Father Sandoval in 1610 seems to offer an insight into the belief system held by the Roman Catholic church in Europe at that time.

> "In the year 1610, a Catholic priest in the Americas named Father Sandoval wrote back to a church functionary in Europe to ask if the capture, transport, and enslavement of African blacks was legal by church doctrine. A letter dated March 12, 1610, from Brother Luis Brandaon to Father Sandoval gives the answer:
>
> Your Reverence writes me that you would like to know whether the Negroes who are sent to your parts have been legally captured. To this I reply that I think your Reverence should have no scruples on this point, because this is a matter which has been questioned by the Board of Conscience in Lisbon, and all its members are learned and conscientious men. Nor did the bishops who were in SaoThome, Cape Verde, and here in Loando—all learned and virtuous men—find fault with it. We have been here ourselves for forty years and there have been among us very learned Fathers. . . never did they consider the trade as illicit. Therefore, we and the Fathers of Brazil buy these slaves for our service without any scruple.[2]"

2. Zinn, A Peoples History of the United States, p29

Gold and diamond deposits were discovered in Brazil in 1690, which sparked an increase in the importation of African slaves to power this newly profitable market. Transportation systems were developed for the mining infrastructure, and population boomed from immigrants seeking to take part in gold and diamond mining.

> *"In the 16th and 17th centuries, they (the Portuguese) could not be expected to be tolerant of Oriental religions, although they soon recognized that wholesale conversion to Catholicism was impossible. Some Africans and Asiatics became Christians and even entered the clergy; but seldom if ever did they rise above the status of parish priests. In other affairs the Portuguese generally treated the dark-skinned peoples as inferiors.*
>
> *1580 Philip II of Spain seized the Portuguese throne, which had fallen vacant and to which he had some blood claim. Portugal remained theoretically independent, bound only by a personal union to its neighbour; but succeeding Spanish monarchs steadily encroached on its liberties until the small kingdom became, in effect, a conquered province. Spain's European enemies meanwhile descended on the Portuguese Empire and ended its Eastern supremacy."*[3]

---

3. Nowell, The Great Discoveries and the First Colonial Empires

6

How European Countries applied the Papal Bulls: Spain

"Living in harmony with their world, the Indians prospered until the fateful day, five hundred years ago, when the Italian explorer Christopher Columbus arrived with his Spanish galleons."

BRITANNICA

EVERY AMERICAN, FROM ELEMENTARY School onwards, learns the Columbus story, and learns it the same way: "*In Fourteen Hundred and Ninety-Two, Columbus Sailed the Ocean Blue.*" This was the traditional history of the 'discovery' of the Americas. This chapter seeks to reveal the truth.

It was not until the union of Aragon and Castile and the completion of the Reconquista that the united country (Spain) became fully committed to looking for new trade routes and colonies overseas. In 1492, the joint rulers of the country decided to fund Christopher Columbus' expedition that they hoped would bypass Portugal's lock on Africa and the Indian Ocean, and instead, reach Asia by travelling west over the Atlantic. Columbus, in his letter to King Ferdinand of Castile and Queen Isabella of Seville, (1492) also recognized the role and significance of the Papacy as an integral component of the contract he was making with them. The transcript of the letter is given below:

(Literally Translated) IN NOMINE D. N. JESU CHRISTI

'Because, Most Christian and very exalted and very excellent and very powerful Princes, King and Queen of the Spains and of the Islands of the Sea, our Lords, in this present year of 1492 after your Highnesses had made an end to the war of the Moors, who were reigning in Europe, and having finished the war in the very great city of Granada, where in this present year on the 2nd day of the month of January, I saw the Royal banners of your Highnesses placed by force of arms on the towers of the Alhambra, which is the fortress of the said City: and I saw the Moorish King come out to the gates of the City and kiss the Royal hands of your Highnesses, and the hands of the Prince, my Lord: and then in that present month, because of the information which I had given your Highnesses about the lands of India, and about a Prince who is called Great Khan, which means in our Romance language, King of Kings,—how he and his predecessors had many times sent to Rome to beg for men learned in our Holy Faith that they might be instructed therein, and that the Holy Father had never furnished them, and so, many peoples believing in idolatries and receiving among themselves sects of perdition, were lost;—your Highnesses, as Catholic Christians and Princes, loving the Holy Christian faith and the spreading of it, and enemies of the sect of Mahomet and of all idolatries and heresies, decided to send me, Christopher Columbus, to the said regions of India, to see the said Princes and the peoples and lands, and learn of their disposition, and of everything, and the measures which could be taken for their conversion to our Holy Faith: and you ordered that I should not go to the east by land, by which it is customary to go, but by way of the west, whence until to-day we do not know certainly that any one has gone. So that, after having banished all the Jews from all your Kingdoms and realms, in the same month of January, your Highnesses ordered me to go with a sufficient fleet to the said regions of India.*[1]

Having received his papers from his highnesses Philip of Seville and Isabel of Aragon, Columbus left the port of Saltes and sailed directly to Gomera, the westernmost island of the Canaries, to complete the preparations of the three vessels for the trip. The Countess of La Gomera offered him vital support in preparations of the fleet, and he ended up staying one month. When he finally set sail on 6 September 1492, she gave him cuttings of sugarcane, which became the first to reach the New World.

---

1. Columbus, The Journal of Christopher Columbus (During his first voyage 1492) Boyd Thacher

HOW EUROPEAN COUNTRIES APPLIED THE PAPAL BULLS: SPAIN

Columbus wrote a log of his journey. The Papal Bull Dum Diversas could be the basis of his decisions and actions. We quote that portion of the Bull that gives specific rights and instructions. They are followed up by the inclusion of certain officials on the voyage to ensure compliance with the Bull itself:

> ...we grant to you full and free power, through the Apostolic authority by this edict, to invade, conquer, fight, subjugate the Saracens and pagans, and other infidels and other enemies of Christ, and wherever established their Kingdoms, Duchies, Royal Palaces, Principalities and other dominions, lands, places, estates, camps and any other possessions, mobile and immobile goods found in all these places and held in whatever name, and held and possessed by the same Saracens, Pagans, infidels, and the enemies of Christ, also realms, duchies, royal palaces, principalities and other dominions, lands, places, estates, camps, possessions of the king or prince or of the kings or princes, and to lead their persons in perpetual servitude, and to apply and appropriate realms, duchies, royal palaces, principalities and other dominions, possessions and goods of this kind to you and your use and your successors the Kings of Portugal."[2]

The date that New World Culture was implemented was Friday; Oct. 12, 1492:

The Landing: When they reached a small island of the Lucayas, (Bahamas) which is called in the language of the Indians, Guanahani, they saw naked people and the Admiral Columbus landed in the armed boat with Martin Alonso Pinzon and Vincente Yañez, his brother, who was captain of the ship "Nina."

The Admiral took the royal banner and the two captains had two banners of the Verde Cruz, which the Admiral carried on all the ships as a sign, with an F. and a Y. The crown of the Sovereigns surmounted each letter, and one was one side of the + and the other the other side. Having landed they saw very green trees and much water, and many fruits of different kinds and they took possession of the land as laid down in the Papal Bull, which said:

> ["... we grant to you full and free power, through the Apostolic authority by this edict, to invade, conquer, fight, subjugate the Saracens and pagans, and other infidels and other enemies of Christ,][3]

---

2. Dum Diversas, www.papalencyclicals.net
3. Dum Diversas, www.papalencyclicals.net

The Admiral called the two captains and the others who landed and Rodrigo Descoredo, Notary of all the Fleet, and Rodrigo Sanchez of Segovia, and told them to hear him witness and testify *that* he:

> " *in the presence of them all, was taking, as in fact he took possession of the said isle, for the King and for the Queen, his Lords, making the protestations which were required, as contained more at length in the depositions which were made there in writing. Then many of the people of the island gathered there.*
>
> *My People—men and women all belong to your Highnesses on this island . . . .as well as on the other islands."—(pagans, and other infidels and other enemies of Christ,]*
>
> *and to lead their persons in perpetual servitude, and*
>
> *to apply and appropriate . . . . possessions and goods of this kind to you and your use and your successors 'the Crowns'."*[4]

The indigenous people he encountered, the Lucayan, Taíno, or Arawak, were peaceful and friendly. (Precedent 2)

Noting their gold ear ornaments, Columbus took some of the Arawaks prisoner and insisted that they guide him to the source of the gold.

From the entry in Columbus' journal of 12 October 1492, in which he wrote of them:

> *"Many of the men I have seen have scars on their bodies, and when I made signs to them to find out how this happened, they indicated that people from other nearby islands come to San Salvador to capture them; they defend themselves the best they can. I believe that people from the mainland come here to take them as slaves. They ought to make good and skilled servants, for they repeat very quickly whatever we say to them. I think they can very easily be made Christians, for they seem to have no religion. If it pleases our Lord, I will take six of them to Your Highnesses when I depart, in order that they may learn our language. Columbus remarked that their lack of modern weaponry and metal-forged swords or pikes was a tactical vulnerability, writing, "I could conquer the whole of them with 50 men and govern them as I pleased."*[5]

Columbus repeated this process in the islands of Cuba and Haiti. In Haiti he experienced a major incident. On Christmas Day the Santa Maria struck a sand bank and had to be abandoned. Columbus wrote in his

---

4. Columbus, The Journal of Christopher Columbus (During his first voyage 1492) Boyd Thacher

5. Columbus, The Journal of Christopher Columbus (During his first voyage 1492) Boyd Thacher

HOW EUROPEAN COUNTRIES APPLIED THE PAPAL BULLS: SPAIN   59

journal about the most sympathetic manner by which the natives supported him in this misadventure:

> ... "and they say that the King wept when he heard of the disaster and sent all his people from the village with many large canoes to unload the ship: and so, it was done and everything was unloaded from the decks of the ship in a very brief space of time, such was the great haste and diligence which that King displayed. And he in person with his brothers and relatives showed great assiduity both in the matter of unloading the ship and guarding what was thrown on land that everything might be in security. From time to time, he sent one of his relatives weeping to the Admiral to console him, saying that he must not feel troubled or annoyed, and that he would give him whatever he possessed. The Admiral certifies to the Sovereigns that in no part of Castile could things be placed in such safety without the loss of so much as a leather strap. The King ordered everything placed near the houses while some houses which he wished to give up were vacated, where everything could be stored and guarded. He ordered armed men placed around everything to watch all night."[6] He continued in his amazement, literally to quote the Bible in his description of these: "He with all the people in the village wept a great deal (says the Admiral): they are an affectionate people and free from avarice and agreeable in everything and I certify to your Highnesses that in all the world I do not believe there is a better people or a better country: they love their neighbours as themselves and they have the softest and gentlest speech in the world and are always laughing. . . .. But your Highnesses may believe that they have very good customs among themselves, and the King maintains a most wonderful state, and everything takes place in such an appropriate and well-ordered manner that it is a pleasure to see it all: and they have good memories and wish to see everything, and they ask what it is and for what purpose."[7]

The Tainos' love and care for these visitors did not end there. They assisted in salvaging the ship and Columbus was able to construct a fort for the thirty-nine men whom he had to leave there to continue their work in establishing relations with the natives and to locate the gold and other resources for future trade and export (the Nina having arrived soon after the incident) back to Spain and the rest of Europe. (Precedent 1, 2) In the

6. Columbus, The Journal of Christopher Columbus (During his first voyage 1492) Boyd Thacher

7. Columbus, The Journal of Christopher Columbus (During his first voyage 1492) Boyd Thacher

few days Columbus had learned the places, where they had gold in such a quantity that little value was attached to it. He had also learned where there were spices of which there was a great quantity and worth more than pepper and "manegueta." He charged those persons who were to remain there to obtain as much as they could.

Thursday, December 27, 1492

At sunrise, the King of that country came to the caravel and told the Admiral that he had sent for gold and that he wished to cover him all over with gold before he went away, and he begged him not to go away before. The King ate with the Admiral, and a brother of his and another near relative, which two told the Admiral that they wished to go to Castile with him. At this time news came that the caravel Pinta was in a river at the head of that island. Then the Cacique, who loved the Admiral so much it was wonderful, sent a canoe there in which the Admiral despatched a sailor. The Admiral was already preparing with as much haste as possible for the return to Castile on the other ship.

Columbus took some more natives captive and continued his exploration, along the northern coast of Hispaniola in the Pinta. He stopped at a port he called Samana Peninsula where he encountered some resistance from the natives. However, he kidnapped some more natives. "Which says the Admiral......... because men and women all belong to your Highnesses on this island especially as well as on the other islands." (*Precedent 1*)

Leaving Hispaniola, Columbus returned to Spain, arriving in Saltes on March 15, 1493, with great fanfare accompanied with the fame and fortune. He is now the Don the great and mighty one and so will be his descendants in perpetuity. And the natives—largely killed, those not dead- slaves in perpetuity, baptised as Catholic Christians and owned by Spain!

Columbus' assessment of this voyage was based on the specifications of *"Dum Diversas."* He had quickly concluded that these fine hospitable hosts would make acceptable servants. With fifty men they could subjugate them all and make them do whatever they wanted. Western culture (Roman Catholic Christianity and European civilisation) would dominate and replace anything that existed in these islands.

With the overwhelming success, Columbus was granted full funding for a subsequent voyage and the fame and honours that were part of his contract. (Precedents 4,7and 9).

Columbus receives re-investment and expansion of powers:

3 November 1493: Columbus' second voyage involved a fleet of 17 ships carrying 1200 men and goods to establish permanent colonies in the New World, with Hispaniola (Dominican Republic and Haiti), being the first. The passengers included priests, soldiers, and farmers to create colonies of settlement from which to launch missions dedicated to converting the natives to Christianity. Having journeyed through the Lesser Antilles, Columbus sighted and named several islands, many of them after Roman Catholic Christian saints and mentors:

- Montserrat (for Santa María de Montserrate, after the Blessed Virgin of the Monastery of Montserrat, which is located on the Mountain of Montserrat, in Catalonia, Spain),
- Antigua (after a church in Seville, Spain, called Santa María la Antigua, meaning "Old St. Mary's"),
- Redonda (*Santa María la Redonda*, Spanish for "St. Mary the Round," owing to the island's shape),
- Nevis (derived from the Spanish *Nuestra Señora de las Nieves*, "Our Lady of the Snows," because Columbus thought the clouds over Nevis Peak made the island resemble a snow-capped mountain),
- Saint Kitts (for St. Christopher, patron of sailors and travellers),
- Sint Eustatius (for the early Roman martyr, St. Eustachius),
- Saba (after the Biblical Queen of Sheba),
- Saint Martin (*San Martín*), and
- Saint Croix (from the Spanish *Santa Cruz*, meaning "Holy Cross").

Columbus later returned to Hispaniola where he had left men from his earlier voyage. He found the fort in ruins and the corpses of the Spaniards. In retaliation for this attack, Columbus ordered that each Taino Indian over fourteen years present a bell full of gold powder every three months or, twenty-five pounds of spun cotton. Tainos had their hands cut off and were left to bleed to death if they failed to deliver the goods.

This decision by Columbus (on behalf of the Crown), established the principle and practice that gave Europeans the right and authority to determine the life of non-European beings in the New World also. The longevity of their life was determined by the quantity of gold (money), or any plant products Columbus deemed valuable from the islands. They must accumulate and deliver for the colonists and for the flag of the sponsoring country. However, he did introduce the age limit of fourteen as being the age for economic production of gold or spun cotton.

On his third voyage: May 30, 1498, Columbus left with six ships from Sanlúcar, Spain, for his third trip to the New World. He was accompanied by the young Bartolomé de Las Casas, who would later provide partial transcripts of Columbus' logs.

Columbus landed on the south coast of the island of Trinidad on July 31. From August 4 through August 12, he explored the Gulf of Paria which separates Trinidad from Venezuela, South America. He explored the mainland of South America, including the Orinoco River. He also sailed to the islands of Chacachacare and Margarita Island and sighted and named Tobago (Bella Forma) and Grenada (Concepcion).

Columbus made a fourth voyage nominally in search of the Strait of Malacca to the Indian Ocean. Accompanied by his brother Bartolomeo and his 13-year-old son Fernando, he left Cádiz, Spain on May 11, 1502, with the ships Capitana, Gallega, Vizcaína and Santiago de Palos. He arrived at Santo Domingo on June 29, but was denied port, and the new governor refused to listen to his storm prediction. Instead, while Columbus' ships sheltered at the mouth of the Jaina River, the first Spanish treasure fleet sailed into the hurricane. Columbus' ships survived with only minor damage, but twenty-nine of the thirty ships in the governor's fleet were lost to the storm. In addition to the ships, 500 lives (including Francisco de Bobadilla's) and an immense cargo of gold were surrendered to the sea. He also discovered on his trips further north, exploring the coasts of Honduras, Nicaragua, and Costa Rica, before arriving in Almirante Bay, Panama on October 16.

In Panama, he learned from the natives of gold and a strait to another ocean. After much exploration, he established a garrison at the mouth of Rio Belen in January 1503. He left for Hispaniola on April 16, heading North he sighted the Cayman Islands on May 10, naming them Las Tortugas after the numerous sea turtles there. He next sustained more damage in a storm off the coast of Cuba. Unable to travel any farther, the ships were beached in St. Ann's Bay, Jamaica, on June 25, 1503. Columbus and his men were stranded in Jamaica for a year. Two Spaniards, with native paddlers, were sent by canoe to get help from Hispaniola. That island's governor obstructed all efforts to rescue Columbus and his men. Grudging help finally arrived on June 29, 1504, and Columbus and his men arrived in Sanlúcar, Spain, on November 7.

By this time Columbus had lost his authority and his wealth as he successfully established Western Culture of the New-World. His successes in obeying the Papal Bulls were such that it even amazed both the clergy and the crowns. However, the love of gold far outweighed the spiritual force of Roman Catholic Christianity, that their protestations when they fell on willing ears, they were powerless to implement many of the changes to the laws thus made.

These practices by the Europeans and the clergy were well documented by Bartholomew de Las Casas, a Spanish citizen and Dominican Friar who arrived in Hispaniola on Columbus' third voyage and stayed. What the Spaniards did to the Indians is told in horrifying detail by Las Casas, whose writings give the most thorough account of the Spanish Indian encounter. The Dominican Friars were the first to condemn the *encomienda* and worked for its abolition, although Las Casas was the outstanding reformer. Las Casas suggested a plan where the Indians would be congregated into self-governing townships to become tribute-paying vassals of the King. He still suggested that the loss of Indian labor for the colonists could be replaced by allowing the importation of African slaves.

> *"Las Casas' gradual response to the call to community life and witness was just one of a series of transformations in his long life. His love of truth was like a thorn in his side, always urging him on toward growth. There is perhaps no greater example of this openness to change than in his understanding of the oppression of the Africans who were being brought to the Americas as slaves. Although the Spanish Crown had legally authorized African slave trade even before Las Casas came to the Americas, Las Casas did, for a time, condone the use of African slaves as a step toward the freedom of the Indians. He thought that the Africans were better disposed for the harsh working conditions imposed on the indigenous people. By 1516, though, Las Casas realized the sinfulness of his well-meaning intentions. He who had seen up close the dehumanizing treatment of the Indians, finally got close enough to see in the enslaved Africans the very same image of the crucified Christ.*
>
> *I soon repented and judged myself guilty of ignorance. I came to realize that black slavery was as unjust as Indian slavery . . . and I was not sure that my ignorance and good faith would secure me in the eyes of God."*[8]

Las Casas's testimony was corroborated by other eyewitnesses. A group of Dominican friars, addressing the Spanish monarchy in 1519, hoping for the Spanish government to intercede, talked about unspeakable atrocities, children thrown to dogs to be devoured, new-born babies born to women prisoners flung into the jungle to die.

Forced labor in the mines and on the land led to much sickness and death. Many children died because their mothers, overworked and starved,

---

8. Pierce, Spirituality Today: Bartolome de las Casas, 4–19

had no milk for them. Las Casas, in Cuba, estimated that 7,000 children died in *three months*.

The Indians became real or nominal Christians, but their numbers shrank, less from slaughter and exploitation than from Old World diseases, frequently smallpox, for which they had no inherited immunity. The aboriginal Caribbean population virtually disappeared in a few generations, to be replaced by black slaves from Africa. The numbers of the population of the Indigenous peoples shrank in all mainland areas: at the beginning of the Spanish settlement there were perhaps 50,000,000 aborigines; the figure had decreased to an estimated 4,000,000 in the 17th century, after which it slowly rose again.

Las Casas, in his book *The Devastation of the Indies*, writes of the Arawaks:

> "...of all the infinite universe of humanity, these people are the most guileless, the most devoid of wickedness and duplicity...yet into this sheepfold...there came some Spaniards who immediately behaved like ravening beasts..... Their reason for killing and destroying...is that the Christians have an ultimate aim which is to acquire gold..."[9]

The cruelties multiplied. Las Casas saw soldiers stabbing Indians for sport, dashing babies' heads on rocks. And when the Indians resisted, the Spaniards hunted them down, equipped for killing with horses, armour plate, lances, pikes, rifles, crossbows, and vicious dogs. Indians who took things belonging to the Spaniards—they were not accustomed to the concept of private ownership and gave freely of their own possessions—were beheaded or burned at the stake.

Howard Zinn in his book "*A Peoples History of the United States*" writes about the content of Columbus' journal:

> "*His journal was revealing. He described the people who greeted him when he landed in the Bahamas—they were Arawak Indians, sometimes called Tainos—and told how they waded out into the sea to greet him and his men, who must have looked and sounded like people from another world and brought them gifts of various kinds. He described them as peaceable, gentle, and said: "They do not bear arms, and do not know them for I showed them a sword—they took it by the edge and cut themselves."*
>
> "*In the standard accounts of Columbus what is emphasized again and again is his religious feeling, his desire to convert the natives to Christianity, his reverence for the Bible. Yes, he was*

---

9. Pierce, Spirituality Today, Bartolome de las Casas, 4-19

HOW EUROPEAN COUNTRIES APPLIED THE PAPAL BULLS: SPAIN

concerned about God. But more about Gold. Just one additional letter. His was a limited alphabet. Yes, all over the island of Hispaniola, where he, his brothers, his men, spent most of their time, he erected crosses. But also, all over the island, they built gallows-340 of them by the year 1500. Crosses and gallows were that deadly historic juxtaposition."[10]

In his quest for gold, Columbus, seeing bits of gold among the Indians, concluded there were huge amounts of it. He ordered the natives to find a certain amount of gold within a certain period. And if they did not meet their quota, their arms were hacked off. The others were to learn from this and deliver the gold. Samuel Eliot Morison, the Harvard historian who was Columbus' admiring biographer and was himself a sailor who retraced Columbus's route across the Atlantic, wrote:

> "Whoever thought up this ghastly system, Columbus was responsible for it, as the only means of producing gold for export.... Those who fled to the mountains were hunted with hounds, and of those who escaped, starvation and disease took toll, while thousands of the poor creatures in desperation took cassava poison to end their miseries."[11] "

However, Columbus could not obtain enough gold to send home to impress the King and Queen and his Spanish financiers, so he decided to send back to Spain another kind of loot: slaves. They rounded up about one thousand, two hundred natives, selected five hundred, and these were sent, jammed together, on the voyage across the Atlantic. Two hundred died on the way, of cold, of sickness.

In his popular book *Christopher Columbus, Mariner*, written in 1954, Morison records the enslavement and the killing of the indigenous people:

> "So the policy and acts of Columbus for which he alone was responsible began the depopulation of the terrestrial paradise that was Hispaniola in 1492. Of the original natives, estimated by a modern ethnologist at 300,000 in number, one-third were killed off between 1494 and 1496. By 1508, an enumeration showed only 60,000 alive.... in 1548 Oviedo [Morison is referring to Fernandez

---

10. 32 An excerpt of "Columbus and Western Civilization" written by Howard Zinn that appears in the Disinformation anthology *You Are Still Being Lied To* edited by RussKick.

11. An excerpt of "Columbus and Western Civilization" written by Howard Zinn that appears in the Disinformation anthology *You Are Still Being Lied To* edited by RussKick.

de Oviedo, the official Spanish historian of the conquest] doubted whether 500 Indians remained."[12]

In Columbus' journal, an entry of September 1498 reads: "*From here one might send, in the name of the Holy Trinity, as many slaves as could be sold...*" To use the name of the Holy Trinity as the source of testimony for the sale of other human beings; and with exclusivity to non-Europeans, into slavery seems to contradict the only purpose that Father God sent His only begotten Son to pay for man's redemption to the Father who sent the Holy Spirit on the day of Pentecost to be in man.

As in many military conquests, women came in for especially brutal treatment. One Italian nobleman named Cuneo recorded an early sexual encounter. The "Admiral" he refers to is Columbus, who, as part of his agreement with the Spanish monarchy, insisted he be made an Admiral. Cuneo wrote:

> *" I captured a very beautiful Carib woman, whom the said Lord Admiral gave to me and with whom...I conceived desire to take pleasure. I wanted to put my desire into execution, but she did not want it and treated me with her finger nails in such a manner that I wished I had never begun. But seeing that, I took a rope and thrashed her well. . ... Finally we came to an agreement."*[13]

As Papal Bull Romanus Pontifex so delicately articulated "peacefully subdued. "

There is other evidence which adds up to a picture of widespread rape of native women. Howard Zinn quotes Samuel Eliot Morison, who wrote, "*In the Bahamas, Cuba and Hispaniola they found young and beautiful women, who everywhere were naked, in most places accessible, and presumably complaisant.*" Who presumed this? Morison, and so many others.

Morison saw the conquest as so many writers after him have done, as one of the great romantic adventures of world history. He seemed to get carried away by what appeared to him as a *masculine* conquest. He wrote: "*Never again may mortal men hope to recapture the amazement, the wonder, the delight of those October days in 1492, when the new world gracefully yielded her virginity to the conquering Castilians*"[14].

12. An excerpt of "Columbus and Western Civilization" written by Howard Zinn that appears in the Disinformation anthology *You Are Still Being Lied To* edited by RussKick.

13. Kick, Russ An excerpt of "Columbus and Western Civilization" written by Howard Zinn that appears in the Disinformation anthology *You Are Still Being Lied To*

14. Kick, Russ An excerpt of "Columbus and Western Civilization" written by Howard Zinn that appears in the Disinformation anthology *You Are Still Being Lied To*

The language of Cuneo ("we came to an agreement"), and of Morison ("gracefully yielded") written almost five hundred years apart, surely suggests how persistent through modern history has been the mythology that rationalizes sexual brutality against non-Europeans in the Western Hemisphere, by seeing it as "complaisant."

This writer hastens to add that that treatment is not confined to the treatment of women but persists as one twenty-first century historian describes "unchangeable status quo" of New World Culture.

All these atrocities were somewhat based on the Papal Bulls "*Dum Diversas*" and "*Romanus Pontifex*": some specifications are here repeated for ease of reference.

In Pope Nicholas V subsequent Bull issued three years later: "*Romanus Pontifex*" 1455 he extended the scope of engagement with non-Europeans from the basis of religion to include people groups. Firstly, he considered an alliance with the (East) Indians, who are said to worship the name of Christ, to aid the Christians (Europeans) against the Saracens and other such enemies of the faith and subdue other gentile or pagan peoples.

However, in their encounter with the Guineamen and other negroes, whose lands they had never visited and who had never invaded them, he re-affirmed the Papal Bull "*Dum Diversas*" and added to the instruction. These additions would prove to be basis of the future of the sub-Saharan African people group in the new world-culture.

The use of the terms:

- subdued and peacefully possessed and
- take them by force, by barter (of unprohibited articles) and by lawful contract of purchase:
- send them away to other kingdoms as the true lords of them.

Updated forms of enslavement, labour intensive single crop agriculture for export and distribution of labour practices and living conditions were also developed and later applied in the New World.

On Columbus' second voyage he also initiated the first transatlantic slave voyage, a shipment of several hundred Taino people sent from Hispaniola to Spain. There were doubts about the legality of their enslavement in Spain. Columbus returned to Spain from his second voyage, carrying around thirty enslaved Tainos. Once again, there are doubts about the legality of their enslavement. The papacy was specific in their instructions about their treatment of non-Africans—"the taking of them by force and by barter and by lawful contract of purchase and sending them away to other kingdoms; as true lords of them." The Tainos and natives of the new continents were not "Guineamen or other negroes" to be transported from their homeland (Hispaniola) to Spain. However as early as 1499 there seemed to be no opposition in Spain when Amerigo Vespucci and Alonso de Hojeda sold more than 200 slaves in Cádiz; taken from the coast of South America.

These exclusive additions to the Papal Bull "*Dum Diversas*" 1452, would prove to be the basis for the new world-culture for the sub-Saharan African people group:

- 1502: Juan de Córdoba of Seville becomes the first merchant we can identify to send an African slave to the New World. Córdoba, like other merchants, is permitted by the Spanish authorities to send only one slave. Others send two or three.
- 1504: a small group of Africans captured from a Portuguese vessel— are brought to the court of King James IV of Scotland.
- 1505: (7 years after Columbus first voyage) first record of sugar cane being grown in the New World, in Santo Domingo (modern Dominican Republic).
- 1509: Columbus's son, Diego Cólon, becomes governor of the new Spanish empire in the Caribbean. He soon complains that Native American slaves do not work hard enough.
- 22 January 1510: the start of the systematic transportation of African slaves to the New World: King Ferdinand of Spain authorises a shipment of 50 African slaves to be sent to Santo Domingo.
- 1516: the governor of Cuba, Diego Velázquez, authorises slave-raiding expeditions to Central America. One group of slaves aboard a Spanish caravel rebel and kill the Spanish crew before sailing home—the first successful slave rebellion recorded in the New World. 1516: in his book *Utopia*, Sir Thomas More argues that his ideal society would have slaves, but they would not be *'non-combatant prisoners-of-war, slave by birth, or purchases from foreign slave markets.*' Rather, they would be local convicts or *'condemned criminals from other countries, who are acquired in large numbers, sometimes for a small payment, but usually for nothing.'*[15] (Trans. Paul Turner, Penguin, 1965)

What follows is the institutionalisation of the New-World Culture as developed and applied by Columbus' in the West Indies. It began with Precedent 1 when an entrepreneur/explorer sought and obtained the authority to conquer new lands in the name of the Crown. Columbus and the Crown

---

15. St Thomas More, Utopia,(Trans Paul Turner)

administration then began to implement the other precedents as identified in the Canaries.

In 1518 (26 years after Columbus 1st voyage) The Spanish government (as Crown administrators in the West Indies) introduced the asiento, to supply the new colonies with slave labor. The asiento was a license to supply a given number of slaves. The Spanish authorities sold the asiento to the highest bidder, and the money went to the Spanish king and queen. The merchant who bought the license could buy slaves in Africa and sell them in the Spanish Americas. They hoped to get back the money they spent on the license and make a good profit. The merchant could also make money by selling shares in the license to other merchants. Any Spanish license holders had to arrange delivery of the enslaved Africans by Portuguese traders. This was because Spanish ships could not legally go to Africa since the Portuguese had the monopoly there. As Spain and Portugal were at that time on good terms, having settled their differences at the signing of the Treaty of Alcacovas & Treaty of Tordesillas 1493, the terms and conditions as of the Bull Dum Diversas and Romanus Pontifex arrangements for the purchase and sale of slaves were still honored. 18 August 1518: in a significant escalation of the slave trade, Charles V grants his Flemish courtier Lorenzo de Gorrevod permission to import four thousand African slaves into New Spain. From this point onwards thousands of slaves were sent to the New World each year. Charles V was born in Belgium. He was Holy Roman Emperor, from 1519–1556 and Archduke of Austria. From 1516–1555 he was Lord of the Netherlands as. titular Duke of Burgundy and inherited a Hapsburg empire extending across Europe from Spain and the Netherlands to Austria and the Kingdom of Naples. He oversaw both the continuation of the long-lasting Spanish colonization of the Americas and the German colonization of the Americas. The union of the European and American territories of Charles V was the first collection of countries across the globe labelled "the sun never sets."

1521 Less than thirty years after Columbus' first encounter with the New World 13 August with the capture of King Cuahutemotzin by Hernan Cortés and the fall of the city of Mexico, the Aztec empire is overthrown, and Mexico comes under Spanish Rule. 1522: A major slave rebellion breaks out on the island of Hispaniola. This is the first significant uprising of African slaves. After this, slave resistance becomes widespread and uprisings common.

The first Spanish-owned sugar plantations were established in the Canaries. The Spanish then transferred this technology including Canarian experts in sugarcane cultivation to the Antilles. The flourishing Caribbean sugar industry overtook the originally prosperous Canary Islands' production, initiating the economic decline of the islands which would ultimately result in heavy emigration to the Americas.

> "These Arawaks of the Bahama Islands were much like Indians on the mainland, who were remarkable for their hospitality, and their belief in sharing (European observers were to say again and again). These traits did not stand out in the Europe of the Renaissance, dominated as it was by the religion of popes, the government of kings, the frenzy for money that marked Western civilization and its first messenger to the Americas, Christopher Columbus." Columbus further wrote:
>
> "As soon as I arrived in the Indies, on the first Island which I found, I took some of the natives by force in order that they might learn and might give me information of whatever there is in these parts."[16]

Spain's mission to build an empire in the New World began with the expeditions of Christopher Columbus who convinced the Spanish royalty he could find a western route across the Atlantic Ocean to the Indies, (Asia). He sailed west in 1492 and six months later landed in islands in the Caribbean Sea. Columbus mistakenly thought he had reached the Indies and brought news of his new route to Spain.

---

16. Zinn, A Peoples' History of the US 1–2

7

Anglo World Culture and Christianity

"The United States of America was established as a white society, founded upon the near genocide of another race and then the enslavement of yet another"[1].

THE BRITISH TRADING IN enslaved Africans became established in the 1500s. In 1562 Captain John Hawkins was the first known Englishman to include enslaved Africans in his cargo. Queen Elizabeth l approved of his journey, during which he captured three hundred Africans. He then sailed across the North Atlantic and exchanged them for hides, ginger, and sugar. He returned to London in 1563. Thirsty for greater profits, he organised another voyage in 1564 to which Queen Elizabeth contributed one vessel. Meanwhile the African presence in England became established to such an extent that attempts were made to limit their numbers. Queen Elizabeth enjoyed the profits of the Atlantic slave trade and employed African entertainers in her court, but she issued a decree to expel Africans from England in July 1596.

Despite this, Africans were to remain a consistent presence in English life.

---

1. Wallis, *America's Original Sin- Racism, White Privilege and the Bridge to a New America 33*

In 1578, Queen Elizabeth1 eventually gave a charter to Sir Humphrey Gilbert and Sir Walter Raleigh to establish a permanent settlement in North America. That attempt resulted in the ill-fated Lost Colony of Roanoke island. These incursions contributed to increasing tensions between England and Spain. Finally, the English destruction of the Spanish Armada in 1588 changed the balance of power in the Atlantic, resulting in a new confidence by English investors and adventurers.

For nearly fifty years, an Anglican priest named Richard Hakluyt had advocated for an English colony in the New World. As an advisor of Queen Elizabeth, he conducted in-depth research on global exploration and wrote and lectured often on the subject. Years before Rev. Hunt landed in Virginia, the driving force behind the founding of Jamestown was Hakluyt—who was also one of the world's leading authorities in navigation and seafaring.

From his extensive research he also wrote his famous "*Discourse on Western Planting*" in which he presented twenty-one reasons why England should pursue the colonisation of North America. The primary reason, in Hakluyt's view, was evangelism. To see the fulfilment of his dream for an English settlement in the New World, Hakluyt gathered like-minded businessmen who worked together to form the Virginia Company. A pamphlet published by the Virginia Company called "*A True Declaration of the State of Virginia*" announced the purposes of the new colony. . . .*our primarie end is to plant religion, our secondary and subalternate ends are for the honour and profit of our nation.*"

Another tract published by the Virginia Company was called a "*True and Sincere Declaration of the Purposes and Ends of the Plantation.*" In this document the leaders of the company state that a motivating purpose of the endeavour was:

> "*First to preach and baptize into Christian religion and by the propagation the Gospel, to recover out of the arms of the devil a number of poor and miserable souls wrapped up unto death in almost invincible ignorance; to endeavor the fulfilling and accomplishments of the number of the elect which shall be gathered from out of all corners of the earth; and add to our myte the treasury of heaven.*"[2]

King James ascended to the throne with the death of Queen Elizabeth in 1603. As he also had with Queen Elizabeth I, Rev. Hakluyt found favor with the new king. It was King James who granted a charter to the Virginia Company and asked Hakluyt to help in the writing of the document. Parson Hakluyt carried his missionary zeal into the task and was able to convince

---

2. Klein Faith of our Fathers: Spirituality in Jamestown, CBN

the king and his colleagues in the Virginia Company to make world evangelism a key objective of this new colony. King James shared the vision for a colony that would carry British civilisation and Christianity to the New World. In the Virginia Charter he declared:

> *"We greatly commend and graciously accept their desires for the furtherance of so noble a work, which may, by the providence of Almighty God, hereafter tend to the glory of His Divine Majesty, in propagating of Christian religion to such people as yet live-in darkness and miserable ignorance of the true knowledge and worship of God and may in time bring the infidels and savages living in those parts to human civility and a settled, quiet government."*[3]

On December 20, 1606, one hundred and five colonists and forty seamen set sail from England to plant this new settlement to the glory of God. Hakluyt, who was now an old man, was forbidden by the crown to make the dangerous crossing. Instead, he chose his secretary, friend, and fellow Anglican priest, Robert Hunt, to be the chaplain of the colony.

The settlers landed on the shores of Virginia on April 26, 1607. Before permitting the colonists to continue inland, Rev. Hunt required that every person wait before God in a time of personal examination and cleansing.

Three days later, on April 29, 1607, the expedition, led by Rev. Hunt, went ashore to dedicate the continent to the glory of God. They carried one item with them from England for the purpose of giving glory to God in the endeavour—a rough-hewn wooden cross. As the party landed on the windswept shore, they erected the seven-foot oak cross in the sand.

The colonists and sailors gathered around the cross, holding the first formal prayer service in Virginia giving thanksgiving for God's mercy and grace. As they knelt in the Virginia sand, Rev. Hunt reminded them of the admonition of the British Royal Council, taken from the Holy Scripture: *"Every plantation, which my Heavenly Father hath not planted, shall be rooted up."* Raising his hands to heaven, Rev. Robert Hunt claimed the land for country and king and consecrated the continent to the glory of God. In covenantal language he declared, *". . .from these very shores the Gospel shall go forth to not only this New World, but the entire world."*

> *Psa 113:3 From the rising of the sun unto the going down of the same the LORD'S name is to be praised.*
>
> *Isa 59:19 So shall they fear the name of the LORD from the west, and his glory from the rising of the sun. When the enemy shall*

---

3. Klein Faith of our Fathers: Spirituality in Jamestown, CBN

come in like a flood, the Spirit of the LORD shall lift up a standard against him.

Mal 1:11 For from the rising of the sun even unto the going down of the same my name shall be great among the Gentiles; and in every place incense shall be offered unto my name, and a pure offering: for my name shall be great among the heathen, saith the LORD of hosts.

Between 1607 and 1696 England established its New-World culture in the Americas and in the West Indies.

From a trickle of one hundred and five souls landing in Jamestown in 1607, it became a deluge of Europeans; mostly Protestants whose ethic was based on the application of Old Testament precepts as described with the Promised Land of Canaan as their basis for addressing non-Europeans who were largely Indigenous Americans and later, Africans. Perhaps they used as their reference the following verses from scripture:

"Num 33:50–54 And the LORD spake unto Moses in the plains of Moab by Jordan near Jericho, saying, 51 Speak unto the children of Israel, and say unto them, When ye are passed over Jordan into the land of Canaan; 52 Then ye shall drive out all the inhabitants of the land from before you, and destroy all their pictures, and destroy all their molten images, and quite pluck down all their high places: 53 And ye shall dispossess the inhabitants of the land, and dwell therein: for I have given you the land to possess it. 54 And ye shall divide the land by lot for an inheritance among your families: and to the more ye shall give the more inheritance, and to the fewer ye shall give the less inheritance: every man's inheritance shall be in the place where his lot falleth; according to the tribes of your fathers ye shall inherit.[4]

This form of evangelism: plunder, murder, and genocide, was never preached in the New Testament, which states in the books Matthew and Mark: referring to 'the great commission':

Matt 28:16–20
16 *Then the eleven disciples went away into Galilee, into a mountain where Jesus had appointed them.*

17 *And when they saw him, they worshipped him: but some doubted.*

18 *And Jesus came and spake unto them, saying, All power is given unto me in heaven and in earth.*

---

4. Bible, King James Version

> *19 Go ye therefore, and teach all nations, baptizing them in the name of the Father, and of the Son, and of the Holy Ghost:*
> *20 Teaching them to observe all things whatsoever I have commanded you: and, lo, I am with you alway, even unto the end of the world. Amen*[5].

Mark 16:14–20
> *14 Afterward he appeared unto the eleven as they sat at meat, and upbraided them with their unbelief and hardness of heart, because they believed not them which had seen him after he was risen. 15 And he said unto them, Go ye into all the world, and preach the gospel to every creature.*
> *16 He that believeth and is baptized shall be saved; but he that believeth not shall be damned. 17 And these signs shall follow them that believe; In my name shall they cast out devils; they shall speak with new tongues; 18 They shall take up serpents; and if they drink any deadly thing, it shall not hurt them; they shall lay hands on the sick, and they shall recover. 19 So then after the Lord had spoken unto them, he was received up into heaven, and sat on the right hand of God. 20 And they went forth, and preached every where, the Lord working with them, and confirming the word with signs following. Amen.*[6]

Rev Robert Hunt died in 1608 and the commitment by the English to propagate the Christian faith was passed on to Sir Thomas Gates who issued instructions that conflicted with: "Matt 28:19 *"Go ye therefore, and teach all nations, baptizing them in the name of the Father, and of the Son, and of the Holy Ghost."* He called for a forcible conversion of Native Americans to Anglicanism and their subordination to colonial administration.

In 1609 Sir Thomas Gates and later Thomas West, baron De La Warr, who the Virginia Company had appointed governor of the colony, gave further instructions to settlers in Virginia to kidnap Native Americans' children to 'educate them with English values and religion.' These instructions also sanctioned attacking the indigenous people, the Iniocasoockes, who were the cultural leaders of the local Powhatans. In England, meanwhile, a propaganda war ensued, and an article published in *Nova Britannia* that year, compared Native Americans to *'wild animals'*—"*heardes of deere in a forest.*" While it did portray the Powhatan as peace-loving, it threatened to deal with any who resisted conversion to Anglicanism as enemies of their country. This is another example of where the English colonizers in the New

---

5. Bible, King James Version
6. Bible, King James Version

World began to implement the precedents which the Spanish had established in the Canaries. (Precedents 1,6,7,10)

Over the next three years tensions arose between the colonizers and the indigenous people as more land was taken. Finally, the first Anglo-Powhatan war broke out in 1610 and for the following four years there were sporadic wars between the settlers and the Powhatan tribes. Their relationship alternated between peace and war. The indigenous people had growing concerns for their own safety and security with the increasing numbers of immigrants in the English settlements. They decided to try and wipe them out. They made a surprise attack on the village and killed 347 men, women, and children. This was a declaration of war!

The English decided to use a strategy that would respond to the relative strengths and weaknesses of the parties. The English had increasing numbers, and unrivalled musket power. The indigenous people were at home in their land. As one historian, Edmund Morgan wrote in his history of early Virginia:

> "Since the Indians were better woodsmen than the English and virtually impossible to track down, the method was to feign peaceful intentions, let them settle down and plant their corn wherever they chose, and then, just before harvest, fall upon them, killing as many as possible and burning the corn. . .. Within two or three years of the massacre the English had avenged the deaths of that day many times over." . . . . .
>
> "Not able to enslave the Indians, and not able to live with them, the English decided to exterminate them."[7]

Jamestown needed people, to replenish its dwindling numbers due to sickness and death and to increase the labor force to defend the project. England was experiencing a major paradigm shift in its own economic and social circumstances. A population boom in England had created food shortages, rising prices, declining wages, and a huge drop in the standard of living in many areas. There was little work to be found and England was anxious to get rid of the vagrants that began to fill its cities. One solution was to exile them to America. Some were sentenced under poor and vagrancy laws to exportation to the colonies.

Indentureship: Some of the indentured servants left willingly because they thought America had to be better than England. Some were kidnapped by ship captains looking for more cargo to take to America. Velasco, the Spanish Ambassador in England said as much in a 1611 letter to his monarch: *"Their principal reason for colonising these parts is to give an outlet for*

---

7. Morgan, *American Slavery, American Freedom*, 100

*so many idle, wretched people as they have in England and thus prevent the dangers that might be feared of them.*⁸"In England, the marketing of Nova Britannia, and the application of the vagrancy laws reaped a harvest for the colony (and later, other colonies). Servitude became the source of labour by which the tobacco plantations would become productive. *"Servitude however in Virginia's tobacco fields approached closer to slavery than anything known at the time in England,"* the historian Edmund S. Morgan wrote. *"Men served longer, were subjected to more rigorous punishments, [and] were traded about as commodities"*⁹beginning in the 1620s. For much of the seventeenth century, those servants were white English men and women—with a smattering of Africans, Native Americans, and Irish—under indenture with the promise of freedom. 1619 marked the year of the importation and purchase of the first Africans into the colony and the English colonies. Historians seem to be ambivalent about the treatment of these Africans. An African American writer, J. Saunders Redding, describes the arrival of a ship in North America in the year 1619:

> *"Sails furled, flag drooping at her rounded stern, she rode the tide in from the sea. She was a strange ship, indeed, by all accounts, a frightening ship, a ship of mystery. Whether she was trader, privateer, or man-of-war no one knows. Through her bulwarks black-mouthed cannon yawned. The flag she flew was Dutch, her crew a motley. Her port of call, an English settlement, Jamestown, in the colony of Virginia. She came, she traded, and shortly afterwards was gone. Probably no ship in modern history has carried a more portentous freight. Her cargo? Twenty slaves."*¹⁰

Howard Zinn in his book *"A Peoples History of the US"* argues that:

> *"There is not a country in world history in which racism has been more important as the United States. And the problem of "the colour line," as W. E. B. Du Bois put it, is still with us. So it is more than a purely historical question to ask. If history can help answer these questions, then the beginnings of slavery in North America—a continent where we can trace the coming of the first whites and the first blacks—might supply at least a few clues. On the other hand, some historians think those first blacks in Virginia were considered as servants, like the white indentured servants brought from Europe. But the strong probability is that, even if they were listed as "servants" (a more familiar category to the*

---

8. Morgan, American Slavery, American Freedom 96
9. Morgan, American Slavery, American Freedom 296
10. Zinn, A Peoples History of the United States, 23

> *English), they were viewed as being different from white servants, were treated differently, and in fact were slaves. In any case, slavery developed quickly into a regular institution, into the normal labour relation of blacks to whites in the New World. With it developed that special racial feeling—whether hatred, or contempt, or pity, or patronisation—that accompanied the inferior position of blacks in America for the next 350 years —that combination of inferior status and derogatory thought we call racism?*[11]

The Virginians of 1619 were desperate for labor, to grow enough food to stay alive. Among them were survivors from the winter of 1609–1610, the "starving time," when, crazed for want of food, they roamed the woods for nuts and berries, dug up graves to eat the corpses, and died in batches until five hundred colonists were reduced to sixty.

In the *Journals of the House of Burgesses of Virginia* is a document of 1619 which tells of the first twelve years of the Jamestown colony. The first settlement had a hundred persons, who had one small ladle of barley per meal. When more people arrived, there was even less food. Many of the people lived in cave-like holes dug into the ground, and in the winter of 1609–1610, they were:

> . . .*driven through insufferable hunger to eat those things which nature most abhorred, the flesh and excrements of man as well of our own nation as of an Indian, digged by some out of his grave after he had laid buried there days and wholly devoured him; others, envying the better state of body of any whom hunger has not yet so much wasted as their own, lay wait and threatened to kill and eat them; one among them slew his wife as she slept in his bosom, cut her in pieces, salted her and fed upon her till he had clean devoured all parts saving her head. .*

A petition by thirty colonists to the House of Burgesses, complaining against the twelve-year governorship of Sir Thomas Smith, said:

> *"In those 12 years of Sir Thomas Smith, his government, we aver that the colony for the most part remained in great want and misery under most severe and cruel laws. . . The allowance in those times for a man was only eight ounces of meale and half a pint of peas for a day. . . mouldy, rotten, full of cobwebs and maggots, loathsome to man and not fit for beasts, which forced many to flee for relief to the savage enemy, who being taken again were put to sundry deaths as by hanging, shooting and breaking upon the wheel. . . of whom one for stealing two or three pints of oatmeal*

---

11. Zinn, A Peoples' History of the United States, 23

had a bodkin thrust through his tongue and was tied with a chain to a tree until he starved."[12]

The Virginians needed labour, to grow corn for subsistence, to grow tobacco for export. They had just figured out how to grow tobacco, and in 1617 they sent off the first cargo to England. Finding that, like all pleasurable drugs tainted with moral disapproval, it brought a high price, the planters, despite their high religious talk, were not going to ask questions about something so profitable.

They could not force the Indians to work for them, as Columbus had done. They were outnumbered, and while, with superior firearms, they could massacre Indians, they would face massacre in return. They could not capture them and keep them enslaved; the Native Americans were tough, resourceful, defiant, and at home in these woods, as the transplanted Englishmen were not.

White servants had not yet been brought over to Virginia in sufficient quantity. Besides, they did not come out of slavery, and did not have to do more than contract their labour for a few years to get their passage and start a new life in the New World. As for the free white settlers, many of them were skilled craftsmen, or even men of leisure back in England, who were so little inclined to work the land that a kind of martial law was declared, to organise them into work gangs, and force them into the fields for survival.

There may have been a kind of frustrated rage at their own ineptitude, at the Indian superiority at taking care of themselves, that made the Virginians especially ready to become the masters of slaves.

Edmund Morgan imagines their mood as he writes in his book" *American Slavery, American Freedom:*"

> *"If you were a colonist, you knew that your technology was superior to the Indians'. You knew that you were civilized, and they were savages. . . But your superior technology had proved insufficient to extract anything. The Indians, keeping to themselves, laughed at your superior methods and lived from the land more abundantly and with less labour than you did. . . And when your own people started deserting in order to live with them, it was too much. . . So, you killed the Indians, tortured them, burned their villages, burned their cornfields. It proved your superiority, in spite of your failures. And you gave similar treatment to any of your own people who succumbed to their savage ways of life. But you still did not grow much corn."*[13]

12. Zinn, A Peoples' History of the United States, 24
13 Morgan, American Slavery, American Freedom 90

African slaves were the answer. And it was natural to consider imported blacks as slaves, even if the institution of slavery would not be regularised and legalised for several decades. Because, by 1619, a million Africans had already been transported to South America and the West Indies, to the Portuguese and Spanish colonies, to work as slaves. Fifty years before Columbus, the Portuguese took ten Africans to Lisbon—this was the start of a regular trade in slaves. Africans had been stamped as slave labor for a hundred years. So, it would have been strange if those twenty blacks, forcibly transported to Jamestown, and sold as objects to settlers anxious for a steadfast source of labor, were considered as anything but slaves. As slaves they were not considered residents and had no stake in the colony except to be the labor force on the plantations of the new cash crop -tobacco. Despite these adjustments, the colony was not a financial success. The Virginia Company declared bankruptcy in 1622. Two years later in 1624, the Crown assumed full control of the settlement, making Virginia the first of the royal colonies. Thus began, for the English the first fulfilment of the doctrine of Colonialism as developed in the Canaries by the Spanish. (Precedent 1,6)

In 1620, a second colony at Plymouth was founded, by a group of Puritan Separatists initially known as the Brownist Emigration, who came to be known as the Pilgrims. It would become the first permanent English settlement in America, and it is located in the New England region.

Despite the colony's relatively short existence, Plymouth holds a special role in American history. Most of the citizens of Plymouth were fleeing religious persecution and searching for a place to worship as they saw fit, rather than being entrepreneurs like many of the settlers of Jamestown in Virginia. The social and legal systems of the colony became closely tied to their religious beliefs, as well as to English custom. Many of the people and events surrounding Plymouth Colony have become part of American folklore, including the American tradition of Thanksgiving and the monument of Plymouth Rock. The colony established a treaty with Wampanoag Chief Massasoit which helped to ensure its success; in this, they were aided by Squanto, a member of the Pawtuxet tribe. Plymouth played a central role in King Philip's War (1675–1678), one of several Indian Wars, but the colony was ultimately merged with the Massachusetts Bay Colony and other territories in 1691 to form the Province of Massachusetts Bay.

John Winthrop, (1588–1649), Boston, Massachusetts Bay Colony was the first governor of the Massachusetts Bay Colony, and the chief figure among the Puritan founders of New England. He was a member of the ruling class; his father having bought land directly from Henry V111 at the time of the Reformation.

Like other Puritans at the time, without the experience of living among other non-European peoples, he dedicated himself to remaking, as far as possible, the wicked world as he saw it, arguing that *"the life which is most exercised with tryalls and temptations is the sweetest, and will prove the safeste."* That Puritan position cost him his court position in 1629. He felt trapped. When, in 1629, the Massachusetts Bay Company obtained a royal charter to plant a colony in New England, Winthrop joined the company, pledging to sell his English estate and take his family to Massachusetts if the company government and charter were also transferred to America. The other members agreed to these terms and elected him governor.

As Winthrop sailed west on the *Arbella* in the spring of 1630, he composed a lay sermon, *"A Modell of Christian Charity,"* in which he pictured the Massachusetts colonists in covenant with God and with each other, divinely ordained to build *"a Citty upon a Hill"* in New England, with *"the eyes of all people"* on them:

> *"If we deal falsely with our God in this work we have undertaken and so cause Him to withdraw His present help from us, we shall be made a story and a byword throughout the world; we shall open the mouths of enemies to speak evil of the ways of God and all believers in God; we shall shame the faces of many of God's worthy servants and cause their prayers to be turned into curses upon us, till we are forced out of the new land where we are going."*[14]

However, on their arrival in New England the Puritans applied the same principles that Columbus had initiated almost one hundred and fifty years earlier in 1492 under the Roman Catholic doctrine (as defined in Papal Bulls *"Dum Diversas"* and *"Romanus Pontifex"*). These principles encouraged the seizure of lands of non-Christians (Non- Europeans) and the enslavement of and wanton murder of such peoples, in the name of the Trinity.

The Puritans were coming not to "vacant" land but to territory inhabited by Native Americans (mistakenly called Indians by Columbus). The governor of the Massachusetts Bay Colony, John Winthrop, used the excuse to take 'Native Americans' land by declaring the area legally unoccupied. The Indians, he said, had not "subdued" the ! *For there is no respect of persons with God."* It seems that they applied Old Testament teaching of when the children of Israel entered the Promised Land, and they replaced the children of Israel with the Church. God did not replace the Jews with the Greek. As Paul writes in his letter to the Romans:

14. Winthrop, A Modell of Christian Charity 1630

Rom 1:16–19

16 For I am not ashamed of the gospel of Christ: for it is the power of God unto salvation to every one that believeth; to the Jew first, and also to the Greek. 17 For therein is the righteousness of God revealed from faith to faith: as it is written, The just shall live by faith.

18 For the wrath of God is revealed from heaven against all ungodliness and unrighteousness of men, who hold the truth in unrighteousness; 19 Because that which may be known of God is manifest in them; for God hath shewed it unto them..

And in Romans 10:12 *For there is no difference between the Jew and the Greek: for the same Lord over all is rich unto all that call upon him.*

It seemed that Protestant Christianity like Roman Christianity at that time was based on European genealogy and that 'conversion by force' was the method of making Christians of non-Europeans. They applied that principle in Jamestown and continued that system in the other locations in and out the Charter!

They held the truth in unrighteousness. These were features of the Roman Catholic culture, teaching, and tradition as practiced in the fifteenth century.

The seemingly non-stop and ever-increasing immigration of Europeans into the country called America gave the Native Americans some cause for alarm. These Europeans came and occupied their land in what is presently called Connecticut, Rhode Island: generally, the region around Massachusetts. The first arrivals were adherents to Anglicanism, Congregationalism, Presbyterianism, Lutheranism, Quakerism, Mennonite and the Moravian church from British, German, Dutch, and Nordic stock. America emerged as a Protestant majority nation, with significant minorities of Roman Catholics and Jews. This invasion of European manpower, gunpower and technological superiority changed the balance of power against the Native Americans. Whatever goodwill that was established at the original Thanksgiving (that the Americans still celebrate) during which the Native Americans brought and shared their food with the Europeans in 1620, was quickly dissipated.

Subsequently, the English applied all measures to take control of the new lands of the Americas. Beginning in 1636, they fought three wars against the native Americans, applying every tactic to secure victory; pre-emptive attacks, including massacre of the villagers, scorched earth policies, divide and rule, and finally with numerical increase into the lands. They introduced its courts of law and imposed English to control prisoners and native Americans.

An event called the "Standish Raid" eventually proved to be essentially the beginning of a process of colonisation that would define the nature of the nation that would become the United States of America. (Precedents 6,7,9,10)

"*The United States of America was established as a white society, founded upon the near genocide of another race and then the enslavement of yet another.*"[15] The murder of a white trader, Indian-kidnapper, and troublemaker became an excuse to make war on the Pequot tribe in 1636.

Myles Standish was the military leader of Plymouth Colony from the beginning. He organized and led the first party to set foot in New England, an exploratory expedition of Cape Cod upon arrival in Provincetown Harbour. He also led the third expedition, during which Standish fired the first recorded shot by the Pilgrim settlers in an event known as the First Encounter. Standish led two early military raids on Indian villages: the raid to find and punish a native, named Corbitant for his attempted coup, and the killing at Wessagussett the former had the desired effect of gaining the respect of the local Indians. Reports reached Plymouth of a military threat to Wessagussett, and Myles Standish organized a militia to defend them. However, he found that there had been no attack. He therefore decided on a pre-emptive strike, an event which historian Nathaniel Philbrick calls "Standish's raid." He lured two prominent Massachusetts military leaders into a house at Wessagussett under the pretence of sharing a meal and making negotiations. Standish and his men then stabbed and killed the two unsuspecting Native Americans." That only served to frighten and scatter them, resulting in the Pilgrims' loss of trade and income, which they needed to repay their loans to their English financiers.

The second event in this process of colonisation, was the Pequot War, from 1636–1638 which resulted in the dissolution of the Pequot tribe and a major shift in the local power structure. The first confirmed account of slavery in the colony came in 1638 when several native prisoners taken during the Pequot War were exchanged in the West Indies for African slaves. Such exchanges became common in subsequent conflicts.

As early as 1669 laws were implemented to protect the white population from any abuse of slaves: October 1669:

> "*Act I: An act about the casual killing of slaves. Whereas the only law in force for the punishment of refractory servants resisting their master, mistress or overseer cannot be inflicted upon negroes, nor the obstinacy of many of them by other than violent means*

---

15. Wallis: America's Original Sin: Racism, White Privilege, and the Bridge to a New America 33.

suppressed, Be it enacted and declared by this grand assembly, if any slave resist his master (or others by his masters order correcting him) and by the extremity of the correction should chance to die, that his death shall not be considered a felony, but the master (or that other person appointed by the master to punish him) be acquit from molestation, since it cannot be presumed that malice existed(which alone makes murder a felony) [or that anything] should induce any man to destroy his own estate."[16]

Finally, the third King Philip's War: 1675-1676:

"The cause of the war stems from the ever-increasing numbers of English colonists and their demand for land. As more land was purchased from the Native Americans, they were restricted to smaller territories for themselves. Native American leaders such as King Philip resented the loss of land and looked for a means to slow or reverse it. Of specific concern was the founding of the town of Swansea, which was located only a few miles from the Wampanoag capital at Mount Hope. The General Court of Plymouth began using military force to coerce the sale of Wampanoag land to the settlers of the town. It had the most dramatic effect on local populations, resulting in the death or displacement of as much as 80% of the total number of Native Americans of southern New England. The other destructive act was the enslavement and removal of thousands of Native Americans to the Caribbean and other locales."[17]

A ray of light had appeared in the original declaration of the First Charter as declared by King James 1. He had proposed the publishing of the Bible, commonly called the KJV Bible. It was in the life and time of one called John Eliot, who later dedicated his life to the evangelisation of the Native Americans and leading them into a kingdom relationship with Jesus Christ.

John Huffman, in his article "John Eliot—Apostle to the Indians" writes about Eliot's calling:

"Who will go to the Indians?" This question hung for a long moment in the assembly hall in Boston. The magistrates of the Massachusetts Bay Colony had decided that they would provide for the annual support of two ministers who would leave their home

---

16. Virginia Slave Codes Excerpts taken from William W. Henning, The Statutes at Large; Being a Collection of all the Laws of Virginia, v.2 (1823)

17. Philbrick, Mayflower a story of courage, community and war p. 57-58, 71, 84, 90, 115, 128, 155f

churches and labor among the Indians of the Massachusetts Bay region. The silence was long and intense. All that had been asked was that two servants of God volunteer."[18]

Huffman continues:

"In the crowded assembly hall, finally there was a stir of activity. One courageous man stepped forward to offer himself for the mission work among the Indians. He knew nothing of the Indian language. He was the pastor of the church in Roxbury and had a comfortable situation and a steady income. This was not a mere novice. The man who stepped forward was in the prime of his life, 42 years old. His name was John Eliot, and he came from a very prosperous family back in England. He was a graduate of Jesus College in Cambridge University and was recognized as an excellent Hebrew scholar. He had cast his lot with the Puritans and crossed the ocean, arriving in Boston in 1631[19].

The impact of Eliot's work was monumental. In assuming his new responsibilities, he resolved that he would continue his work as pastor in Roxbury, but travel on a regular basis into the western woods to minister in the Indian villages. Leaving his comfortable home on a regular basis, John Eliot faithfully served simultaneously as pastor, missionary, husband, father, and medical doctor in the Indian villages. His ministry reflected the command Jesus Christ gave us in Matt 28:19-20,

> Mat 28:19 Go, then, to all peoples everywhere and make them my disciples: baptize them in the name of the Father, the Son, and the Holy Spirit,
> Mat 28:20 and teach them to obey everything I have commanded you. And I will be with you always, to the end of the age."

He focused on every component/aspect of that command: 'all the peoples everywhere'; "make them disciples" (followers of Jesus Christ). The peoples whom the Lord gave him firstly were the Europeans who came to America. He continued his pastoral work in Roxbury. Secondly, the other people in America were the Native Americans. He would regularly travel to the woods to minister to the Indian villages. His original missionary outreaches were as he put it 'a disaster'. Not put off, he decided to use his talents of understanding linguistics and immersed himself in the language of the natives. Within a few months, he had learned the language to the extent that

18. Huffman, John Eliot Apostle to the Indians
19. Huffman, John Eliot Apostle to the Indians

he was able to haltingly preach in their language. A few months later, he began the translation of the Word of God into the language of the Indians of Massachusetts, and his wife catechized the children, rewarding them for good work. Eliot taught them to obey the Ten Commandments, to have only one God—not to practice witchcraft or 'paw pawing' as they called it. He taught them new skills to facilitate their life opportunities in a changing world: they learnt how to salt their fish to preserve it and how to use iron tools to their advantage.

In preaching to the Indians, Eliot *"believed that the Gentile nations ought to obey and submit to the Law of God. He patterned the Christian Indian villages after what he found in the Old Testament, appointing officers and judges in each village to hear cases and administer Biblical law."*[20]

This was one of the few times that Europeans described non-Europeans who were not Jews as "Gentiles," all of whom Jesus came to reconcile to Himself. This set the basis for evangelising the nation. Eliot assisted in the foundation of settlements of believing Indians or *Praying Indians* as they were called, to become self-sustaining according to Biblical teaching. He took that instruction literally and instituted the teaching of not only how to get to heaven but also how to govern a home Biblically; how to farm Biblically; how to punish crime Biblically; how to wage war Biblically; and how to govern a village Biblically. He patterned the Christian Indian villages after what he found in the Old Testament, appointing officers, and judges in each village to hear cases and administer Biblical law. This also included provision for their own schools, churches and the preaching of the Gospel in their own language. The first such settlement, Natick, was begun in 1650 and 13 others followed, surviving until the rebellions of the 1670s. This Native American Mariner Culture were among the first eastern Tribal Nations converted to Christianity.

Elliot continued his work among the Europeans and the native Indians for the rest of his life. He died in 1690 at age of 86. It is noteworthy that by 1661 he completely translated the book of Psalms (The Bay Book of Psalms) and the bible. They were also the first books printed in America; the Western Hemisphere; the New World and they were in the language of the Algonquin!

John Winthrop, (1587/88—1649) the Governor of Massachusetts Bay Colony, gave this glowing report of John Eliot's work among the Indians:

"God prospered his endeavors. Some of the Indians began to be very seriously affected and to understand the things of God and they were generally ready to reform whatever they were told to be against the word of God."

---

20. Huffman, John Eliot Apostle to the Indians

Cotton Mather, 1663—1728 (New England clergyman, graduate of Harvard College and writer) singled out the Indians before their conversion as "doleful creatures, the veriest ruins of mankind," whose way of living was "infinitely barbarous," now had this to say about Eliot's work:

> "It is above forty years since that truly Godly man, Mr. John Eliot . . . not without very great labor, translated the whole Bible into the Indian Tongue. He gathered a church of converted Indians in a Town called Natick; these Indians confessed their sins with tears, and professed their faith in Christ, and afterwards they and their children were baptized; and they were solemnly joined together in a church Covenant. The Pastor of that church now is an Indian, his Name is Daniel. Of the Indians there are four and twenty who are preachers of the Word of God."[21]

Eliot became known as 'The Indian Apostle and Waban (at Natick, MA) was the first Indian chief to embrace Christianity and entertained John Eliot in his wigwam when Eliot first went among the Nipmuc as a preacher in their own language on October 28, 1648.

Although the colonials did raise a Praying Indian Company, composed of fifty-two Native Mount Hope campaign, a certain segment of the English population distrusted all Native Americans and felt that the Praying Indians would always be more loyal to the hostile tribes than to the English.

By August 30, 1675, the Governor, and Council of the Massachusetts Colony, in response to public demand, disbanded all Praying Indian companies, confined these Christian Indians to the Old Praying Indian towns, and restricted their travel to within one mile of the centre of those towns and only then when in the company of an Englishman. If a Native American broke these rules, he could be arrested or shot on sight. Most Englishmen were unwilling to reside in these towns because of the prejudice directed toward any Englishman supporting the Praying Indian cause.

Christian Indians were caught between two warring factions: the English and the hostile tribes fighting with King Philip.

They pledged their loyalty to the English who refused to trust them and, at the same time, faced the enmity of their own people. Their loyalty was rewarded with such public hatred toward them that in August 1675, the General Council in Boston began to consider removing the Praying Indians to Deer Island in Boston Harbor. Finally, in October 1675, the order passed for removal; by December of that year, there were over five hundred Christian Indians confined to the island:

---

21. Huffman, John Eliot: Apostle to the Indians

> "*The enmity, jealousy, and clamors of some people against them put the magistracy upon a kind of necessity to send them all to the Island. ...*" where they "*... lived chiefly upon clams and shell-fish, that they digged out of the sand, at low water; the Island was bleak and cold, their wigwams poor and mean, their clothes few and thin; some little corn they had of their own, which the Council ordered to be fetched from their plantations, and conveyed to them by little and little.*"[22]

There they stayed until released in 1677, but the world to which they returned was totally changed. The English had defeated the warring tribes, leaving the Native Americans strangers in their own homeland.

The following is a twenty-first century testimony by the descendants of the Praying Indians who were evangelised by John Eliot:

> "Descendants of the Praying Indians from Natick have organized as the Praying Indian Tribe of Natick, currently under the leadership of Rosita Andrews or Caring Hands from Stoughton, Massachusetts, who received her title of chief from her mother. The Praying Indian members live within a radius of twenty miles (32 km) around Stoughton. According to Caring Hands, in 2011 there were just under fifty members of Natick Praying Indians.
>
> On 11 August 2012, members of the tribe celebrated a public service in Eliot church, South Natick, the site of the original church of the Praying Indian town of Natick, for the first time after almost three hundred years.
>
> Although we are not the only descendants, we are the only existing Praying Indian Tribe. The blood of a praying Indian is both physical and spiritual. Our lineage of both is unbroken. We have seen our brothers and sisters, descendants of shared heritage deviate from the path and acknowledge the weight of an overwhelming history. In suffering the loss of family and brethren we recognize the difficulty of the walk of our praying Indian ancestors. We have understood that boundaries are spiritual as well as physical. Shunned for years by the Native community, we are rewarded in now witnessing resurgence of our praying Indian brethren."
>
> "As the earth reclines under the grass, so too does the earth recline under the Great Spirit of God. Therefore the chosen habitations thereof are a principle of God understood by all indigenous people (moskhet kutoo). We are mindful of our past, of all our native brothers and sisters suffering and the wish of all non-natives of good hearts to reconcile. This can be done only through the people wronged, forgotten and holding out the scepter of reconciliation.

---

22. The Christian Indians, Archaeologia Americana, Vol 2, 1836.djvu/521

> *True restoration is more than a word. As a chief honored in the spiritual lineage of Waban, first indigenous minister of light and a remnant surviving the physical and spiritual holocaust of a blessed people, the Praying Indians stand as first ambassadors of this country to the world. In an inordinate display of reconciliation we extend our hand to our captors. As we hold out the scepter understand that restoration is more than a word.*
>
> *I am proud to be Chief of the Mother Village of all Praying Indians. I am proud of the tribe which has stood by my leadership and against the tide of suffering and misunderstanding. We do not apologize for our belief in love of The Father God and His Son First Spoken Word of Light. Even those who do not agree must honor the strength of standing for one's beliefs. As a chief watching her people suffer the isolation of a social Deer Island, I see as Waban saw in facing his people on Deer Island. Waban, can you see me? In an echo from the past do we stand alongside all our ancestors and welcome our brethren in the name of Word Faithful and True. We are who we are. We stand where we stand. We are the Massachusett Praying Indians. In thoughts ever toward peace I say Aho. I have spoken. I am Naticksquaw Chief Caring Hands, she who speaks for her people."*
>
> Looking into the past. . . "Waban, can you see me. . ."
>
> The Answer. . . "The end is the beginning in His Love. . ." We love you and it is all about love."[23]

Despite their church being burned down several times, they stated their belief which is:

> Jas 4:17 *So then, if we do not do the good we know we should do, we are guilty of sin.*

The Natick here has expressed a godly offer of love to the descendants of their 'captors', the Europeans, in their desire for reconciliation in the family of Christ.

"*America's other original sin*" according to Jim Wallis was the enslavement of the Africans, by the English and implemented by the Puritans and later Anglicanism and Protestantism. Anglo-America's slave trade began in 1636 with the Puritans. "*Desire*" was the first American-built slave ship. She was constructed and armed in Marblehead, Massachusetts, her belly outfitted with leg irons, bars, and racks. In 1637, a year after the founding of Harvard University, seventeen years after the landing of the Pilgrims at Plymouth Rock, that "*Desire*" set sail for the British West Indies, and

---

23. natickprayingindians.org

returned seven months later with cotton, tobacco, and enslaved Africans who laboured on Caribbean plantations. The Africans were quickly bought up by enterprising Massachusetts citizens. These Puritans threw the gauntlet down at the English navy as they not only built a slave ship but entered the slave trading business.

In 1640, John Punch, a runaway black servant, was sentenced to servitude for life. His two white companions who ran away with him, were given extended terms of servitude. Punch is the first documented African sentenced for life. This decision marks the establishment of 'unequal treatment before the law' in America, based on John Punch's ethnicity defined as being a 'Guineaman.'

Massachusetts was the first colony in 1641, to legalise slavery in the American colonies. Two years later in 1643, the New England Confederation of Plymouth, Massachusetts, Connecticut, and New Haven was established. They covenanted to support each other and themselves against invasions from native tribes, the Dutch and other European insurgents.

Some of the other major areas of agreement were as follows:

Corporate defence: Since the Massachusetts Bay Colony was the largest, it was required to send one hundred men while the other colonies were required to send forty each.

Domestic Policing: As far as policing was concerned, the individual colonies were encouraged to avoid war as much as possible and to keep peace within its own colony to prevent enemies from taking advantage of internal problems.

Citizens' (Ethnic) Arrests: In addition, runaway servants and slaves escaping to other colonies within the confederation, were to be returned to their masters. Escaped prisoners were also to be returned. Could this have been the birth of institutional discrimination against people of colour?

> "*This society comprised many of the descendants of the people (Europeans) who could have participated in the Crusades against the Saracens. Their ancestors could have had their beliefs shaped by the Lutherans in Germany or the Huguenots in Holland and France, or from other Protestants in England and those who wanted to go further away from the doctrines of the Roman church at that time, including the Puritans, Quakers, the Presbyterians, and others.*"[24]

Jamestown had been established in 1607 as a Christian colony as declared by Rev John Hunt. After his early death De Warr assumed power in 1609 and introduced a scorched earth policy. It was declared financially

---

24. Wallis, *America's Original Sin*

bankrupt in 1624 despite its production and export of that carcinogenic substance—tobacco. The Crown therefore assumed full control of the colony and it was subsumed into the Massachusetts Bay Colony. It became the English first colony in the New World in 1624, just seventeen years after the first landing.

Thanksgiving Day, which is an annual national holiday in the United States is modelled on the 1621 harvest feast shared by the English colonists (Pilgrims) of Plymouth and the Wampanoag people. It was because of the Wampanoag's welcome and generosity in helping the Pilgrims to find food during the winter months, following the death of almost fifty percent of the original group of Pilgrims.

8

Barbados, the West Indies and Anglo-America

WHAT IS THE HISTORY and significance of this little island, that is called Barbados and "Little England," where cricket is the celebrated national pastime and of its people whose brogue is that of an old British accent? At one time this little island had more resident Church of England vicars, than any other colony in North America!

King James 1, of England, claimed Jamestown in 1607, Bermuda in 1609; the Plymouth Colony in 1620; in 1623 St. Kitts and several islands in the Leeward Islands. Following the death of King James 1, King Charles 1, continued the mission of acquiring more lands and expanding English occupation of the islands of the West Indies. Barbados was among the first cluster of colonies claimed in the name of King Charles 1 of England, 1625—1649 followed by other English settlements in both North America and the West Indies; 1628: Nevis, 1632 Montserrat and 1632 Antigua.

In the seventeenth century, Barbados was established as a 'proprietary colony' which was similar to those established by the British in North America and other parts of the West Indies. It was funded by Sir William Courten, a City of London merchant who acquired the title to Barbados and several other islands. So, the first colonists were tenants and most of the profit from their labor returned to Courten and his company. (Precedent 1)

At that time in history, all land belonged to the monarch, and it was his prerogative to divide. Therefore, all colonial properties were partitioned by royal charter into one of four types: royal, joint stock, covenant or proprietary. King Charles II used the proprietary solution to reward allies and focus his own attention on England. He offered his friends colonial charters which facilitated private investment and colonial self-government. The charters made the proprietor the effective ruler, albeit one responsible to English Law and the King. In 1664, Charles II gave New Netherland to his younger brother The Duke of York, who named it New York. He gave an area to William Penn who named it Pennsylvania in 1681.

The first English people to arrive in Barbados were originally eighty yeoman farmers who were also adventurers. En-route to Barbados the English ship intercepted another vessel and captured ten Africans who they took to Barbados. They finally arrived in Barbados on 17 February 1672, landing at Holetown on the west coast of the island. As farmers, they immediately got to work clearing the thick virgin forests and planted cotton, indigo and tobacco. They lived off the land and wild boar that were roaming around the island earlier released by passing Portuguese sailors.

However, the staple cash crop of tobacco experienced major competition from other English Colonies, both in the West Indies, and in Virginia, Anglo America. To facilitate the demise of tobacco production in Barbados, the English government imposed an increased import tax on Barbadian tobacco entering England. Many tobacco planters, some of whom had acquired land at the end of their indentureship, sold off their plots and emigrated to North America; with Carolina, being the most popular destination. Others remained in Barbados. One of the remaining plantation owners was Sir James Drax who accumulated extraordinary wealth as a pioneer of the sugar trade in the English colonies. The Caribbean sugar plantations established by James Drax and those who followed his example, would be at the epicenter of the growing English and French empires, helping to fuel economic growth and imperial expansion.

According to author Matthew Parker, who writes in his book, "Sugar Barons";[1] James Drax was the son of William Drax, a gentleman of the village of Finham, in the parish of Stoneleigh, Warwickshire. In the late 1620s, James Drax became one of the earliest English migrants to the island of Barbados. He and his companions arrived and lived for a time in a cave, hunting for provisions, and clearing land for the planting of tobacco, which soon became the agricultural focus of the island. Drax later claimed that he had arrived with a stock of no more than £300, and that he intended to stay on the island until he had increased his first investment into a landed fortune worth £10,000 a year back home.

---

1. Parker, Sugar Barons, 13

Drax, together with his brother, William, had accumulated a substantial portion of land in Barbados, by the late 1630s. Owing to a slump in tobacco prices, the late 1630s saw considerable economic difficulty in England's fledgling colonies in the Caribbean, and white colonists began to turn to other crops. According to tradition, Drax was one of the pioneers of the introduction of sugar to the island and was reportedly the first planter successfully to cultivate sugar cane on a large scale. Matthew Parker writes:

> "Concurrent with the rise of sugar came large-scale and intensive exploitation of slave labor, with Drax being was one of the pioneers of slavery in the Caribbean. Prior to 1640, the primary source of labor in Barbados had been European indentured servants. Although there were enslaved Africans in Barbados before that time, it was only after 1640, and frequently in tandem with the cultivation of sugar, that slave labor began to supplant indentured servitude as the main workforce. By 1641 he had over 400 acres, making him nearly the greatest landowner on the island. Just as he was getting involved in sugar, he acquired twenty-two Africans in early 1642 at a time when nobody else had even a handful of slaves. In 1644, he purchased another thirty-four enslaved Africans. By the early 1650s, his plantation, Drax Hall Estate, was worked by some 200 enslaved Africans. Drax was known by his contemporaries to provide his slaves and servants well, unlike James Holdip who was known to be so cruel and oppressive, that his servants burnt his entire plantation to the ground."[2]

This model of intensive slave labor organized into work gangs, and disciplined through ubiquitous violence, also quickly spread through the West Indies, going together with sugar production.

> "Drax profited spectacularly from his sugar enterprise, allowing him to live "like a prince." With wealth and power came political controversy. He emerged during the 1640s as a supporter of the Parliamentarians and during the civil war and became a Colonel in the island's militia. As a result, when a royalist faction seized control of Barbados in 1650, James and William Drax were exiled from the island, along with other prominent parliamentarians. They returned to London, where they lobbied the House of Commons to send an expedition to retake the island. In 1651, Drax sailed in the fleet designed to re-conquer Barbados, and he was part of the team that went ashore to negotiate the surrender of

---

2. Parker, Sugar Barons, 30

the island. Restored to his estates and power, Drax once again assumed a leading role in the governance of the colony."[3]

Drax also played a role as patron of explorers of the North American coast, including Robert Sandford. In 1658, Drax was rewarded for his loyalty with a knighthood from the Lord Protector, Oliver Cromwell.

> "By this point, Drax had returned to England, where he acquired a series of estates, pursuing his original ambition of setting himself up as a landed magnate at home, while continuing to profit from his plantations and estates in Barbados. He survived the transition of the Restoration, but died in early 1662, and was buried in the parish of St. John Zachary, London. After his death, his son Henry continued to own and manage the family estate in Barbados. The Drax descendants were particularly active in the development of Jamaica where there is a Drax Hall Estate in St Ann's parish, Jamaica."[4]

In 1789, Drax's grand nephew established Jamaica College, a public Christian Secondary School and sixth form for boys in Kingston, Jamaica.

As mentioned earlier, sugarcane was originally grown in Barbados in 1637 on a small scale and was used mainly for animal feed and for making rum. It was a labor-intensive industry. The laborers for this period came from the same source as that of the Virginia settlements; indentured laborers, of people who were enticed, kidnapped, or sentenced (by the Law Courts) to Barbados for some petty crime from England, Ireland, and Europe. The other sources of labor came from the settlements in Virginia—Native American Indians captured in war, or sentenced into slavery to Barbados, by the Law Courts in Anglo America. London merchants who were already investing in transoceanic commerce pioneered a slave trade to the island directly from Africa. Richard Rugemer in his book: "Making Slavery English writes:

> "By 1643 there were six thousand four hundred Africans on the island, about one-fourth of a population of at least twenty-five thousand, and by 1650 the European population had grown to about thirty thousand while the number of Africans had increased to twelve thousand eight hundred."[5]

Throughout British North America, slavery evolved in practice before it was codified into law. The Barbados Slave Code of 1661 marked the

---

3. Davis, The Cavaliers and Roundheads of Barbados, 1650-52 145-149, 178-190
4. https://en.wikipedia.org/wiki/James_Drax—cite_note-14
5. Rugemer, Making Slavery English, 5

beginning of the legal codification of slavery. "*Romanus Pontifex*" 1455, by Pope Nicholas V was the original Papal Bull that initiated that specific dictum against 'Guineamen and other negroes'. He first issued it to King Afonso V of Portugal. The Portuguese later applied this practice to their only New World colony, Brazil. The Dutch rule was short-lived, 1630 and 1654, but they were able to make legal changes permitting religious freedom for the various faiths, including Jews, Roman Catholics, and Non- Catholic Christians.

Rugemer writes:

> "In 1654 John Birkenhead wrote that: Barbadians killed their slaves with impunity and ranked them with "dogs." Henry Whistler described a multi-ethnic servant population of "English, French, Duch, Scotes, irish" and Spanish Jews, along with the "miserabell Negors borne to perpetuall slauery thay and thayer seed." Whistler's remarks are particularly suggestive; they reflect a broad catchment region for European indentured servants and they indicate the Barbadian adoption of hereditary slavery. The Council in 1636 had not described slavery as hereditary and the transition by the 1650s simply followed the practice of the Iberians who emulated Ancient Greece and Rome, among whom slave status was hereditary. This transformation took place simultaneously with emergence of sugar production and the rise in the African population, which grew mostly from importation.
>
> Social relations between planters and their workforce had never been good, but they seem to have worsened with the emergence of sugar."[6]

Lauren Kramer, an award-winning Canadian journalist writing about the Jewish presence in Barbados, (which was a direct consequence of the Spanish Inquisition) records:

> "The history of the Jews in Barbados has existed almost continually since 1654, when Sephardic Jews arrived on the island as refugees from what was formerly Dutch Brazil after it was captured by the Portuguese colonisers who were consolidating their hold over Brazil. The Jewish refugees brought with them expertise in the production and cultivation of sugar cane and coffee, expertise which contributed to the development of Barbados as a major producer of sugar."[7]

---

6. Rugemer, Making Slavery English 6
7. Kramer, The Nidhe Israel Synagogue Mikveh: A Barbados Treasure from 1654

> The majority of Jews that settled in Barbados in the seventeenth century were of Sephardic origins. In 1654, the Jewish community in Bridgetown, the capital was formally established and a Sephardic synagogue K.K. Nidhei Israel ("the dispersed ones of Israel"), was consecrated.
>
> Once in Barbados, many Jewish settlers engaged in sugar and coffee cultivation. Whilst the British Government considered Jews to be good businessmen and tradesmen, British merchants did not like the Jews and accused them of committing illegal business transactions. Jews were accused of trading more frequently with the Dutch, than the British merchants. "[8]

In October 23, 1668, the Jews of Barbados were banned from all forms of trade. Jews were forbidden from purchasing slaves and were forced into living in a Jewish Ghetto in Bridgetown. By 1679 nearly three hundred Jews lived in Barbados.

African slaves had already become a source of free labor within the English economy. Another source of labor came in their thousands; Irishmen defeated by Cromwell in 1652 and thousands of Scots following Bonnie Prince Charlie's Rebellion a century later were *"Barbadosed"* to work as indentured servants alongside the slaves from West Africa.

The Lesser Antilles islands of Barbados, St. Kitts, Saint Vincent and the Grenadines, Antigua, Martinique, Guadeloupe, Saint Lucia and Dominica were the first important slave societies of the Caribbean, switching to slavery by the end of the seventeenth century as their economies converted from tobacco to sugar production. Barbados, Jamaica (1655) and other Caribbean colonies became the center of wealth and the focus of the slave trade for the growing English empire.

A new generation of wealthy investors, and those with political affiliations, joined and finally led the existing plantocracy in the 1600's, with a strategy of political control. This basically marginalised the poor whites and excluded the Africans not only from the political infrastructure but also from humanity within the society. With the success of this strategy, the largest white population of the fledgling English empire settled in Barbados and as it were established the cultural norms of New World society.

Russell Menard (historian) estimates that by 1660 Barbados had become a black majority society. A year later the English devised a code to supposedly protect the slaves. Nevertheless, Menard notes:

> "The Barbados Slave Code of 1661 was a law passed by the colonial English legislature to provide a legal base for slavery in the

8. Scheib, The Virtual Jewish World

> Caribbean island of Barbados. The code's preamble, which stated that the law's purpose was to "protect them [slaves] as we do men's other goods and Chattels, established that black slaves would be treated as chattel property in the island's court."⁹

The Barbados Slave Code required masters to provide each slave with one set of clothing per year, but set no standards for other aspects of life, including diet, working conditions or housing. It also denied basic rights as was the practice under English common law, such as the right to life. Owners were allowed to do entirely as they wished, including mutilating their slaves, burning them alive, without fear of reprisal. (Precedent 6)

In his book, "Making Slavery English," Richard Rugemer describes the appalling treatment of Barbadian laborers."

> "*The sugar regime was more brutal and profitable than either cotton or tobacco, and the combination of more arduous labor and greater profits seems to have deepened the exploitation of Barbadian labourers, enslaved, or indentured. Richard Ligon believed that servants were treated worse than the slaves. He described "their poor diet of potatoes, the inadequate lodging, and the cruelty of overseers who would "beat a Servant with a cane about the head" until the blood flowed freely. Father Antoine Biet's 1654 account concurred about the diet and lodging for both groups of labourers, but he described the treatment of black slaves with far more gruesome language. "Servants and slaves were both beaten viciously, but slaves could be "brand[ed] all over their bodies which makes them shriek with despair," and one cruel overseer sliced off one of his slave's ears, roasted it, and forced the poor man to eat it.*¹⁰"

The Barbados Assembly reenacted the slave code, with minor modifications, in 1676, 1682, and 1688. The Barbados slave code also served as the basis for the slave codes adopted in several other English colonies, including Jamaica (1664), South Carolina (1696), and Antigua (1702).

A census carried out in 1684 showed that there were almost 50,000 black slaves, 19,861 whites including only 2,381 white indentured slaves in Barbados. By this time Barbados had shifted from an island that enjoyed a healthy system of government made up of representative members of the eleven parishes; to being controlled by a small number of European plantation owners who ran the parliament to protect themselves and suppress the black slaves through brutal repression.

---

9. Wikipedia
10. Rugemer, Making slavery English 6–7

In his book; *"The First Black Slave Society"* Dr. Hilary Beckles, Pro Vice-Chancellor of the University of the West Indies, described the structure of the society that the English created in Barbados which was designed to maintain and:

> *"to sustain intergenerational wealth creation and assured elite status and social privileges, monarchs, the upper class and merchants, purchased colonial produce in the market all benefited from the Barbados bonanza."*

They proceeded to protect their wealth and position by instituting new laws that would, in effect, remove all competition:

> *"This new Barbadian hierarchy used the House of Assembly to protect themselves against the black slaves and the Parliament in England. The rules were changed so that the only people eligible to stand vote or hold a position of office had to be British subjects and Christians, owned a minimum of 10 acres or have a house with a taxable valuable of at least £10 per year. Not only did this prevent the black slaves from any form of representation, but it also prevented the poor white servants from even voting.*
>
> *As the smaller farmers continued to leave, the rich aristocracy on the island took more and more control. The plantation aristocracy, or plantocracy was born and the sugar industry was in full force."*[11]

The following names of members of the plantocracy are significant' in that they constitute the significant persons and families among whom were the early promoters of the sugar industry and consequently, English Slavery in the West Indies and Anglo America.

They are as follows:

- Sir James Drax died 1662
- Colonel Sir Thomas Modyford (c.1620—2 September 1679)
- Christopher Codrington 1 (1606-1656) (He emigrated to Barbados, during the reign of King Charles I.)
- Christopher Codrington 11: 1640 -1698.
- Christopher Codrington 111: 1668—1710

Sir Thomas Modyford was another member of the English aristocracy (with connections to the Duke of Albemarle) who emigrated to Barbados

---

11. Callaghan,1637–1702 From Tobacco to Sugar: From White Servants to Black Slaves

with the rest of his family in 1647 during the beginning of the English Civil War. He went on to become one of the many evangelists of English slavery in the Anglo New World. He was a Barbados plantation owner and eventual Governor of Jamaica. He presided over Port Royal when it was a known pirate haven and even helped launch the career of the notorious Henry Morgan.

Being a wealthy landowner, Modyford soon got involved in local politics and quicky rose through the ranks to become Speaker of the House of Assembly. He was also involved with the local slave trade on the island through a company called the Royal Adventurers. Originally known as the Company of Royal Adventurers Trading to Africa, by its charter issued in 1660 it was granted a monopoly over English trade along the West Coast of Africa, with the principal objective being the search for gold and later in 1663, for trade in slaves. With the help of the army and navy, it established a strong presence, controlling all trade between the West African coast and the West Indies and responsible for seizing any English ships that attempted to operate in violation of the company's monopoly (known as interlopers). In the "prize court," the King received half of the proceeds and the company half from the seizure of these interlopers.

In 1655 the English soldiers captured Jamaica, which island was not considered much by the Spaniards who were more interested in finding gold. However, the English realised the financial potential of sugarcane plantations and immediately implemented the plantocracy system recently developed in Barbados.

> "On February 15th, 1664. Thomas Modyford was appointed Governor of Jamaica by commission, and he arrived on the island on June 4th. He arrived with seven hundred plantation owners along with their slaves to create a plantation driven economy on the island. To help with his administrative duties he appointed his brothers Col. Sir James Modyford and Col. Thomas Modyford to help oversee the island. He even maintained contacts with the Royal Adventurers Company and used them to import slaves onto the island until 1669. In addition to help get the island started, Sir James was given a license to ship convicts from England to the island to be indentured servants. Around 2,800 of these labourers arrived on the island to assist with its construction.
>
> By the 1670s his title according to the commission he gave to the pirate, Henry Morgan was: Governor of His Majesty's Island of Jamaica, Commander-in-Chief of all His Majesties Forces within

the said Island and in the Islands adjacent Vice-Admiral to His Royal Highness the Duke of York in the American Seas."[12]

Despite some political and legal challenges which he had to address in England, Modyford was acquitted. He returned to Jamaica and lived out the rest of his days in relative luxury on the island, spending another nine years before dying at his estate 1679.

The Codringtons are an example of a family that impacted on the life of the English/British Empire and on the Church of England. The Codrington family's rise to wealth and prominence in Barbados paralleled what Richard Dunn has called the "rise of the planter class." Studying the consolidation of capital and power in the English West Indies, Dunn noted that of the one hundred and fifty-nine families that constituted the planter "elite" in 1680, sixty-two of them already held property on the island in 1638. Codrington and Drax were among those elite families whose timely investment in sugar cultivation and early entrance into the political sphere allowed them to take full advantage of the economic boom that made Barbados the wealthiest colony in the English empire by the late seventeenth century. Following the lead of the Portuguese and Dutch in Brazil and Surinam, they imported large numbers of enslaved Africans to feed the demand for labor on the newly founded sugar plantations. White indentured servants were quickly replaced with Black slaves as planters purchased items of luxury, such as tables, silver, cushions, carpets, and four-poster beds, to show off their newly acquired wealth.

Accordingly, Christopher Codrington, (1668–1710) the elder son of Christopher Codrington (1639/40–1698) wrote in his will that his plantations should serve as a college to train "Professors and Scholars" who were under "vows of Poverty, Chastity and Obedience."

The reference to vows of poverty, chastity and obedience were identical to those taken by Jesuits and exposed the depth of Codrington's admiration for French Catholic practices. They also embodied Codrington's accumulated insight into the culture of slavery in the English Caribbean. Like the concerned Anglicans he befriended in England, he believed that English slaves needed to be Christianized. Yet his upbringing in Barbados and familiarity with planter ideology gave him a realistic sense of the challenges facing any missionary endeavor. He found the local clergy to be hopelessly unprepared to convert slaves to Christianity and he feared that baptizing slaves wantonly would be "pernicious." His solution emerged from his experiences bridging divides: between colony and metropole, between French and English, and between Protestant and Catholic.

12. Wikipedia

The Codrington Plantations were two historic sugarcane producing estates on the island of Barbados, established in the seventeenth century by Christopher Codrington (c. 1640—1698) and his father of the same name. Sharing the characteristics of many plantations of the period in their reliance on slave labor, their particular significance was as a part of a charitable bequest in 1710, on the death of the third Christopher Codrington (1668—1710), to the Society for the Propagation of the Gospel in Foreign Parts. (SPG).

Between 1633–1635 Charters were obtained for Carolina in America. A group of Barbadians led by John Yeamans, attempted to establish a settlement on the Cape Fear River (now North Carolina). This settlement did not last, but Yeamans later became one of the first governors of Carolina from 1672 to 1674.

In 1699 a Fundamental Constitution of Carolina encouraged African slavery based on the West Indian model. The Constitution granted every freeman 'absolute Power and Authority over his Negro slaves which assured West Indian planters they could continue using enslaved African labor when they emigrated to Carolina to establish plantations.

This started the Anglo-American plantation societies which would later be led by Jamaica after it was fully developed. At its peak production between 1740 –1807 Jamaica received 33% of the total slaves that were imported to keep up its production.

By 1800 ten to fifteen million Africans had been transported as slaves to the Americas, representing perhaps one third of those originally seized in Africa.

Howard Zinn in his book "A people's History of the United States," describes in graphic detail the passage made from their capture to the arrival of Africans in Virginia:

> "In fact, it was because they came from a settled culture, of tribal customs and family ties, of communal life and traditional ritual, that African blacks found themselves especially helpless when removed from this. They were captured in the interior (frequently by blacks caught up in the slave trade themselves), sold on the coast, then shoved into pens with blacks of other tribes, often speaking different languages."[13]

The marches to the coast, sometimes for one thousand miles, with people shackled around the neck, under whip and gun, were death marches, in which two out of every five blacks died. On the coast, they were kept in cages until they were picked and sold. One John Barbot at the end of the seventeenth century, described these cages on the Gold Coast:

---

13. Zinn, A Peoples History of the United States 28

> "As the slaves come down to Fida from the inland country, they are put into a booth or prison... near the beach, and when the Europeans are to receive them, they are brought out onto a large plain, where the ship's surgeons examine every part of everyone of them, to the smallest member, men and women being stark naked... Such as are allowed good and sound are set on one side... marked on the breast with a red- hot iron, imprinting the mark of the French, English or Dutch companies... The branded slaves after this are returned to their former booths where they await shipment, sometimes 10–15 days."[14]

Elmina and Cape Coast Castles on the west coast of Africa were the holding places for Africans waiting to be shipped across the Atlantic Ocean. Men and women were kept in separate dungeons, in the dark, with little ventilation and water and no sanitation. Food was thrown into the dungeon from a small opening near the ceiling in the dungeon.

Sometimes people were kept in these conditions for up to six weeks until there were sufficient captives to fill a ship. Then they were taken out at night through the *"gate of no return"* to board the slave ship, so that locals would not see what was happening.

In Jamaica from 1829 to 1832 the average mortality rate for slaves on sugar plantations was 35.1 deaths per one thousand. The most dangerous part of the sugar plantation was the cane planting. The cane planting part of sugar production during this era consisted of clearing land, digging the holes for the plants, and more. The slaves were forced to work under the punishment of pain usually. Overseers were used to motivate and punish the slaves by using the whip or other methods of flogging. The slaves themselves were also working and living with barely adequate nourishment and in times of hard work would often be starved. This contributed to low birth rates and the high mortality rates for the slaves. Some experts believe that the average birth rate mortality at plantations to be roughly 50% and above. This extremely high rate of infant mortality meant that the slave population that existed in the Lesser Antilles was not self-sustaining thus requiring a constant importation of new slaves. Living and working conditions on the other non-sugar plantations were better for slaves however it was only marginally better.

The English treated their slaves (indentured or otherwise; white, brown or black) not really dissimilar to that of the Muslims. However, what was different was the increasing compromise of biblical truth to accommodate the financial imperative of the plantocracy and various sectors of the upper classes, as the basis of their faith.

14. Zinn, A Peoples History of the United States, 28

> "Successful rice production coincided with the Assembly's dominance by a faction known as the Goose Creek men, Anglican Barbadians who were some of the colony's first settlers. In 1691 the Assembly adopted Jamaica's 1684 Slave Act as South Carolina's own. They added "Indian" to the definition of slave and dropped a few of the provisions in the Jamaica law that were not applicable. The rest of the Act—word for word—was taken from the Jamaica legislation. It should not be surprising that Carolinians turned to Jamaica rather than Barbados for its slave code. The two colonies were intricately linked through trade and correspondence and the Jamaica Assembly had made important innovations in the law. They had consolidated the slave court system and established a legal structure for catching runaways that was far more compatible with Carolina geography. And unlike the Assemblies in Barbados and Jamaica that passed the first slave codes, the South Carolina Assembly did not pass a Servant Act at the same time. There were relatively few white servants in South Carolina at this time, moreover, by 1691 the distinctions in status and treatment between white indentured servants and enslaved Africans had already been codified. This political work had been done and Carolinian slaveholders reaped the benefits. In contrast, the Barbados Assembly had enacted five new provisions in 1688 that must not have appeared particularly useful to Carolinians. Barbadians had extended the list of property crimes committed by slaves and made the punishments for those crimes more severe; adopted a provision ground requirement that Jamaica had developed in 1684; and added to the search provision "Drums, Horns, or any other loud Instruments."[15]

The South Carolina slave code served as the model for other colonies in North America. In 1770, Georgia adopted the South Carolina slave code, and Florida adopted the Georgia code. The USA won their Independence from Britain in 1776.

The 1712 South Carolina Slave Code included provisions such as:

- *Slaves were forbidden to leave the owner's property unless they were accompanied by a white person or had permission. If a slave left the owner's property without permission, "every white person" was required to chastise such slaves.*

- *Any slave attempting to run away and leave the colony (later the state) received the death penalty.*

---

15. Rugemer, Making Slavery English

- *Any slave who evaded capture for 20 days or more was to be publicly whipped for the first offence, branded with the letter R on the right cheek for the second offence, and lose one ear if absent for 30 days for the third offense, and castrated for the fourth offense.*
- *Owners refusing to abide by the slave code were fined and forfeited ownership of their slaves.*
- *Slave homes were to be searched every two weeks for weapons or stolen goods. Punishment for violations escalated to include loss of ear, branding, and nose-slitting (for the fourth offence, death)*
- *No slave was allowed to work for pay; plant corn, peas or rice; keep hogs, cattle, or horses; own or operate a boat; buy or sell; to wear clothes finer than 'Negro cloth.'*

The South Carolina Slave Code was revised in 1739 with the following amendments:

- *No slave is to be taught to write, to work on Sunday, or to work more than 15 hours per day in summer, and 14 hours in winter.*
- *Willful killing of a slave exacts a fine of £700, "passion"-killing £350.*
- *The fine for concealing runaway slaves is $1,000 and a prison sentence of up to one year.*
- *A fine of $100 and six months in prison are imposed for employing any black or slave as a clerk.*
- *A fine of $100 and six months in prison are imposed on anyone selling or giving alcoholic beverages to slaves.*
- *A fine of $100 and six months in prison are imposed for teaching a slave to read and write, and death is the penalty for circulating incendiary literature.*
- *Freeing a slave is forbidden, except by deed, and after 1820, permission of the legislature (Georgia required legislative approval after 1801).*

Northern colonies: Slave codes in the northern colonies, before slavery was abolished, were less harsh than slave codes in the southern colonies but contained many similar provisions, such as forbidding slaves from leaving the owner's land, forbidding whites from selling alcohol to slaves, and specifying punishment for attempting to escape.

> "The significance of these early comprehensive slave laws is not in their novelty, but in the political work they did in making slavery English. It may well have been an "unthinking decision" in 1636

that led the English in Barbados to enslave Africans and Indians, for as Winthrop Jordan observed long ago, the English simply emulated the practices of the Iberians and the Dutch. But the Restoration marked the culmination of a socioeconomic transition whereby the profits gained through slavery had begun to change habits on Barbados, and to attract the interest of some of the most powerful men of England. The Barbadian laws of 1652 suggest that Europeans were encouraged to treat enslaved Africans with especial severity and the comprehensive acts of 1661 enhanced the distinctions made between European and African labourers. Moreover, in 1661 these distinctions were justified with language that adumbrated racial thinking, specifically, the naming of "Negroes." And as the political economy of slavery spread into Jamaica and South Carolina, racial language became more sophisticated with the naming of "white" people. Through a decades-long struggle fraught with blood, terror, sweat, and considerable investment, these English colonial Assemblies used the power of the law to forge an English political economy of slavery that would last for two hundred years."[16]

Andrea Stuart, author of "*Sugar in the Blood: A Family's Story of Slavery and Empire*" insists Barbados, with its long history of slavery, matters more than we know.

"On a day-to-day basis," she writes, slavery "was sustained by a campaign of violence and brutality, random whippings, mutilation and branding, mobilized to remind the slave who he was." Slaves like John Stephen never found out who their mothers were. Stephen did know who his father was, though Cooper owned him, and Stephen had to call him "Massa." Slavery's racial legacy affects Stuart's life to this day, like it does most blacks: "My color still enters the room before I do," she writes. "And in some situations I have to work inordinately hard to make others put it aside." Stuart argues that: "Slavery and its legacy—race—still shape our world. But more specifically, the creation of Barbados, the British empire's earliest, most profitable settlement in the New World, provided the blueprint for all its future slave colonies: South Carolina, North Carolina, Virginia, Georgia, you name it."[17]

Over the course of thirty-five years the Assemblies of Barbados, Jamaica, and South Carolina forged the political foundation for slavery in the English Empire. For Englishmen in the seventeenth century this was quite

16. Rugemer, Making Slavery English
17. Stuart, Sugar in the Blood

new, but in the longer flow of human history their actions were as old as slavery itself. The Hammurabi code did not recognize the killing of a slave as murder and male slaves were castrated in ancient Rome, medieval Egypt, and in sixteenth century Peru. Laws ordered payments for slave catchers in ancient Rome and in sixteenth century Mexico, just as they did in the English colonies. Assertions of the biological difference of slaves were not new either. Aristotle wrote of the "natural slave" and likened them to "tame animals," (note that this was how the Papacy and the Portuguese/Spanish explorers viewed the indigenous peoples and Africans)

As highlighted by the words of Eric Williams, the first Prime Minister of Trinidad and Tobago, and author of the 1944 book "*Capitalism and Slavery*":

"*Slavery was not born of racism: rather, racism was the consequence of slavery. Unfree labour in the New World was brown, white, black, and yellow, Catholic and Protestant and pagan.*"[18]

However, the status of the African was unique in that his future was determined since 1455 by the Papal Bull, Romanus Pontifex and, first, fully realised in Barbados.

> "*English investors were prepared to enslave whoever they could, once they were classified as poor, landless and therefore subject to labour coercion. It did not matter to these aggressive profit-seekers whether those persons were black, white, or brown. They intended all workers to be placed in bondage to achieve the full potential of their capital investments, though it was understood that the deepest end of this bondage—lifelong status—was reserved exclusively for Africans.*"[19]

As white labor became more troublesome and expensive to acquire, (because of opposition to this practice in England) more African slaves were imported. This prolonged importation of slaves for over the next two hundred years was caused by the high mortality rate on the island due to overwork, bad food and disease, and some from loss of hope. During the 1600's, there were three unsuccessful rebellions in Barbados; 1649, 1675 and 1692. Except for the 1649 rebellion which was about insufficient food, they all ended with mass arrests and torture. Many of those found guilty of rebellion were executed. Some committed suicide, while others were beheaded or burnt alive[20].

---

18. Williams, Capitalism and Slavery p7
19. Beckles, Hilary, McD *The First Black Slave Society*. 37–38
20. Wikipedia

9

The Role of the Church in the Anglo New-World

WE MENTIONED IN CHAPTER seven of this book that along with the adventurers and the state, the Church of England was an integral part of the colonisation process of the Anglo New World.

The extent of the Church of England's involvement in the Transatlantic Slave Trade has only recently been made public following research which was initiated by the Church Commissioners in 2019—before the death of George Floyd sparked the Black Lives Matter movement.

The Commissioners worked with forensic accountants and the historians Dr Helen Paul and Professor Arthur Burns to review early ledgers and other original source documents from Queen Anne's Bounty. Queen Anne's Bounty invested significant funds in the South Sea Company which traded in enslaved people. It's main commercial activity between 1715 and 1739 when it transported 34,000 people in "crowded, unsanitary, unsafe and inhumane" conditions over ninety-six transatlantic voyages. The initial report, dated June 2022 states that:

> "The Bounty "also received numerous benefactions, many of which are likely to have come from individuals linked to, or who profited from, transatlantic chattel slavery or the plantation economy," the researchers write.
>
> About 14 per cent of its income between 1708 to 1743 was given by benefactors, among them Edward Colston, a slave trader whose statue in Bristol was toppled and pushed into the harbour

during protests in 2020. The Bounty used this money to buy land and property to augment clergy income or pay the church's running costs. Of this land, "most if not all" is no longer in the Commissioners' property portfolio, the report says.

From 1723 to 1777, funds that were not used to buy land were invested almost exclusively in South Sea Company annuities. By the time the Company ceased slave-trading in 1739, these investments were worth £204,000, which may be equivalent to about £443 million today, the report states.

Archbishop Welby, who chairs the Commissioners, said on Thursday that these links were "a source of shame" for the church. "I am deeply sorry for the links with transatlantic chattel slavery that the church Commissioners has identified. This abominable trade took men, women, and children created in God's image and stripped them of their dignity and freedom. The fact that some within the church actively supported and profited from it is a source of shame.

"It is only by facing this painful reality that we can take steps towards genuine healing and reconciliation—the path that Jesus Christ calls us to walk. This is a moment for lament, repentance, and restorative action. I pray for those affected by this news and hope that we may work together to discern a new way forward."[1]

At the beginning of the seventeenth century there were three groups of professing Christians in England. Officially there were no Roman Catholics. They had then been banned by law. If they were there, they were practising their religion in secret. There were two groups within the Church of England. The two groups were the Church of England (Anglicans) and the Puritans. Anglicans accepted a slightly modified version of the Roman Catholic teachings as a kind of compromise, a mixture of things that were done by the Roman Catholics but also things that the Reformers did. Within the Church of England was another group of people represented by Richard Baxter who were called Puritans, because they desired to see a much purer Church of England. They wanted worship to be plain, simple, and pure. Above all they wanted the Word of God to be central to their doctrine. They were committed Bible readers in their own homes, as families, or as individuals, above all they wanted to see Bible study in the church. The Puritans sailed to Virginia in the Mayflower in 1620 as part of the second phase of the Charter, because they were being persecuted.

---

1. www.churchofengland.org/media-and-news/press-releases/church-commissioners-research-identifies-historic-links-transatlantic-slavery

In 1611 the King James Bible was published and was to become a feature in the growing English Empire. In the West Indies, the history of the fledgling English Empire, with special reference to Barbados, provides information on the challenges and victories (and failures) of the church in obedience to "the great commission." The Church of England has the spiritual authority over the land and the reigning monarch is head of the church. England is defined as a Protestant nation in which its stated beliefs and culture are based on the Authorised King James' Version of the Bible and the Anglican thirty-nine Articles.

The Church of England, or as it is called, the Anglican Church has been present in Barbados since the seventeenth century and is one of its oldest institutions. It was taken to the West Indies in the early part of the seventeenth century by English settlers. It was the church of the Englishmen who resided in the colony and the clergy came largely on their own to minister to the settlers. The Bishops of London were regarded as having responsibility for the churches in the colonies in the early seventeenth century. Prior to 1824 the functions of the Bishop of London were limited to ordaining those candidates who presented themselves and licensing Clergy; appointment and dismissals of clergy remained the responsibility of the Governor of the Colony. (Precedent 6)

At this point it is important to consider similarities between Christianity which is viewed as a state/ethnic/cultural religion and Islam and to take a brief look at how both were involved in slavery (and were also engaged in major confrontations). The Muslims took Europeans as slaves justifying it on the grounds of religion. The Christians took Africans into slavery, justifying it on the definition given in the Papal Bull Romanus Pontifex, which identified them as 'Guineamen and negroes.'

Portugal had managed to expel the Moors (Muslims) of North Africa in thirteenth century and the Spanish in 1492. Nevertheless, the Muslims continued to pillage those countries and those of the Mediterranean and western Europe into the nineteenth century.

Concurrent with the development of the English (British) Empire in the seventeen hundreds, were the battles which were fought in the North Atlantic and Mediterranean between the Christians (Roman Catholic and Protestant nations) and the Muslim pirates from the Barbary Coast of North Africa; authorised by their governments. These pirates attacked shipping owned by the Christian countries, grabbed ships with their sailors, and sold the sailors into slavery. In his book: British Slaves on the Barbary Coast Ohio State University Professor Robert Davis writes:

> "Admiralty records show that during this time the corsairs plundered British shipping pretty much at will, taking no fewer than 466 vessels between 1609 and 1616, and 27 more vessels from near Plymouth in 1625. As 18th-century historian Joseph Morgan put it, 'this I take to be the Time when those Corsairs were in their Zenith'.
>
> Unfortunately, it was hardly the end of them, even then. Morgan also noted that he had a '...List, printed in London in 1682' of 160 British ships captured by Algerians between 1677 and 1680. Considering what the number of sailors who were taken with each ship was likely to have been, these examples translate into a probable 7,000 to 9,000 able-bodied British men and women taken into slavery in those years."[2]

The pirates seemed to have a free for all along the coasts of England. They often raided coastal settlements, and with guerrilla efficiency would sometimes run their craft onto unguarded coastal beaches, creep up on villages in the dark, kidnap the victims and take them away before any alarm was made. Many such attacks were made along coastal villages in Devon, and Cornwall and in Ireland.

Samuel Pepys, (an administrator of the English Navy and Member of Parliament, famous for his diary) gives a vivid account of an encounter with two men who had been taken into slavery, in his diary of 8 February 1661. This was the same year that the Bible was first printed in America and in the New World, and, paradoxically, the printing of the first Barbados Slave Code).

> '... to the Fleece tavern to drink and there we spent till 4 a-clock telling stories of Algier and the manner of the life of Slaves there; and truly, Captain Mootham and Mr Dawes (who have been both slaves there) did make me full acquainted with their condition there. As, how they eat nothing but bread and water.... How they are beat upon the soles of the feet and bellies at the Liberty of their Padron. How they are all night called into their master's Bagnard, and there they lie.'[3]

Coastal dwellers and fishermen's lives in England and Ireland in the seventeenth century was one of terror of being kidnapped by the pirates and sold into slavery in North Africa on the Barbary Coast, where many of them met wretched deaths. These stories have unfortunately not had much

---

2. Davis, British Slaves on the Barbary Coast
3. Samuel Pepys 23 February 1633—26 May 1703

publicity over the centuries. Life for the Christian slaves in Barbary was horrendous. It should be noted that the word Christian for the Muslims was synonymous with Europeans, including those from the islands off the western shores of Europe and including Iceland. Richard Davis further describes the conditions under which these European slaves lived:

> "They were the property, first of the ruling Pasha, who had claim to 25 percent of all Europeans captured and a first lien on the others at a negotiated price. His personal slaves were housed in large prisons in terribly overcrowded conditions. They were used as unpaid labour for rowing the corsairs as they went in pursuit of more loot (and more slaves). The work so intolerable that thousands died or went mad while chained to the oar. In the off season, during the winter months, they worked on other state projects-quarrying stone, building walls or harbour facilities, felling timber, and constructing new galleys. Those who faltered on the job, due to exhaustion or malnutrition, would be beaten until they got up and went back to work. They were fed two or three loaves of bread That the dogs would not eat) and limited water. They received one change of clothing per year. The Pasha also bought women slaves, women of whom were taken into his harem where they spent the rest of their days or ransomed. The majority were however acquired for their ransom value. Those slaves owned by the private sector, faired no better. Their treatment depended on the circumstances of their master. Some were well treated and even became virtual companions of their owners."[4]

Europeans sometimes attempted to buy their people out of slavery. These pirate invasions and kidnappings were so commonplace and regular, that systematic methods for paying ransoms were finally arranged, often involving the state. The clergy were the usual negotiators; collecting funds from the villagers and the state and voyaging to the Barbary to negotiate with the slave owners. Some church Religious Orders were detailed to effect these transactions, especially in Spain and Italy. The Roman Catholic Church impressed on their parishioners that ransoming slaves was the best charitable work they could do for their poor brothers in bondage, 'Their [only] fault, their crime, is recognising Jesus Christ as the most divine Saviour... and of professing Him as the True Faith, writes Richard Davis.

By the seventeen hundreds, ransoming payments by the Roman Catholics significantly reduced their slave populations in the Barbary. However, according to Davis, thousands of Dutch, German and English people:

---

4. Davis, *British Slaves on the Barbary Coast*

> ... "languished for years in the chains of Barbary..." (Richard Davis) without the aid of organised clergy or state funds for their release. England did set aside its 'Algerian Duty' from Customs income to finance the reparation payments, but much of it was diverted to other uses. In 1646 Edmund Casson freed 244 men, women, and children- a rare feat among the English. One slave is recorded as saying: 'All of the nations made some shift to live, save only the English, who it seems are not so shiftful as others, and... have no great kindness one for another. The winter I was in [captivity], I observ'd there died above twenty of them out of pure want.'[5]

For five hundred years, the Muslims of the Ottoman Empire enslaved Europeans, having expelled the last Christian armies in 1302 ending the era of the Crusades. That empire continued into the twentieth century until the Turkish war of Independence and the abolition of the Ottoman monarch in 1924.

The Barbary Coast states of Algiers, Tunis & Tripoli, and the independent Sultanate of Morocco operated with the blessings of the Ottoman Empire.

The American War of Independence from Great Britain in 1776-1783 saw its ambassadors operating in the world sphere, the focus of which was Europe and the Mediterranean. The first country the ambassadors approached was the independent state of Morocco who sought trading links beyond their existing zone.

> " Sidi Muhammad ibn Abdallah, Sultan of Morocco, opened his ports to trade with the fledgling United States in 1777, making Morocco the first country whose head of state publicly recognized the United States. Abdallah saw the future for his country in foreign trade, and actively sought a treaty relationship with the US, well before war ended with Great Britain. The treaty signed by Thomas Barclay and Sultan Muhammad III in 1786 and ratified by the Confederation Congress the following July is still in effect today, the longest continuous treaty relationship in United States history."[6]

Despite the overtures by the Americans, the Barbary pirates began to harass American shipping as early as 1785. They captured eleven American vessels in 1793 alone, holding the ships and crew for ransom.

---

5. Davis, *British Slaves on the Barbary Coast*
6. todayinhistory.blog/tag/barbary-pirates/

In March 1786, two future presidents met with an ambassador from the pirate nations of North Africa. Thomas Jefferson, who was the U.S. ambassador in France, and John Adams, the ambassador to Britain, met with the ambassador from Tripoli in London. They asked why American merchant ships were being attacked without provocation. The ambassador explained that Muslim pirates considered Americans to be infidels and they believed they simply had the right to plunder American ships.

In 1794 the US Congress passed the Naval Act, appropriating funds to build a fleet of six three-masted heavy frigates for the United States Navy. The act included a clause halting construction, in the event of a peace treaty with Algiers. No such treaty was ever concluded. The United States of America paid tribute to the Barbary pirates (1790s) to keep them quiet, but this ended in 1800. Professor Robert Davis estimates that Barbary corsairs captured as many as 1—1¼ million Europeans between the sixteenth and nineteenth centuries alone, kidnapped from seaside villages along the Mediterranean coast, England's coastal areas and as far away as the Netherlands, Ireland, and Iceland. Some 700 Americans were held in conditions of slavery in North Africa, between the period of the American Revolution and the War of 1812.

Davis argues that "*The Arab slave trade was never racialised in the way of trans-Atlantic, chattel slavery. Black Africans and white Europeans alike, were fair game. Some historians assert that as many as 17 million entered the Arab slave markets, from Western Asia, North Africa, the Horn of Africa, Southeast Africa and Europe.*"[7]

It is most remarkable that this area of history: 'The Barbary Pirates', deals with 'religious slavery', in that anyone who was not a Muslim would be fair game for enslavement. Whilst on the other hand, in the sixteenth century, the Pope made slavery racial in Romanus Pontifex, by targeting Guineamen and Negroes for perpetual slavery. Could the seemingly strategic omission of this narrative have given licence to the rulers of European Catholic nations of Spain and Portugal and eventually the missionaries of New World Christianity? Yet the American battle song 'From the Halls of Montezuma to the shores of Tripoli' commemorates this early period of the United States of American history.

In contrast, English slavery in the New World was confronted with the application of the Charter as the reference given by King James 1, in 1606. Later Protestant English, with the King James Bible and the ensuing plethora of other Protestant denominations, created an environment where both belief systems (enslavement of colonised peoples and Kingdom

7. todayinhistory. blog/tag/barbary-pirates/

Christianity) could co-exist under the same legal system. Tensions arose between the Church and the State Administration over the issue of conversion of slaves to become Christians. The tension being based on a different understanding of what it means to be a follower of Jesus Christ. Kingdom Christianity references Jesus telling his disciples to go and teach all nations and baptise them, as the following texts illustrates: The Great Commission in Matt 28:18 –20

> Mat 28:18 *And Jesus came and spake unto them, saying, All power is given unto me in heaven and in earth. 19 Go ye therefore, and teach all nations, baptizing them in the name of the Father, and of the Son, and of the Holy Ghost: 20 Teaching them to observe all things whatsoever I have commanded you: and, lo, I am with you alway, even unto the end of the world. Amen.*
>
> Mark 14–20 *Afterward he appeared unto the eleven as they sat at meat, and upbraided them with their unbelief and hardness of heart, because they believed not them which had seen him after he was risen.*
>
> *15 And he said unto them, Go ye into all the world, and preach the gospel to every creature. 16 He that believeth and is baptized shall be saved; but he that believeth not shall be damned. 17 And these signs shall follow them that believe; In my name shall they cast out devils; they shall speak with new tongues; 18 They shall take up serpents; and if they drink any deadly thing, it shall not hurt them; they shall lay hands on the sick, and they shall recover. 19 So then after the Lord had spoken unto them, he was received up into heaven, and sat on the right hand of God. 20 And they went forth, and preached everywhere, the Lord working with them, and confirming the word with signs following. Amen.*
>
> Luke 24:44—49
>
> *Luk 24:44 And he said unto them, These are the words which I spake unto you, while I was yet with you, that all things must be fulfilled, which were written in the law of Moses, and in the prophets, and in the psalms, concerning me. 45 Then opened he their understanding, that they might understand the scriptures, 46 And said unto them, Thus it is written, and thus it behoved Christ to suffer, and to rise from the dead the third day: 47 And that repentance and remission of sins should be preached in his name among all nations, beginning at Jerusalem. 48 And ye are witnesses of these things.*
>
> *49 And, behold, I send the promise of my Father upon you: but tarry ye in the city of Jerusalem, until ye be endued with power from on high.*

Further, the Bible clearly states that unless one is born again one cannot see and enter the kingdom of God John 3: 3–9. Later in John 15 Jesus tells his disciples that He must leave but He will send from the Father, another Helper, the Comforter, the Spirit of Truth. At Pentecost, the disciples were all filled with the Holy Spirit. So were three thousand persons from across the Roman Empire: Africa, Asia, Europe.

In Matt 7: 15 -Jesus had warned the people that there would be many false prophets coming in His name. He therefore explained how to recognise his true followers:

> Matt 7:15—23
>
> *15 Beware of false prophets, which come to you in sheep's clothing, but inwardly they are ravening wolves. 16 Ye shall know them by their fruits. Do men gather grapes of thorns, or figs of thistles? 17 Even so every good tree bringeth forth good fruit; but a corrupt tree bringeth forth evil fruit. 18 A good tree cannot bring forth evil fruit, neither can a corrupt tree bring forth good fruit. 19 Every tree that bringeth not forth good fruit is hewn down, and cast into the fire. 20 Wherefore by their fruits ye shall know them. 21 Not every one that saith unto me, Lord, Lord, shall enter into the kingdom of heaven; but he that doeth the will of my Father which is in heaven. 22 Many will say to me in that day, Lord, Lord, have we not prophesied in thy name? and in thy name have cast out devils? and in thy name done many wonderful works? 23 And then will I profess unto them, I never knew you: depart from me, ye that work iniquity.*

How did missionaries and evangelists navigate around the challenges of a system so far removed from the Bible they proclaimed? A report by Richard Ligon (1757), an Englishman who lived on the island of Barbados gives practical insight into the challenges the missionaries and evangelists had to overcome as they sought to apply the great commission of Jesus Christ as stated in Matt 28:18—20.

During the construction of a roadway as part of a public works project, Richard Ligon is questioned about the use of a compass by a slave, which he describes in an extract from his work *"A true and exact history of the Island on Barbadoes'* below:

> *"[He] comes to me, and seeing the needle wag, desired to know the reason of its stirring and whether it were alive: I told him no, but it stood upon a point, and for a while it would stir, but by and by stand still, which he observ'd and found it to be true.*

> *The next question was, why it stood one way and would not remove to any other point, I told him that it would stand no way but North and South, and upon that show'd him the four Cardinal points of the compass, East, West, North, South, which he presently learnt by heart, and promis'd me never to forget it. His last question was, why it would stand North, I gave this reason, because of the huge Rocks of Lodestone that were in the North part of the world, which had a quality to draw Iron to it; and this Needle being of Iron, touch'd with a Loadstone, it would always stand that way.*
>
> *This point of Philosophy was a little too hard for him, and so he stood in a strange muse; which to put him out of, I bade him reach his axe and put it near to the Compass, and remove it about; and as he did so the Needle turned with it, which put him in the greatest admiration that ever I saw a man, and so quite gave over his questions, and desired [asked] me that he might be made a Christian; for, he thought to be a Christian was to be endued with all those knowledges he wanted.*
>
> *I promised to do my best endeavor; and when I came home, spoke to the Master of the Plantation, and told him that poor Sambo desired much to be a Christian. But his answer was, that the people of that Island were governed by the Laws of England, and by those Laws we could not make a Christian a Slave. I told him my request was far different from that, for I desired him to make a Slave a Christian. His answer was, That it was true, there was a great difference in that: But, being once a Christian, he could no more account him a Slave and so lose the hold they had of them as Slaves by making them Christians; and by that means should open such a gap as all the Planters in the Island would curse him. So I was struck mute, and poor Sambo kept out of the church; as ingenious, as honest, and as good natur'd poor soul, as ever wore black, or eat green.*"[8]

Christianity and slavery were diametrically opposed categories for the Master of the Plantation, for he defined Christianity in racial and legal terms. He stated that a Christian could not be made a slave because English law was credited with providing Christians with their freedom. It was the belief that English people were both Christian and free within the bounds of the English Empire. The term 'Christian slave' during the seventeenth century was linked to the Barbary pirates. As a result, to be a Christian slave within the English domain was impossible—*"being once a Christian,"* one

---

8. Ligon, Slavery on the English Island of Barbados, A True and Exact History of the Island of Barbadoes

could *"no more [be] account[ed] a Slave,"* Ligon was told. Compounding the issue was the threat to the social order. Making the jump from the particular to the abstract, the planter feared that the master class would *"lose the hold they had of them as Slaves, by making them Christians."* This 'gap' would cause *"all the Planters in the Island [to] curse him."*

Karen Kuppermann, in "True and Exact History of the Island of Barbados" writes:

> *"For the slave master, then, Christianity was intimately tied to both Englishness and freedom. While it was not inconceivable for a slave to become a Christian, it was undesirable because it would shake the social order and deprive the planters of their most captive labourers. To be a Christian was to claim contested terrain in the early modern Atlantic world. The enslaved man, his master, and Richard Ligon all articulated divergent ideas about the meaning and accessibility of Christian practice. While the enslaved man viewed Christianity to access knowledge and power, his master sought to build walls around his religion, which was bound closely to his ethnic identity as an Englishman as well as the sense of freedom and order that came from English law. Ligon, while not stating his position explicitly, was clearly more amenable to the idea of slave conversion.*
>
> *Ligon's belief that an Afro-Caribbean slave should, if desired, have access to the Christian religion, represented the general view of slave conversion in Protestant Europe. Over the course of the seventeenth century, this pro-conversion stance grew stronger, as reports of planter intransigence and anti-conversion sentiment became infamous among concerned Protestants in Europe."*[9]

That report (and others) gives an insight into the reality of the role missionaries faced as they struggled to negotiate the complex fabric of being in the world (of English/British mercantilism and slavery) 'but not of' that world. This challenge was compounded by the fact that many of the missionaries were Englishmen (and Europeans) and as such may have had a vested interest in the success of their country and their kin. As far as the peoples whom they were evangelising- well they were visibly different- religiously described as heathens and culturally described as savages. These reports were first scripted by Columbus in Hispaniola about the native Tainos 1492 and repeated by the English in Jamestown, after their first encounter with the indigenous people in 1606.

---

9. Ligon, *True and Exact History of the Island of Barbados*, ed. Karen Kupperman (Hackett Publishing, 2011), 101 n. 120.

What were the Christian evangelists bringing to the people, both free and slaves and how did their attitudes and doctrine change?

> *Php 1:15 –18 Some indeed preach Christ even of envy and strife; and some also of good will:*
>
> *16 The one preach Christ of contention, not sincerely, supposing to add affliction to my bonds:*
>
> *17 But the other of love, knowing that I am set for the defence of the gospel.*
>
> *To live Is Christ*
>
> *18 What then? notwithstanding, every way, whether in pretence, or in truth, Christ is preached; and I therein do rejoice, yea, and will rejoice.*

Most Protestant slave owners fiercely guarded their religion and churches from these non-whites (blacks, Afro Caribbean and Africans and North American Indians). As such they vigorously conflicted with the Quakers and Moravians missionaries and used every instrument (in law and practice) they had to maintain their status quo which was: 'A Christian cannot be a slave' according to English law. Despite the persistence of the plantocracy, the churches persevered and over the years there were many non-whites being baptised in the Anglican Church. Despite planter intransigence, a small number of enslaved and free Africans advocated and won access to Protestant rites, for example, many slaves who had personal relations with their masters; drivers, house servants, and women whom they met on more intimate encounters. As such children of mixed heritage and their mothers were also baptised. Herein lies a major anomaly as the church accepted the immoral behaviour of the Planters and their double standards.

The Quakers and Moravians were not sponsored by the State but were supported by church members in their own countries and were missionaries in the New World. Their desire was to convert the slaves to Christianity in the first instance and later to be born again. They had church meetings with both black and white slaves teaching them to read the Bible. Many planters objected to this, arguing that the slaves should not learn to read. However, the missionaries countered this by reasoning that if they were able to read the Bible, they would be more productive as slaves. Consequently, over time the missionaries compromised by having separate meetings for whites only and separately for blacks. The teaching to the blacks was usually edited to 'slaves obey your masters', forgiveness etc. There are reports that huge portions of the bible given to the blacks to read, were removed.

From Christian to White

One such Moravian missionary was Rebecca Protten, born a slave in 1718 and kidnapped at an early age from the island of Antigua, was converted at an early age. Rebecca was regarded as being the "Mother of Modern Missions" or perhaps more significantly, the "Mother of the Black Reformation." In his article "*Why the Enslaved Adopted the Religion of Their Masters—and Transformed It*" Dante Stewart, a student at Reformed Theological Seminar and a graduate of Clemson University, writes:

> "In the 1730s, the birth of one of the earliest African Protestant churches found pivotal momentum in a seemingly unlikely place: the rugged roads through the hills of St. Thomas, a Danish sugar colony in the West Indies, known to the enslaved as "The Path." Though kept from popular nightly meetings due to violent animosity, black men and women would press their way along these rugged roads to hear the gospel."
>
> "Protten would eventually gain her freedom and join a group of German missionaries from the Moravian church in 1736. Freidrich Martin, a Moravian missionary, wrote that Protten had done "the work of the Savior by teaching . . . and speaking." Protten didn't just give her voice to the mission of God; she gave her life. As she and others took the gospel from plantation to plantation "St. Thomas suddenly became the Americas' new axis of Afro-Protestant conversion." Fuelled by the message of liberating grace, they put "themselves at the forefront of an indigenous black movement that was birthed in the slave quarters."[10]

A further example of how blacks adopted the religion of their masters and transformed it is the testimony of Richard Allen who was born into slavery in 1760. Allen became a Methodist preacher, an outspoken advocate of racial equality and a founder of the African Methodist Episcopal (AME), one of the largest African American denominations in the US. At age seventeen, Allen converted to Methodism after hearing a white itinerant Methodist preacher. Allen's owner, a Delaware planter, also converted and allowed Allen to buy his freedom in 1783. Allen bought his freedom for $2000 and received a bill of manumission. He gave himself a last name, Allen. In 1786 Allen settled in Philadelphia went into business and attended St George's Methodist Church where blacks and whites were allowed to worship together. Allen became an assistant minister, preaching at an early morning service which attracted a large following. The church constructed a balcony

---

10. Stewart, Why the Enslaved Adopted the Religion of Their Masters—and Transformed It

to accommodate its growing membership. In November 1787, Allen and other blacks were instructed to move into the balcony during the Sunday Service. Stewart writes:

> "Unfortunately, in 1787, racial tensions got the best of the congregation of St. George's. One morning while attending the church, segregated seating was instituted. Allen, not one to lack courage, believed this was a sign that a separate church was necessary for black congregants. Allen and the black congregants walked out and formed what would become Bethel A.M.E Church. This ministry would not just struggle for the advance of the gospel; it would also struggle for racial justice in America, be home for the benevolence of African American peoples and would be a church that would support missions in several countries overseas."

Bethel Church was very successful with a membership of over four hundred by 1810. The church had become black Philadelphia's most important institution. The success of the church angered and worried white Methodist preachers, incensed by Allen's refusal to allow them to control the church. They tried to take over the church and when that failed, they went to Court and won a lawsuit enabling them to sell the building and the land. Not put off Allen raised the funds quickly and bought back the very church he had built. In 1816 Allen and representatives from other black Methodist churches formally broke with the Methodist Church and established a new denomination the African Methodist Episcopal Church where he was appointed Bishop. Blacks elected to form their own, separate denominations in major Northern and Southern cities. Black clergy began speaking out against slavery and established organisations aimed at social reform and self-improvement.

> "Allen's principal biographer Richard Newman, assesses Allen's historical significance in two ways. He was clearly a 'black founder' who established black institutions and engaged in black politics. But in a larger sense, he can be considered an American founder, on a par with the white Founding Fathers. He had a vision of what America could—and should—become: a place where the promise of equality set forth in the Declaration of Independence and the Constitution was not simply a shining example of principles but a living reality. Allen's vision has echoed throughout history, influencing activists and thinkers including Frederick Douglass and Martin Luther-King Junior.[11] "

---

11. PBS People & Ideas: Richard Allen

Abolition of the slave trade

In England in 1787 the Society for Effecting the Abolition of the Slave Trade was formed, with nine of the twelve founder members being Quakers. During the same year, William Wilberforce was persuaded to take up their cause; as a Member of Parliament (MP), Wilberforce was able to introduce a Bill to abolish the slave trade. At the same time at the beginning of the nineteenth century The Clapham Sect who were a group of evangelical Anglicans based in Clapham, London, were focused on the abolition of the slave trade and liberation of slaves. Members of the Clapham group were chiefly prominent and wealthy Christians who shared common political and social views and who worked laboriously towards the abolition of slavery. They were motivated by their Christian faith and concern for social justice and fairness for all. Members of the Clapham sect were Thomas Fowell Buxton MP, William Dealtry, Edward James Eliot, Thomas Gisborne, Charles Grant, Zachary Macaulay, Hannah More, Granville Sharp, Charles Simeon, James Stephen, Lord Teignmouth, Henry Thornton MP, Henry Venn, John Venn, William Smith MP and William Wilberforce MP.

Thomas Clarkson was another English Christian abolitionist and a leading campaigner against the slave trade in the British Empire. In 1785 Clarkson entered a latin essay competition that was to set him on the course for most of the remainder of his life. The topic of the essay was *Anne liceat invitos in servitutem dare* (is it lawful to make slaves of others against their will?),[11] and it led Clarkson to consider the question of the slave trade. He read everything he could on the subject, as well as first-hand accounts of the African slave trade. He also researched the topic by meeting and interviewing those who had personal experience of the slave trade and of slavery.

After winning the prize, Clarkson had what he called a spiritual revelation from God as he travelled by horse between Cambridge and London. He broke his journey at Wadesmill in Hertfordshire. He later wrote:

> "*As it is usual to read these essays publicly in the senate house soon after the prize is adjudged, I was called to Cambridge for this purpose. I went and performed my office. On returning however to London, the subject of it almost wholly engrossed my thoughts. I became at times very seriously affected while upon the road. I stopped my horse occasionally and dismounted and walked. I frequently tried to persuade myself in these intervals that the contents of my Essay could not be true. The more however I reflected upon them, or rather upon the authorities on which they were founded, the more I gave them credit. Coming in sight of Wades Mill in Hertfordshire, I sat down disconsolate on the turf by the*

roadside and held my horse. Here a thought came into my mind, that if the contents of the Essay were true, it was time some person should see these calamities to their end. Agitated in this manner I reached home. This was in the summer of 1785."[12]

This experience and sense of calling ultimately led him to devote his life to abolishing the slave trade and helped found The Society for Effecting the Abolition of the Slave Trade and helped achieve in 1807 the passage of the Slave Trade Act[13]. Although it did not abolish the practice of slavery, it did encourage British action to press other nation states to abolish their own slave trades which ended the trade in British slaves.

A National Archives publication on the abolition of the slave trade, draws attention to the role white women played in the abolitionist movement:

> *"Recent studies show that, in addition to the more well-known abolitionists Mary Birkett, Hannah More and Mary Wollstonecraft, a considerable body of working and middle-class women in Britain were involved in the campaign from the early stages. These white women spoke out against the slave trade, boycotted slave-grown produce and wrote anti-slave trade verses to raise awareness of the violation of family life under slavery. The strength of their support for the campaign can also be gauged through their subscriptions to the Abolition Society; as the historian Clare Midgley reveals, 10% of the 1787–8 subscribers were women.*
>
> *In England, Josiah Wedgwood, the famous potter, and abolitionist, produced a ceramic cameo of a kneeling male slave in chains with the slogan "Am I not a man and a brother"? Later, women campaigners secured production of a similar ceramic brooch, with the caption "Am I not a Woman and a Sister"?*[14]

Wilberforce's involvement in the abolition movement was motivated by a desire to put his Christian principles into action and to serve God in public life. He and other evangelicals were horrified by what they perceived was a depraved and un-Christian trade, and the greed and avarice of the owners and traders. Wilberforce sensed a call from God, writing in a journal entry in 1787 that "God Almighty has set before me two great objects, the suppression of the Slave Trade and the Reformation of Manners [moral

---

12. Clarkson, An Essay on the Slavery and Commerce of the Human Species, Particularly the African

13. Clarkson, The History of the Rise, Progress, and Accomplishment of the Abolition of the African Slave-Trade by the British Parliament.

14 (National Archives: Black Presence: Asian and Black History in Britain, 1500–1850).

values]." The conspicuous involvement of evangelicals in the highly popular anti-slavery movement served to improve the status of a group otherwise associated with the less popular campaigns against vice and immorality.

William Wilberforce first attempted to abolish the trade in 1791 but could only muster half the necessary votes in Parliament. However, after transferring his support to the Whigs, it became an election issue. Abolitionist pressure had changed popular opinion, and in the 1806 election, enough abolitionists entered parliament for Wilberforce to be able to see the passing of the Slave Trade Act 1807. The Royal Navy subsequently declared that the slave trade was equal to piracy, the West Africa Squadron choosing to seize ships involved in the transfer of slaves and liberate the slaves on board, effectively crippling the transatlantic trade. Throughout the region, enslaved people engaged in revolts, labour stoppages and more everyday forms of resistance, for example, in 1730 the Maroons were victorious against the British in Jamaica, resulting in peace treaties in 1739 and 1740. The Haitian Revolution (1791–1804) was the only successful slave uprising in the Americas and heightened British sensitivities to the potential outcomes of insurrection. In 1816 Bussa's rebellion was the largest slave revolt in Barbadian history. It was the first of three large scale rebellions in the British West Indies that shook public faith in slavery in the years leading up to the abolition.

A further rebellion against slavery was instigated by Samuel Sharpe, who was a well-known preacher and leader in the Burchell Baptist Church in Jamaica. His pastor was Rev. Thomas Burchell, a missionary from England. Sharpe spent much of his time travelling to different parishes in Jamaica, educating the enslaved about Christianity, which he believed promised freedom. Where possible the enslaved closely followed the British Parliament's discussions surrounding the abolition of slavery in the mistaken belief that emancipation had already been granted by the British Parliament. When Sharpe was just thirty-one years old, he initiated a plan of passive resistance, a general strike against slavery. The plan was that slaves would refuse to work after their Christmas holiday in 1831 (one hundred years after the Maroons' victories). The enslaved Africans would continue to strike until the state owners and managers listened to their grievances. Sharpe felt that the owners might listen to the slaves as the strike was timed for the key sugar cane harvest and if the ripe cane was not cut then it would be ruined. Sharpe hoped to inspire a peaceful resistance, indeed he encouraged the slaves to only fight physically if the managers didn't agree to their demands. Yet Sharpe probably knew that their strike would not succeed, and he made military preparations for the rebellion.

As the idea for the strike spread throughout the island to St. James, Trelawny, Westmoreland, and beyond, the plan reached the ears of some of the slave owners. As Sharpe anticipated they did not react favourably. Troops were sent to St. James and warships were anchored in Montego Bay and the Black River with their guns trained on the town.

On December 28 1831, the Kensington Estate Great House was set alight as a signal that the rebellion had begun. Other fires broke out and it soon became clear that the Sam Sharpe's hope for peaceful resistance was impossible. The rebellion lasted for eight days and resulted in the death of around 186 slaves and 14 white overseers or planters. Retribution for the resistance was swift and merciless. Over 500 slaves were convicted, and many were executed, most were hanged, and their heads were cut off and placed around their plantations. Those who escaped the death penalty were treated brutally and many did not survive. Sam Sharpe was named as the key figure behind the resistance, and he was captured.

> 'When reminded that the Scriptures teach human beings to be content with the station [status] allotted to them by Providence, and that even slaves are required patiently to submit to their lot, til the Lord in His providence is pleased to change it, Sharpe responded, "If I have done wrong in that, I trust that I shall be forgiven for I cast myself upon the Atonement . . . I would rather die upon yonder gallows than to live in slavery."[15]

Sam Sharpe was hanged in Montego Bay on a square now called Sam Sharpe Square. Sharpe's owners were paid the sum of just £16.00 for their 'loss of property'.

These rebellions and the brutality of the plantocracy against the enslaved, established a contemporary platform for the parliamentarians, to consider legislating widespread abolition. By this time, they were eager to create peace and economic stability in the Colonies. In addition to the slave resistance, Enlightenment thought, and evangelism led members of the British public to question the morality of slavery and the slave trade. In addition, the Industrial Revolution and advances and improvements in agriculture were benefiting the British economy. Since profits were the main cause of starting a trade, it has been suggested, a decline of profits must have brought about abolition because the slave trade ceased to be profitable. Religious, economic, and social factors contributed to the British Empire's abolition of slavery in the West Indies.

In 1833 they passed the Slavery Abolition Act. Slavery was abolished in most British colonies freeing more than 800,000 enslaved Africans in the

15. *Bleby, Death Struggles of Slavery,* 116–17) Sam Sharpe Project

Caribbean, South Africa and other countries. The passing of this Act was met with such joy that Wilberforce was moved to utter the following words of victory:

> "When God is with his people, he will give them power of a destructive kind. Do not be frightened. Here is the text for it: "Behold, the people shall rise up as a great lion, and lift up himself as a young lion"— that is, as a lion in the fulness of his vigour,—"he shall not lie down until he eat of the prey, and drink the blood of the slain." God has pat into his church, when he is in it, a most wonderful, destructive power as against spiritual wickedness. A healthy church kills error, and tears in pieces evil. Not so very long ago our nation tolerated slavery in our colonies. Philanthropists endeavoured to destroy slavery; but when was it utterly abolished? It was when Wilberforce roused the church of God, and when the church of God addressed herself to the conflict, then she tore the evil thing to pieces. I have been amused with what Wilberforce said the day after they passed the Act of Emancipation. He merrily said to a friend when it was all done, "Is there not something else we can abolish?" That was said playfully, but it shows the spirit of the church of God."[16]

However, before actual emancipation, the slaves were forced to engage in what was called the apprenticeship programme. This meant that they had to give the slave master forty-five hours per week of unpaid hours of labor for a period of four years.

The slaves would in fact be paying the slave masters for their freedom! The former masters found other ways to control the labor force and developed a system of dependency, for example, only white men could own land and former slaves could not. Land was to be sold at one pound per acre, which was too expensive for the ex-slaves. There was no freedom of movement to other areas of the country. Former masters continued to ill-treat and exploit them.

Life became more difficult for the former slaves as they received their freedom from the system of slavery, with limited opportunity to support themselves outside of employment on the same estates. Many ex-slaves however, moved to the urban centres to look for work, setting up shanties on the outskirts of towns. Others were forced to squat; to illegally occupy land and cultivate it as a means of securing some form of independence. In other words, they were still outside the embrace of the community, the society and of the letter of the law. Incredibly, when slavery was abolished

---

16. Spurgeon. 'The Best Warcry a prominent Baptist opponent of slavery (Wikipedia)

in 1838, the former slave owners were further compensated for the loss they experienced, while the enslaved peoples received no compensation, financial or otherwise. Professor Hilary Beckles, in his book "The First Black Slave Society," explains the issue of compensation:

> "First the state did not wish to capitulate to the demand for compensation. The government had long been an important part of the slaveocracy. As a slave-owner in its own right, it could not separate itself from its private-sector partners. Second, in order to compensate itself and other enslavers, the government first had to agree to a definition of enslaved Africans as property, and therefore non-human. Only then could it instruct the Treasury to pay for "loss of use" compensation to all enslavers, now branded by the abolitionists as common criminals."[17]

Thomas Clarkson alone, as it seems, promoted the fact that the enslaved were stolen people and, according to Hilary Beckles "... "that enslavers were receivers of criminally acquired bodies which they had converted to property." Beckles continues:

> "If compensation, said Clarkson, was to be considered part of the emancipation process, then it would be the African, he insisted, who should receive such reparations. Clarkson understood the extent to which racism had poisoned the political discourse. He spoke passionately to his fellow parliamentarians: "In all other countries, except in defenseless Africa, or the colonies of nations planted on the discovery of the New World, you would have been condemned to death had you gone there on the same errand."[18]

Behind the scenes, in 1837, a plantation owner called John Gladstone who was representing other sugar plantations in the West Indies requested a meeting with the Colonial Secretary Lord Glenelg.

This was to consider ways of providing a system of producing the cultivation of sugar cane, through a regular, continuous labor force. Gladstone put forward a proposal to import workers from Bengal in Indian, under a system of indentured labor, for a period of five years. In reply, the Colonial Government posed the question of whether this experiment *"could free labor successfully deliver profitability to the British West Indian sugar plantations in competition with the slave producing sugar colonies."*?[19]

---

17. Beckles, *The First Black Slave Society*, p200
18. Beckles, *The First Black Slave Society*, p205
19. A new system of slavery and the origins of Indian indenture, National Archives

As the enslaved Africans were considered to be the property of the slave owners, there was never any consideration given to restoring their humanity; family life, land ownership and safety under the law, the British introduced an Indian indentureship scheme to satisfy the planter class. That scheme provided the East Indians with a contract and other conditions that secured and maintained family life in all its cultural norms.

> "Gladstone was promptly granted permission by Order in Council to recruit indentured labourers from his agent in India. Each indentured labourer signed a 'girmit' or indenture contract. The labourer was agreeing to work for a plantation owner for the period of five years as a 'free labourer' and with 'mutual consent', in return for accommodation, food and medical attention. Theoretically, the labourer would secure free passage back to India after five years. Gladstone's ship, the Hesperus, sailed from Calcutta to Georgetown, British Guiana in September 1837." A 'new system of slavery'? The British West Indies and the origins of Indian indenture."[20]

The Indian indentured laborers were able to retain their religion, language, food, and all their cultural norms as practiced in India. On May 5th, 1838, almost three months before the emancipation of the enslaved Africans on August 1st 1838, in the British West Indies, a small batch of three hundred and ninety-six Indian immigrants popularly known as the 'Gladstone Coolies' landed in British Guiana (Guyana) from Calcutta. This was the beginning of the indenture system and which was to continue, with modifications for over three-quarters of a century and whose essential features were reminiscent of slavery. Despite the original contract, life for the Indians proved in practice to be totally unacceptable.

Less than three years later, however, a new Colonial Secretary, Lord John Russell, under pressure from the metropolitan members of the British and Foreign anti-Slavery Society (BFSS) suspended the Indian Indenture scheme to British Guiana stating:

> "I am not prepared to encounter the responsibility of a measure which may lead to a dreadful loss of life on the one hand, or, on the other, to a new system of slavery (. . .) "Lord Russell, the Colonial Secretary, had to be careful not to antagonise anti-slavery activists, as well as give practical application to Britain's declared imperial mission to uplift and civilize less-privileged people throughout the world. Less than four years later, the argument that indentured migration gave Indians an opportunity to improve their moral

---

20. A new system of slavery and the origins of Indian indenture. National Archives

and material condition and solve labour shortages had won over. Soon a proper legal and regulated framework, enacted in the British Parliament, would, it was believed, secure both the economic and social wellbeing of the British West Indian colonies. immigration was deemed essential."[21]

The reforms proposed 1859 to the Indians were similar to the contract conditions implemented to the white indentured servants in the 1650s: contract period between five and seven years; guaranteed passage paid, and on arrival, be maintained for the duration, at the expense of the planter. When their term of contract had expired, they would either receive ten pounds sterling, or a piece of land equivalent in value. In Radica Mahase's book, "A brief History of Indentureship in Trinidad" she describes the content of the contract:

> "Under the commutation grant in 1859, Indians who had completed their five years contracts and seven years residence in the colony, opted for ten acres of land in lieu of a return passage. This scheme was modified in 1873, to offer a choice between ten acres of land or five acres of land and £5 in cash. A total of eleven thousand nine hundred and thirty three persons commuted their return passages. In total, about 25% of all those who came, returned to India while the majority settled here. While most of them may have opted to stay because the economic situation in Trinidad was seen as much better than what they had experienced in India, large numbers were forced to stay since they could not afford the return passage or ships were not readily available to take them back to their motherland. "[22]

The Government of India finally banned the Indian indenture system in 1917.

To summarise this chapter, we have seen that in the early seventeenth century, the pioneers who travelled to the New World had conflicting interests. The adventurers, entrepreneurs, venture capitalists were accompanied by the Church of England clergy who had a vision of the New World being the 'promised land' of the Bible. They completely underestimated the challenges they encountered in Jamestown and in the first year many starved or died from disease. The early settlers had a very 'prickly' relationship with the indigenous people and in the end tried to evangelise them by force. Much later, the Puritans who were the founding fathers of Massachusetts and they

21. *Russell to Governor Light, 15 February 1840. Parliamentary Papers. Volume XVI (No56)*
22. Mahase, A brief history of Indian Indentureship in Trinidad

too started well but ended up competing with England in engaging with the acquisition of African enslavement. The Puritans used their musket power, legal instruments, and shipping industry in capturing North American Indians and shipped them as slaves to the West Indies in exchange for African slaves whom they brought on their return trip. They had two competing aims gold and God. In their search for wealth (as they did not find gold), they cultivated tobacco and traded with the indigenous people.

As the demand for labor increased in the New World, the West Indian island of Barbados became the first 'slave society in the world', as the English imported thousands of Africans to work on the plantations. The slave system, which was developed by the planters, met with resistance initially by the Church of England because of the inhuman and ungodly treatment of the Africans. English law determined that a person could not be a slave and a Christian, so a conflict arose as many of the African enslaved people were already baptised or were responding to the call to become Christian. However, the Church of England compromised its position by accommodating the practices of the plantocracy and actually participating in the enslavement of Africans.

Nevertheless, as more Africans became Christian, the planters sought to put a stop to the English legal requirement that determined that a Christian could not be a slave by defining 'whiteness' as being Christian. Therefore, a slave, despite his religious belief as being Christian, could not claim the right to be a free man.

From the late eighteenth century, Quaker, Methodist, Baptist, Moravian missionaries arrived and sought to bring the Gospel of Jesus Christ to the white as well as the enslaved people. They met with opposition from planters and had to be very circumspect in their teaching of the Word of God. They decided to make some compromises in order to have access to the plantation.

In the meantime, an abolitionist movement began in the early 19th century by groups of black and white Christians, in England and in the West Indies. This led to the end of the slave trade in 1807 and eventually to the so-called abolition of slavery in 1838 in the British colonies. Could the decision about whiteness being Christian become a religious belief embedded as the root of the culture of society and the root of racial division within the church?

10

New-World Culture in Great Britain

*The 20th & 21st Century Experience:
from colonialism to in-migration*

THIS CHAPTER EXPLORES THE experience of West Indians on their arrival in the "Mother Country"; the United Kingdom.

One might ask: Who are the West Indians? What is their story? Why are they here? What are they to do with us?

Afro-West Indians are the descendants of the Africans who were taken from their land, sold into slavery and shipped to the Caribbean and the New World by the Europeans between the 15th and the 19th century. They survived the degradation of imprisonment in the dungeons of West Africa, such as Cape Coast and Elmina Castles in Ghana, the tomb-like conditions of the slave ships which transported them through the Middle Passage to the West Indies and the trauma of landing in the strange environment of the West Indies. On their arrival they were subjected to a further process of dehumanisation as they were put up for auction and sold to the highest bidder; they then became their property. This is where the practice of 'chattel slavery' was created. As chattel, the African man had no authority over his own life, nor that of his wife and children. The Europeans bought and sold individuals with little regard for their family connections. Men, husbands, fathers, children were sold off and made to work in the various plantations. Slave codes were devised by the English plantation owners and approved by the English Parliament. The lives of enslaved people in the colonies became English 'property'. Barbados was a 'proprietary country', owned by the English investors, under the authority of the Crown, so everything that happened was subject to the Crown. Once placed on to an English slave ship people became English property.

The owners of the plantations in the colonies were not concerned about the welfare of the people, they were only interested in the production of crops. Consequently, people were literally worked to death and the average life span was seven years due to overwork and the cruel conditions on the plantations. Those that survived this unspeakably barbarous regime were eventually freed by the Abolition Act of 1833, but they were left having to pay for their freedom by working free of charge to the plantation owners for a period of four years. Eventually, in 1838 they were made homeless, landless, and illegal. They were forced to squat on any land they could occupy.

It is a remarkable story of a people whose ancestors survived these horrors and overcame every challenge. They did so because they had a faith in God and an ability to overcome. Subsequent generations of West Indians have since gone out into all the world, and this is some of their history in the UK.

West Indians are the people from the archipelago of islands that surround the Caribbean Sea. They also include Guyana, formerly British Guiana in South America and Belize formerly British Honduras, in Central America. They also include Bermuda, the Bahamas and the Turks and Caicos Islands, and the Cayman Islands, which are in the Atlantic Ocean.

They comprise peoples largely of African heritage but also include people from India, Europe France, Netherlands, Spain and Italy, Middle East—Syria and Jews, to name a few. Great Britain owned many of the islands as colonies of the British Empire. They were sometimes settled by the English, Scots, Irish and Welsh.

Little mention is made in history of the indigenous peoples; Caribs, Arawak, Tainos, Siboneys whom Columbus and the early conquistadores met. Their populations were all but decimated within the first fifty years from 1492. However, traces of Carib and other indigenous peoples can be found among many of the descendants of the people groups brought to the West Indies.

The consequences of the transatlantic slave trade in terms of its impact on the British economy and indeed history are well documented. These documents are being researched, published, and debated. They form the basis for confronting a belief system of white supremacy, that exists to this day. The Understanding Slavery Initiative (USI) is a national learning project supporting the teaching and learning of transatlantic slavery and its legacies using museum and heritage collections. USI is funded by major companies and interests such as: National Maritime Museum, Hull City Council, American Museum in Britain, British Museums Galleries, and the Museum of London Docklands has produced much work in exposing information that was hither to obscured.

> *"When you look at the environment, the built environment and all the other things that came out of this history, there are really not that many areas in Britain that you can look at that haven't been touched in some way by this history or built by the wealth made by this history. So it really is kind of embedded within the building of Britain as a great nation. By the end of the 18th century, in 1798, the West Indies. . .what we would call the Caribbean, Britain's Caribbean colonies were slave systems, slave-holding system was very much entrenched. They contributed about a quarter of Britain's sort of global imports. So, the imports coming into Britain from America, Asia, and Africa, about a quarter of the value of those was coming from the slave-holding economies. So I think that gives us a sense of the importance of this trade, and the results of the trade to Britain's economy. Well, transatlantic slavery, and. involvement in transatlantic slavery contributed directly to the wealth and success of Britain, because you are talking about approximately at one stage, 1 million human lives which were working continuously in islands in the Caribbean, in particular owned by the British, when. . . at a time when the population of the British Isles was barely 5 million. So, it's an enormous boost to the economy in terms of free labour, to the extent that in the 1780s, one pound in ten moving through the British economy was coming not just from Caribbean plantations and their products, but from the island of Jamaica alone."*[1]

With the passing of Emancipation Laws between 1834 –38, there followed the economic system of colonialism during which the colonies were ruled by the Crown Colony system. The people of the West Indies were then nurtured with an identity of being British and as an integral part of the British Empire. Their laws, language, education, and religion were all British. Even their passports were British. The British West Indians are British.

Subsequently, as British colonials, these West Indians considered themselves to be an integral part of Great Britain and sought to engage in the wars in which Britain fought.

One such war was the Crimean War 1853—1856, in which one West Indian lady stands out for her commitment and dedication to the soldiers— Mary Seacole: 1805 –1881. In 1854 she travelled to England asking the War

---

1. Understanding Slavery Initiative

Office to be sent as an Army Nurse to the Crimea. She was refused. She went anyway and set up a hotel, where she provided comfortable nursing care for sick and convalescent soldiers wounded on the battlefield. She was posthumously honored by the British government in 2016.

Later, when WWI broke out in 1914, the British colonies in the West Indies quickly pledged their support to Britain in men, money, and materials. King George V called for assistance in the two world wars (as volunteers, soldiers from the British Empire, including the British West Indies) West Indians fought and died alongside the British.

A new regiment

The young men from the West Indies who joined up were keen to prove their worth on the battlefield. Their enthusiasm was not shared by Britain's War Office, which did not want black men in its army. But on the personal intervention of King George V, the War Office eventually relented. On 3 November 1915, the British West Indies Regiment (BWIR) was established by Royal Warrant. In addition to the BWIR, the West Indies contributed men through the West India Regiment (WIR), which had served Britain since 1795. A recruitment poster for the First World War was produced and displayed across the countries in the British West Indies and an example of one from the Bahamas reads:

"YOUNG MEN OF THE BAHAMAS

The British Empire is engaged in a Life and Death Struggle.

Never in the History of England, never since the Distant Past of 2000, years ago, has our beloved country been engaged in such a conflict as she is engaged to-day

To bring to nothing this mighty attack by an unscrupulous and well prepared foe. His most gracious Majesty King George has called on the men of his empire.

Men of every class, creed and colour to come forward to fight

That the Empire may be saved and the foe may be well beaten

This call is to YOU, young man; not your neighbour, not your brother, not your cousin, but just YOU.

Several hundreds of your mates have come up, have been medically examined and have been passed as "fit."

What is the matter with YOU?

Put yourself right with your King: put yourself right with your fellowman: put yourself right with your conscience.
ENLIST TO-DAY."

"*Troops were recruited from the West Indies using leaflets, posters and films, and rallies such as the one pictured above in the Bahamas. In addition, the authorities used financial incentives such as tax concessions and the fact that wages were higher in the army than in many civilian jobs. Moral persuasion was used by many churches, who cast the war between Britain and Germany as a battle between good and evil.*"[2]

Thousands of West Indian young men came forward as volunteers, to answer that call. They wanted to be a part of this great struggle and to prove their loyalty to the king.

'The formation of the BWIR did not give soldiers from the West Indies the opportunity to fight as equals alongside white soldiers. Instead, the War Office largely limited their participation to 'labour' duties. The use of BWIR soldiers in supporting roles intensified during the Battle of the Somme as casualties among fighting troops meant that reinforcements were needed in the front line.

BWIR troops were engaged in numerous support roles on the Western Front, including digging trenches, building roads and gun emplacements, acting as stretcher bearers, loading ships and trains, and working in ammunition dumps. This work was often carried out within range of German artillery and snipers. In July 1917, 13 men from the BWIR were killed by shell fire and aerial bombardment. In 1917 Field Marshal Sir Douglas Haig said of the BWIR, '[Their] work has been very arduous and has been carried out almost continuously under shell-fire. In spite of casualties the men have always shown themselves willing and cheerful workers, and the assistance they have rendered has been much appreciated by the units to which they have been attached and for whom they have been working. The physique of the men is exceptional, their discipline excellent and their morale high."[3]

Accounts of West Indians' involvement and participation in both world wars are not widely known, for example:

---

2. Imperial War Museum, London

3. *Imperial war museum* https://www.iwm.org.uk/history/the-story-of-the-british-west-indies

> "The Palestine Campaign was far away from the main conflicts of the First World War in Europe. However, the battle here against the Turks was a vicious affair because . . . ." the Turks were ferocious fighters." It was not long before the machine gun crews of the West Indian regiment were tested out. They were sent into action against a large body of Turkish soldiers and showed great coolness and self-discipline under fire.
>
> The commanding officer of 162 Machine-gun Company praised the work of the West—Indian gunners: "The men (in machine-gun section) worked exceedingly well . . . showing keen interest in their work, cheerfulness, coolness under fire and the ability to carry out under difficulties."
>
> General Allenby also highlighted the machine-gun crews' outstanding achievements. He wrote to the Governors of Jamaica and the other British West Indian colonies: "I have great pleasure in informing you of thee excellent conduct of the machine-gun section of the BWIR during two successful raids on the Turkish trenches. All ranks behaved with great gallantry under heavy rifle fire and contributed in no small measure to the success of the operation."[4]

However, in 1918 BWIR soldiers were denied a pay rise given to other British troops on the basis that they had been classified as 'natives'. The increase was eventually granted following protests by serving soldiers and the various island governments.

Tensions brought about by this sort of treatment eventually came to a head in Taranto, Italy in December 1918. Frustrated by their continued use as laborers whilst waiting for demobilisation, men of the 9th Battalion attacked their officers in a mutiny that lasted four days before being quelled. Around sixty men were tried for mutiny, receiving sentences from three to five years, with one man getting twenty years, and another was executed by firing squad.

The war ended with one hundred and eighty-five BWIR men killed in action and another one thousand and seventy-one who died from sickness. It is a sad to report that more West Indian soldiers were killed by 'friendly fire' than by enemy bullets. Despite the conditions of war for the West Indians the official report of the BWIR by The Memorial Gates Trust stated that :"15,600 men of the British West Indies Regiment served with the Allied forces. Jamaica contributed two-thirds of these volunteers, while others came from Trinidad and Tobago, Barbados, the Bahamas, British Honduras, Grenada, British Guiana (now Guyana), the Leeward Islands, St Lucia and

---

4 Caribbean Participants in the First World War: Memorial Gates Trust

St Vincent. Nearly 5,000 more subsequently volunteered to join up." During World War One, BWIR soldiers fought in various battles, in Palestine, Egypt and Europe. Over 1,200 were killed and 2,500 injured out of a population of 1,700,000 from West Indian colonies of the British Empire. Awards for bravery were received by eighty-one men and forty-nine, (including the future Prime Minister of Jamaica, Norman Manley,) were mentioned in despatches.

Reni Eddo-Lodge, in her book "Why I'm No Longer Talking To White People About Race" describes in graphic detail, how, despite the heroism displayed by BWIR soldiers who remained in Britain after WWI, they were denied acceptance within British society because of their skin color. They were treated as enemies in many of the towns and cities. Things came to a head when white men attacked the homes of black citizens, and a black man was stabbed by a white man in Wales in 1919. Fights between white and black men also broke out in other cities. Even the Police got involved and vandalised many homes of black people. Subsequently, some white men threw Charles Wootton, a West Indian into the sea. As he tried to get back to safety, they threw bricks at him until he drowned. As more white men ran amok in cities, attacking black men, it was decided by the Government that they would bring to an end to this rioting. They sent the West Indians back to where they came from, and six hundred black men were deported.[5]

Ironically, in World War II, (WWII) when the British armed forces realized that the war could be lost to the Germans, they laid aside their racial prejudices against black West Indians and called on them to fight for the Mother Country. This time they were assigned to regular duties and positions as befitting their abilities. Consequently, many West Indians became officers in the armed forces and again, some received awards for bravery.

Following WW2, the shortage of labour in Britain, resulted in invitations being extended to West Indians to work in the transport system and the newly established NHS. Britain again encouraged immigration, which resulted in the Windrush Generation in 1948. The same year, the government of Great Britain, passed the British Nationality Act; a law that effectively gave Commonwealth citizens the same rights to reside as British subjects.

For many centuries, in the West Indies, people lived under a legal system that was British: laws, language, economy, religion, and education. The West Indians were British citizens. They had British passports, an English system of education—Cambridge and Oxford Certificates at the end of secondary education, and access to tertiary education in the UK and other

---

5. Reni Eddo-Lodge; "Why I'm No Longer Talking To White People About Race."

countries. The British way of life was the way of life for the British West Indians.

Daniel Trilling is the author of "*Lights in the Distance: Exile and Refuge at the Borders of Europe and Bloody Nasty People: the Rise of Britain's Far Right* asks the question, "Why have the 1947 riots been forgotten"?

> "*In 1947 Britain, there were widespread anti-Semitic riots across the country from Glasgow to Liverpool, Manchester, and London. No one died but the British politicians were keen to sweep things under the carpet. James Chuter Ede, the post-war Home Secretary, dismissed the rioting as mere "hooliganism . . . rather than an indication of public feeling," while magistrates condemned rioters as "un-British" and "unpatriotic."*
>
> *Yet the riots were neither an aberration nor the product of an unruly working class. Britain was experiencing an identity crisis: it had won the war but appeared to be losing the peace, with recession at home and the break-up of its Empire abroad, in which the events in Mandate Palestine played only a small part. As colonised peoples increasingly demanded independence, Britain turned to a more inward-looking nationalism. Along with it came the question of who would be included and who would be left out.*
>
> *In 1948, with cross-party support, the Labour government passed the British Nationality Act, marking a shift from a situation where all those living in the Empire—in theory, although quite evidently not in practice—were equal subjects under the Crown to one where each country in the Commonwealth could determine its own version of citizenship. Although in the years to come it would be non-white immigrants from the Commonwealth who would most strongly challenge received notions of Englishness and Britishness and who would bear the brunt of racism, Jews, too, were caught up in this, for a brief period.*"[6]

Seventy years ago, on June 22, 1948, the first wave of West Indians (five hundred) on the Empire Windrush embarked on a trip that originated in Trinidad and travelled to Barbados and Jamaica before landing in England. In London those who did not have accommodation were settled in an air raid shelter underneath Clapham Common. They came in response to the call to assist in rebuilding Britain after the war. They came to work and live in the mother country.

Employment: There was work in the rebuilding of the country because of the bombing by the Germans during the war. Many West Indians were

---

6. Trilling, Why have the 1947 riots been forgotten?

employed in the construction industry and in factories as laborers and general workers.

This was the first time that West Indians, (African heritage descendants of slaves) had ever come to live in the UK in such large numbers at any time. Many had been in the UK during the WWII as personnel in the Armed Forces (some of whom afterwards returned to their various islands in the West Indies). But this was different. These came to stay! The British population was faced with the question of how to relate now to these colored foreigners. The different sectors of society very quickly expressed their positions.

The West Indians' reception in the mother country, the UK, was largely unexpected. As a result of housing shortages, the state provided emergency housing in various parts of the country in London, Sheffield, and Liverpool. Long term accommodation in particular parts of the cities: London—Brixton, Harlesden, Stonebridge, Dalston, Tottenham and Lewisham. In many of these towns in London, there was a London Transport Bus Terminus.

Ten years later, in the mid-50s, the economy had changed. Mass employment had all but dried up and there were long queues of unemployed people. *'The battle lines drawn in this atmosphere were often racial."* (Wikipedia)

Indeed, some black employees were denied work in Nottingham's factories.

> *"In 1958 Nottingham was the scene of one Britain's most bitter and ugliest racial conflicts. Animosity began between the black and white communities in the St Anns district and on 23 August simmering resentment erupted in a scuffle in a local pub and escalated into fighting involving 1500 people. Widespread media coverage spotlighted the problem and the following week a crowd of nearly 4,000 whites gathered seeking revenge. The black community stayed indoors, and the whites fought among themselves. In the aftermath the local Labour party voiced the concerns of the black community who felt that the police had acted in an unfair and prejudicial manner.*
>
> *There was similar flare up of trouble in 1981, not only in Nottingham but nationwide. In July underlying tensions flared up in the Hyson Green area and there were several confrontations between black and white youths and the police. Peace was restored but not before much damage had been done to the Hyson Green flat complex."*[7]

---

7. Amos, The Nottinghamshire Heritage Gateway, Black community history

Over time, permanent accommodation for the West Indians proved to be a major challenge, especially in London. The rental market was littered with signs such as "No Blacks, No Irish, No dogs." The West Indians however, found accommodation in many buildings the like of which other people would not live. They often found themselves victims of slumlords. This shortage of housing meant that many West Indians would find themselves having to live in overcrowded rooms with poor sanitation and overstretched services.

West Indians At Work

Many West Indians came from rural areas in their countries and would have had a trade or some skill and willing to work as laborers. Others had secondary education with Ordinary & Advanced Level Certificates, some even left their jobs and came to better their life chances in the land of opportunity. They came to work. In the workplace they found employment in London Transport in a variety of positions—cleaners, laborers, carpenters and upholsterers, mechanics and even front-line jobs as conductors and drivers on the buses. The other source of employment easily available for them, especially for women was in nursing. Accommodation was part of the package and many women, and some men took up this opportunity. Indeed, many were recruited directly from the West Indies.

SEN (State Enrolled Nurse), SRN (State Registered Nurse), Midwifery, district nursing and even theatre nurses were recruited by the NHS. Those girls who did not have secondary education or who had GCE O Levels were assigned to SEN streaming depending on the need. Others were offered the SRN training which led to the other qualifications in the Nursing career.

Promotion up the ladder to become ward sisters and higher was difficult, yet some eventually achieved, even the position of Matron in hospitals by the late 1960s.

Obtaining careers outside the confines of public transport and Nursing options were more challenging. Despite presenting their 'O' & 'A' level qualifications, applicants would invariably be offered jobs such as laboring or cleaning. Some women however were given typing or other secretarial positions, provided they were not seen by the public.

West Indians had a practice of coming together in the tradition of trade unions, while negotiating for better working conditions and pay. On arrival in the UK and entering the labor force, West Indian workers and tradesmen naturally sought to join a trade union.

West Indians: Race and Trade Unions

Wilf Sullivan, a Trade Union Congress Race Equality Officer writes:

> "However, despite black workers joining trade unions in large numbers, they were not welcomed by the UK trade union movement or the TUC. While the immigrant workers did not constitute a threat to the jobs of British workers because of acute labour shortages following the war, the TUC argued during the 1950's and 1960's that black workers did not integrate with white workers. This helped to stereotype black migrant workers as a "problem" and "others." Even though during the 1969 TUC Congress, rank-and-file trade union members challenged the immigration controls and supported government's plans in calling for positive action to combat discrimination, the TUC General Council prevented the motion receiving majority support, thereby opposing government plans for anti-discrimination legislation.
>
> During this period, the UK trade unions' position could be categorised as 'racist exclusive'. Some trade unions' preference was to, first, keep migrant workers out of the labour market, second, (since that wasn't possible) keep them out of the union, and third, since many became union members, exclude them from the entitled union benefits. In addition, during the 1950s there were a number of race riots, or attacks on immigrants by white youths and the Oswald Mosley's Union Movement. This culminated in the riots in Nottingham and London's Notting Hill in 1958 where black people were attacked in the streets and in their houses."[8]

West Indians at school

Children of the first wave of immigrants from the West Indies were taken to school but were wrongly assessed by Educational Psychologists as being ESN (Educationally Sub Normal) and many were sent to special schools. This was largely because they spoke with a different accent or dialect while at the same time suffering from emotional trauma because of the upheaval of leaving home and family, living in poor housing conditions, and experiencing racism both within school and wider society.

By the summer of the same year, 1958, Notting Hill in London was the center of brewing unrest, as gangs of Teddy Boys were becoming increasingly violent toward anyone who was black. They also attacked Caribbean shops and business.

---

8. Sullivan, *Race and trade unions, TUC Race Equality Officer*

On 24 August, 1958 there were two incidents in Shepherd's Bush and Notting Hill, involving white youths who had assaulted West Indian men, of whom were seriously injured. 'Keep Britain White" fueled the movement of violence against black people. In the week that followed, a group of white youths, armed with knives, iron bars, and other weapons, and intent on finding trouble ran amok through the streets of Notting Hill. After their rampage they left several black men injured in hospital. Also, among the injured was a white Swedish woman called Majbritt Morrison, who was married to a Jamaican, who was hit with an iron bar and pelted with stones.

Following these incidents, a crowd of West Indians, armed with knives and assorted weapons, retaliated shouting abuse and threatening whites in Ladbroke Grove. The riots continued over four nights until they finally ended on 5th September. Those arrested were sent for trial at the Old Bailey where the Judge sent nine white youths who had gone "nigger hunting" to goal for four years each. Of the one hundred and eight people arrested and charged with offenses, seventy-two were white and thirty-six were black.

The Metropolitan Police tried to assert that the riots were not racially motivated, but witnesses disagreed as their statements gave evidence of the motives of the mobs, sometimes a thousand strong, roaming around Notting Hill and attacking any West Indians they could find. This denial has also given rise to the level of mistrust of the Police by West Indians and black people in general.

Notting Hill Carnival

The roots of the Notting Hill Carnival that took shape in the mid-1960s had two separate but connected strands. A "Caribbean Carnival" was held on 30 January 1959 in St Pancras Town Hall as a response to the problematic state of race relations at the time; the UK's first widespread racial attacks, the Notting Hill race riots in which 108 people were charged, had occurred the previous year. The 1959 event, held indoors and televised by the BBC, was organised by the Trinidadian journalist and activist Claudia Jones (often described as "the mother of the Notting Hill Carnival") in her capacity as editor of influential black newspaper, The West Indian Gazette, and directed by Edric Connor; showcasing elements of a Caribbean carnival in a cabaret style. An article in Wikipedia charts the development of the street Carnival in Notting Hill in 1959:

> *While these events were successful, their impact was to be fully realized by the involvement of Ms. Rhaune Laslett, a social worker. She lived in Notting Hill and co-founded in collaboration with*

> John Hoppy Hopkins, the London Free School, a community action group. The Notting Hill riots propelled her into a commitment to heal the racial tensions in her community. She established an adventure playground and a voluntary neighborhood service offering free 24-hour legal advice and other institutional assistance to the immigrants, residents and the homeless. She had a vision in which she saw streets with thousands of people, in brightly dressed costumes, dancing and following bands parading in the streets. They were women and men, children from all nationalities—black , white, brown; all laughing. She shared this vision with her West Indian friends, Guyanese Andre Shevington who was enthused with the idea. They contacted Russ Henderson, a well-known Trinidadian musician and pan man and his band of fellow artists who were veterans of the Claudia Jones carnival events, but more importantly they were from Trinidad and aware of the dynamics of the street carnival and the excitement it generated. "It was the attendance of his band that changed the course of what might otherwise have become a traditional English pageant, albeit with a multicultural theme." [9]

The objective of the Carnival was to entertain the local children, to lift the spirits of those who lived in poor slum conditions, to ease racial tensions and to demonstrate the spirit of co-operation common to the progressives and activists who lived and operated in the area.

In a 1966 interview with The Grove magazine, edited by Hoppy and published by the London Free School, Laslett said: "*We felt that although West Indians, Africans, Irish and many other nationalities all live in a very congested area, there is very little communication between us. If we can infect them with a desire to participate, then this can only have good results.*"

Laslett's first Carnival featured a cornucopia of participants, all residents but hailing from many places: India, Ghana, Czechoslovakia, Ukraine, Cyprus and elsewhere. Performers included Nigerian musician Ginger Johnson and his Afro-Cuban band, Agnes O'Connell and her Irish Girl Pipers and a white New Orleans-style marching band. Horse-drawn carts were borrowed from traders in Portobello Road to make floats and there was even an inter-pub darts.

When Henderson's group arrived and began playing "pan," West Indians—hearing the familiar sounds from home—flooded the streets. In line with the Trinidad carnival tradition of "making a round" where steel-pan players lead a procession that wove up Portobello Road towards Notting Hill Gate and back again, gathering new revelers along the way. Henderson

---

9. Laslett, Wikipledia

had inadvertently put a Caribbean hallmark on the festival and word quickly spread to the other West Indian communities in England about what had taken place."

Notting Hill Carnival since its inception in 1966 has become the largest street festival in Europe, the most multicultural event with the widest age participation in the whole of Europe, regularly attracting approximately two million people for many years.

West Indians in the churches

West Indians have a long history of Bible teaching; from the slave castles in Africa, to the slave plantations in the West Indies and Anglo-America. This continued after Emancipation including the period of colonialism and the present day. Their understanding of the Bible was one that challenged the prevailing church teachings which accepted slavery as a biblical principle. However, there were many Abolitionist missionaries who bucked the system of slavery that prevailed in the church. Rev. Thomas Burchell, a Baptist missionary, assigned to Montego Bay, Jamaica was one such person and an ardent supporter of Wilberforce in the movement to abolish slavery. In Jamaica he mentored Sam Sharpe, a slave who became a deacon in the Baptist Church. Sam Sharpe spent most of his time travelling to different estates in St. James' area educating the slaves about Biblical Christianity and freedom.

It was only in the second half of the twentieth century that Britain had the opportunity to choose Kingdom Christianity or New World Christianity. This choice is well documented by Dr Clifford Hill in his work to commemorate the 150th anniversary of the abolition of Slavery in the British Empire. His book 'Free At Last?'(with a question mark) documented the most unjust treatment of the West Indians. What was more disturbing were the reports of the treatment they received from the church (by the various denominations) on their arrival as in-migrants to the UK in the 1950s, where instead of welcome; they often rejected and advised not to come back.

> *Looking back today in the aftermath of the 2011 riots, I have to say that as a nation we might never have reached this point if the white churches had responded to the Immigration in accordance with the principles and beliefs of the Christian gospel. It grieves me to say this, but I know there many churches where black faces were not welcome. This is something in which we must return in the final chapter.*"[10]

---

10. Hill, *Free at Last?*

The generational sins of classism, racism and anti Semitism are reflected in so many areas of human interaction. The facility for excluding colored or blacks from society has remained a feature of society to this day. The birth of the so-called black church, a term that has no equal within the teaching of the bible became a consequence of the rejection of West Indians of the Windrush Generation by the church in the UK.

Nevertheless, it was not all bad. West Indians survived in whatever and wherever they were placed. For example, Bill Morris (now Baron Morris of Handsworth) in 1992 became General Secretary of the Transport and General Workers' Union and the first black leader of a major British trade union. Many men and women came to study and eventually gained their degrees or other certification at the Tertiary level. Many were given good jobs according to their certification and ability.

The joy experienced by West Indians who were coming to the Mother Country in the 1950s began back in the West Indies when they bought their clothes, new macs, gloves (clothes you'd not need to wear at home because of the hot weather). It was like coming home, so they all put on their Sunday best! The disappointment at seeing the grey weather and smokey sky only added to their amusement—having come from bright, colorful, sun filled lives.

The reality that they were not welcome in Britain was a shock, but they shrugged this off by being together in the place of their dreams. Buckingham Palace, Trafalgar Square, Houses of Parliament, and the Queen were all part of this. Despite the rejection by many people in Britain, there were countless others with whom long-lasting friendships were made.

My own experience, which was on my first visit to the Church of England in Tufnell Park, when the vicar shook my hand and then wiped it down his cassock, was not dissimilar to descriptions I heard from other West Indians when they visited churches of other denominations. Although it put me off Christianity for twenty years, I am grateful to God that He brought me back into relationship with Him.

In all of this I am mindful of God's purposes in bringing us, as West Indians to Britain, which is expressed in Acts 17: 26—27: *"And He has made from one blood every nation of men to dwell on all the face of the earth and has determined their preappointed times and the boundaries of their dwellings, so that they should seek the Lord, in the hope that they might grope for Him and find Him, though He is not far from each one of us."*

11

From These Very Shores

"From these very shores the Gospel shall go forth to not only this New World, but the entire world."

Rev. Robert Hunt

The outpouring of the Holy Spirit in Anglo America, (USA) in 1906 brought that prophecy *"from these very shores the Gospel shall go forth to not only this New World, but the entire world." Rev. Robert Hunt* to fruition. It happened three hundred years (1606–1906) after the English set out for Jamestown, the first permanent English settlement in the New World.

What man meant for evil God meant it for good to save many people alive. Gen 50: 15—21

> *Gen 50:15 And when Joseph's brethren saw that their father was dead, they said, Joseph will peradventure hate us, and will certainly requite us all the evil which we did unto him. 16 And they sent a messenger unto Joseph, saying, Thy father did command before he died, saying, 17 So shall ye say unto Joseph, Forgive, I pray thee now, the trespass of thy brethren, and their sin; for they did unto thee evil: and now, we pray thee, forgive the trespass of the servants of the God of thy father. And Joseph wept when they spake unto him. 18 And his brethren also went and fell down before his face; and they said, Behold, we be thy servants. 19 And Joseph said unto them, Fear not: for am I in the place of God?*

20 But as for you, ye thought evil against me, but God meant it unto good, to bring to pass, as it is this day, to save much people alive. 21 Now therefore fear ye not: I will nourish you, and your little ones. And he comforted them, and spake kindly unto them."

The Azusa Street awakening was an outpouring of the Holy Spirit in a small church in California, USA. The presence of the Holy Spirit was so powerful that people came from all over the world and received the gift with evidence of speaking in tongues, healing, and miracles. This happened in 1906 at a time when the US was segregated and black people were excluded from worshipping together with white people in churches, on public transport, education, and every sector of life. What made Azusa Street unique was that God chose to anoint William Seymour who was the son of an African American slave, to lead that congregation. William believed that the church of Jesus Christ was not segregated but was inclusive of the Holy Spirit and every nation, tribe, and tongue. As if to make the point, to confirm Rev. 2: 9—10, those who came rejected their beliefs and practices based on the teachings they had received over the generations, came, and received the outpouring of the Holy Spirit. They included white Americans, Europeans, Latin Americans, Jews, Chinese and people from all over the globe.

> *"Azusa's inter-racial fellowship was no accident, rather it was a defining mark related to the vision of a man that spent his entire life, searching for true Christian fellowship without limitations. For Seymour, racial inclusiveness was the sign of the true church, that was birthed on the day of Pentecost as people from all nations gathered to hear the Gospel in their own native language."*[1]
>
> *"From Azusa Street, Pentecostalism spread across the globe and found its way to the West Indies through the instrumentality of a godly lady in St Croix named Lawrencina Joseph (later Hurley, who she married after the death of her first husband) p44. On one occasion, she distinctly heard a "Macedonian Call" Acts 16:9—a voice commissioning her to the Gospel message to Montserrat. At that time, she did not know the geographical location of the island, but she and her husband arrived on the island a year later (possibly in 1907/ 1908) in answer to her Divine instruction. There they laboured faithfully for many years. Eventually, by 1946, the Pentecostal Assemblies Of Canada, Executive of the West Indies District (located in Trinidad) commissioned Elizabeth Corbett who was a pastor in Trinidad to return to her homeland, Monserrat to assist Lawrencina. Monserrat became the cradle of the Pentecostal movement in the English-speaking Caribbean.*

---

1. Synan & Fox Jnr, William J Seymour: Pioneer of the Azuza Street Revival. 104

> Many of her sons and daughters took the Gospel message to other islands. H.R. Thomas and other members went to Bermuda in 1919. The Pentecostal ministries in Antigua, Barbados, Trinidad also owe a debt of gratitude to Montserrat."[2]

In a letter dated September 1907, Seymour clearly recognised the Holy Spirit as the only heavenly authority; and there could be no legal religious assembly without His presence and His transaction. The Holy Spirit being the Teacher of Teachers.

> *"It is the office work of the Holy Spirit to preside over the entire work of God on earth (Joh 10:3) Jesus was our Bishop while on earth, but now He has sent the Holy Ghost, amen, to take His place—not men (John 14:16, 15:26; 16:7-14). Praise His holy name!"*[3]

Pentecostalism developed into an international missionary effort almost immediately. The movement spread first among all the ethnic communities in North America and was quickly transferred to Europe. By the end of 1906, missionary work had begun in Norway, and in 1907 it reached the rest of Scandinavia and Germany, Italy, and Holland. Latinos who took part in the Azusa Street revival helped spread the movement to Mexico, and a vital Spanish-speaking church movement developed there and in the southwestern United States. The Assemblies of God and the Church of God developed large Spanish-language branches, and completely new autonomous denominations formed in both Mexico and Puerto Rico. From these groups, Pentecostalism spread into the rest of Latin America, where it became especially popular in the latter decades of the twentieth century.

Missionaries from Azusa Street, who were African-Americans, West Indians and Africans, as well as white Canadians and Americans, went out into all the world, Hong Kong. China, Taiwan, Korea, India, and East, West and South Africa.

Liberia was the first African country in 1906, to receive the Pentecostal message, directly from Azusa Street Revival. One American missionary related directly to William Seymour about her ability to speak the Kru language and that she found her mission field. By 1916, the Methodist Episcopal church reported on the thousands of young people had become Pentecostals across the country.

American Pentecostal missionaries to South Africa, received the teaching of 'Spirit baptism' at Azusa Street. Thomas Hezmalhalch and John

---

2. Maginley, *Ablaze, The Pentecostal Assemblies of the West Indies 1910–2010*
3. Synan & Fox Jnr, *William Seymour: Pioneer of the Azuza Street Revival* 208

Lake carried Seymour's Pentecostal message to South Africa. They moved throughout South Africa and in 1913 Lake established the Apostolic Faith Mission of South Africa (AFMSA}. Their mission to South Africa came at the same time as Apartheid which was instituted by the British Government. The AFM of South Africa started as a non-racial church. Early attempts to introduce racial separation in worship were resisted by the founding missionaries. When the missionaries left the country to return to their homelands, the church was set on a course of racial separation in compliance with the racial ideology of the country.

Pentecostalism was still a minority denomination in the West Indies when the first West Indians came to the UK in the late 1940s. Most people in the West Indies would have grown up in the denominational churches; Church of England, Roman Catholic, or other Protestant churches. However, their faith was severely tested in England.

Clifford Hill writes,

> "The faith of Pentecostals actually survived the shock of migration better than Anglicans and Baptists and others, because they had been used to being regarded as 'different' in the West Indies. Although Pentecostal churches were few and far apart in England in the 1960s, they did expect to be accepted in the British Pentecostal Assemblies, but even there they were not welcome, and those who had formerly held positions of responsibility as pastors and evangelists in the West Indies were not recognised as leaders in Britain. They felt the bitterness of rejection. It was not long before they began to form small assemblies of their own. They began meeting for prayer, worship and fellowship in their homes, the British black churches were born, but most were born in a vale of tears."[4]

By the mid-1960s the in-migrant Pentecostal churches were enjoying enormous numerical success, by attracting people who had come from traditional British denominations in the West Indies. Clifford Hill in this book *"Free at Last"?* recounts:

> "The success of the Pentecostals wholly organised and led by immigrants, underlies the tragic failure of the traditional English churches to hold the allegiance of those immigrants who were already established Christians, before coming to England. To see this failure in its true perspective one must bear in mind that in Jamaica, Pentecostals represent only 5% of the total Christian community."[5]

4. Hill, Free at Last? 235
5. Hill, Free at Last? 79

Clifford Hill recalls a time when he was a special envoy of the British Council of churches, visiting Barbados, Trinidad and Jamaica in 1962. The purpose of the visit was in part fact-finding and in part relationship building. The particular concern in Britain was that large numbers of immigrants were coming from the islands where they had strong links with churches of all the mainline denominations, but once they reached cities in England, they lost all contact with the church. On his visit he noted that Barbados and Jamaica were very British with many place names of towns and streets being British as well as all the major social institutions of government and education. This was less evident in Trinidad with its Spanish colonial influence which was still strong. In schools he was surprised to note that the teaching of history was all about the kings and queens of England and little on their own social history. While he was in the West Indies; in Jamaica he was moved to record his experience of Kingdom Christianity:

> "I had fully expected to meet with resentment at the injustice they had suffered at the hands of my British forebears. It was only some 120 years after emancipation. The grandparents of some of them I met had known slavery. But far from a cold hostile attitude, I was met with warmth and generosity everywhere except in the ganga-smoking Rasta community in west-Kingston, some of whom were remnants of the former war-like Maroons. A small, outlawed group who were by no means representative"[6]

When reflecting on his visit to the West Indies, Hill reported that people were aware of their history, the slavery that they suffered by former generations, but declared that although it was in the past, it was not forgotten, but it was forgiven. He was amazed that everywhere he went that people knew the Bible and its teaching that God loves us and forgives our sins. Here were living out the word of God:

> "This keeping of no record of wrongs which is one of the marks of the true Christian faith was clearly something that most of the Jamaican population had put into practice. . . . . . . .I had hundreds of conversations with people who demonstrated this kind of love in their lives and actually showed this kind of love to me, a stranger, from a nation that had committed such unspeakable cruelty and injustice towards their forbears.. This forgiveness and generosity is of enormous significance in understanding what happened to the first generation of immigrants settling in Britain in the 1950s and 1960. "[7]

6. Hill, Free at Last? 236
7. Hill, Free at Last? 79

One of the earliest examples of a Pentecostal church established in Britain in 1953, is the New Testament church of God (NTCG) which serviced the Windrush Generation just five years after they arrived. They now have one hundred and thirty branches and missions in most of the major cities of England and Wales, with a registered membership of one hundred and ten thousand, representing the diversity of ethnicity of the communities they serve. They have an imaginative training programme for pastors and leaders and do valuable work in the community. NTCG provided much needed spiritual sustenance to the socially and spiritually abused West Indians in the UK who had remained after their duty as soldiers in the Second World War.

The churches of the Windrush Generation grew as their children grew up and many followed in their fathers' footsteps or rather their fathers' pulpits, with ever increasing success in locations and numbers. The following are some examples of churches which demonstrate this succession and a tradition of bible teaching which comes from the Anglo New World:

Ruach City church: Bishop John Francis, consecrated to the office of a Bishop on Sunday, 7th June 1998, is pastor of Ruach City church, which was founded in South London. His father, the late *Bishop T G Francis* was a leading pioneer in the establishment of black-led Pentecostal churches in the UK and was leading national conferences as late as 1993.

Starting with only eighteen faithful members, Ruach City church in Brixton, South London, has transitioned from one church to one church in many locations with over seven thousand congregants regularly attending its services each Sunday. His son, Bishop John Francis is also the International Director of the Ruach Network of churches which he overseas approximately fifty churches in the UK & Overseas.

Worldwide Mission Fellowship's *Pastor Dennis Greenidge* is another second generation Windrush descendant. Pastor Greenidge is the Senior Pastor of the *Worldwide Mission Fellowship* in London, England; a fast growing multicultural, multiracial church with members from over twenty nations which demonstrates a passionate commitment to the principles of God's word.

His father, Dennis Greenidge Snr planted the church over forty years ago and the ministry has grown and flourished under Pastor Dennis' dynamic leadership. Pastor Dennis wears the mantle of an apostle. He has taken the gospel of Christ to over forty nations and actively mentors pastors and leaders in many walks of life in those nations. He is a prolific communicator of biblical truth and a renowned international conference speaker.

His personal life of humility, intense prayer and unceasing integrity has been an inspiration to many people around the world. His overwhelming passion is to preach 'The Living Word to a dying world'.

Rev Carmel Jones founded the *Pentecostal Credit Union (PCU)* in 1979. It is now the second largest credit union in the country. Rev Jones, a COGIC minister, is a member of the Windrush Generation who arrived in Britain from the Caribbean between the late 1940s and 1960s.

Over the years, the PCU has provided loans for pastors to buy churches as well as make essential high-priced purchases, and for individuals to start businesses. Now under new leadership, the PCU is on a mission to support entrepreneurship and wealth-building in the Black community. Rev Jones is still heavily connected to the PCU, and talks about its origins, his life, and his hopes for the PCU's future.

In an interview with Marcia Dixon of Keep the Faith Publications, Rev Jones was asked what had inspired him to start the Pentecostal Credit Union (PCU)?

Rev Jones said that the inspiration came from his concern about the lack of preparedness of mainstream banks to lend money to Black and ethnic communities, and to Black people in particular; but worst still, to purchase places of worship for the people of God. For example, people had to hire places that were used for all sorts of social activities, which resulted in:

> "*Us more than often than not having to clean up after the previous user and, boy oh boy, that means beer cans and bottles and, even worse, people being sick all over the place. Then said I, "Lord, Your people deserve better than this. Help me to help ourselves."*
>
> "*After I received divine sanction to set up the credit union and approach the 20 people who were needed to start, there was 100% unanimity that I should go ahead. All of us met the CEO of the Credit Union League of Great Britain in my 'front room' on Sunday 14th October 1979. Thereafter I began to encourage people to join me in this venture. There were a few that preferred the 'pardner' system, and waged strong resistance against me establishing a credit union. That pre-existing ideology, pre-dating slavery, is still with us today with some of our elderly folks, but on a much lesser scale.*"[8]

Rev Jones was asked about the main challenges and successes he had experienced during the PCU's early years?

He replied:

---

8. Dixon, Keep the Faith Publications

> "A senior prominent minister, on learning about what I was doing, remonstrated with me over the phone for nearly one hour, demanding that I should not pursue calling the organisation the 'Pentecostal Credit Union', because "when it fails, as it surely will, it will bring the entire Pentecostal church organisation into disrepute," and she was having none of it. My reply was this, "Are you saying that I am going to fail?" "Yes," she said, "because Black people always fail, especially where money is involved." I said, "You will be proven wrong."[9]

One of the things the PCU was renowned for, was helping pastors buy their church buildings. Rev Jones was asked why they opted to use the PCU instead of a bank? He explained:

> "Pastors wanting to buy a place of their own, or thinking of purchasing a place, would always come to the credit union first. It is commonly appreciated that where some banks would say 'No', the Credit Union would say 'Yes'. The credit union has faith in the Pentecostal Movement, because of its driving force that it is a disgrace to borrow and not pay back. PCU works with pastors by drawing up business plans, making projections and advising how and when plans may be implemented."[10]

The above reports were some of many testimonies of the descendants of slaves and of colonialism from the West Indies who, in Christ were more than conquerors in the face of the hostile environment which they confronted.

Africans were part of the British Empire and Commonwealth Forces during WWII. During their time together, they came face to face with West Indians for the first time in over five hundred years of separation.

Out of this meeting, came the music of Highlife from Ghana. Indeed, many doctors from the West Indies stayed in Ghana and for some time, they provided medical services to people from Tumu in the north to Accra in the south. Some of their descendants settled and made their homes there.

During the post war period many African and West Indian intellectuals met and discussed their future as a people and as independent nations. From these meetings came the pan-African movement which eventually led to many African countries achieving independence from Britain and later, West Indian countries in the 1960s.

However, it was during the 1970s and 1980s that significant numbers of people from Ghana and Nigeria migrated to the UK. Many of them came

---

9. Dixon, Keep the Faith Publications
10. Dixon, Keep the Faith Publications

to the UK already filled with the Holy Spirit and the experience of Pentecostalism. In Congo, Ghana, and Nigeria Pentecostalism had already taken on different African names.

In July 1937 Sydney Elton, an English missionary, his wife and only daughter settled in Nigeria. Ruth came to join him for the divine missionary adventure. During his fifty years in the ministry in Nigeria, he changed the landscape of Christianity. In the 1970's, he became the father of the Pentecostal/Charismatic movement that emerged in the nation's University campuses. Elton operated with a prophetic unction, and his strategy was to concentrate on the campuses to "catch them young." He succeeded remarkably with breeding budding evangelists. *Pastors Enoch Adeboye (Redeemed Christian Church of God) and William Kumuyi were also two of Elton's mentees.*

The Redeemed Christian Church of God (RCCG) is a Pentecostal church founded in Lagos, Nigeria in 1952 by *Rev. Josiah Olufemi Akindayomi* (1909—1980). Rev Akindayomi chose *Dr Enoch Adeboye* as his successor. Enoch Adeboye was a lecturer in Mathematics, at the University of Lagos, as at the time he joined the church in 1973. Adeboye initially became one of the interpreters, translating his predecessor, Akindayomi's sermons from Yoruba to English. He was ordained a pastor of the church in 1975, and his appointment as leader, (General Overseer) of the church was formalised by the posthumous reading of Akindayomi's sealed pronouncement. In 1990, Redeemed Christian Church of God Bible School was founded.

Andrew Rice, writing in The New York Times, calls the RCCG "one of [Africa's] most vigorously expansionary religious movements, a homegrown Pentecostal denomination that is crusading to become a global faith." The church's leaders preach that in the future "In every household there will be at least one member of Redeemed Christian Church of God (RCCG) in the whole world." News Week, the international news magazine, named Dr. Adeboye as one of the 50 most influential persons on the planet. Currently the RCCG is active across continents with thousands of parishes of which a little over eight hundred and fifty are in the UK.

Kingsway International Christian Centre's (KICC) journey began in 1992 when *Rev. Matthew Ashimolowo* (of Nigeria) and three hundred members rented a hall in Holloway Boys' School in North London. These humble beginnings reflect the persistent prayer, faith and patience of a church that was destined for great things. In three years, the membership grew from three hundred to three thousand. By utilising the professional skills of church members and staff, KICC began to build support networks and provide sound practical advice to address everyday issues. As a result, they began to offer legal counselling (professionally managed by registered legal practitioners who were members of KICC), careers counselling (run in partnership with a local London Borough) and educational counselling (supplied by qualified teachers to GCSE and A level students).

The church's membership grew rapidly, and it was necessary for KICC to move premises a number of times until in 2012 they finally acquired a twenty-four-acre site in Chatham, Kent to house their headquarters/church, and educational facilities.

These are only two examples of the many African led churches in the UK today but there are many others which have joined with pastors from West Indian churches to confront racism in Britain, as a body united in Christ.

The Africans and West Indians (Guineamen and other negroes) have continued to experience the unrelenting abuse of racism within the British society even in the twenty-first century. Prior to the election of 2014, they came together as a National Church Leaders Forum (NCLF) to present their 'manifesto' to the British public. The forum represents the concerns of leaders and members of African and Caribbean churches in the UK. It is supported by key church and denominational leaders, including, Rev Father Olu Abiola, Special Apostle John Adegoke, Bishop Doye Agama, Rev Esme Beswick, Bishop Alvin Blake, Bishop Eric Brown, Rev Celia Appiagyei-Collins, Bishop John Francis, Bishop Paul Hackman, Pastor Agu Irukwu, Bishop-elect Delroy Powell, Bishop Wilton Powell, Dr Michel Sacramento, Rev Nezlin Sterling, Pastor Ian Sweeney, Apostle Alfred Williams. Ade Amooba was co-author of the Manifesto.

The NCLF wrote in 2014 a 'Political manifesto' describing the circumstances of life in the UK, for the members of their congregations and their people groups. This information came as the penultimate broadsheet in 2014. It can be found in the following document—NCLF (National church Leaders Forum), A Black Christian Voice, Published May 2014, Authors: R. R. David Muir & Abe Omooba. It addresses the challenges that black people have experienced for the seventy years in the UK, since 1958. In it they highlight the eight areas of highest need, as follows:

How is this work defined? NLCF in their document: 'Black church Political Mobilisation—A Manifesto for Action' in 2014 highlighted eight sections for active consideration in the UK: Policing and Criminal Justice, Prisons, Mental Health, church and community, Voting and Political Mobilisation, Family and Marriage, Youth and Education, International Aid and Development. The chapter 'Introduction', page 7, ended with the question: 'What We Seek?'

However, their concerns were not confined to their ethnic members, but extended to include the spiritual well-being of the nation as a whole and to all kindred and tongue and people and nation.

Nigerian *Rev Ade Omooba* was co-author of the Manifesto and has been involved in social action projects in Africa and in the UK for over thirty years. Along with Andrea Minichiello Williams, Rev Omooba co-founded *Christian Concern* which is a UK Lobby/Campaign Group on Public Policy and the Christian Legal Centre, addressing Christian liberty issues.

Another example of Christian national participation by Africans and West Indian Believers is *Pastor Les Isaacs* who founded *Street Pastors* in Brixton, London in 2003. He was born in and grew up in Antigua the island with Lord Nelson West Indian dockyard and of Betty's Hope a slave plantation (that is being restored). As a lad he grew up in church in obedience to his mother. Les Isaacs, as a youth, coming into the hostile environment of the British society, experienced gangs, and street violence. In his search for hope he rejected the Christian religion and became a Rastafarian. That also conflicted with his upbringing; he later accepted Jesus Christ as his Saviour. This life changing experience inspired him to seek ways to engage with the same abused and rejected hard-to-reach communities of the societies into which he was embraced. His conversion led him to a Saul/Paul like passion for seeing people set free from the bondage of life without Christ. He went back into the streets.

Street Pastors began in Jamaica and in the UK is an initiative of the Ascension Trust, a registered charity established in 1993. The initial activities of street pastors in areas such as Lewisham, and Hackney focused mainly on confronting gang culture and the use of knives and guns. As Street Pastors started to operate in other areas of the UK, the initiative responded to other local issues, including anti-social behavior and drunkenness.

By 2008 there were *Street Pastors* groups in seventy locations, with another fifty being established. As of January 2015, the official website states that there are over two hundred and seventy active groups.

The aim of *Street Pastors* is to provide a reassuring presence in local communities. Individual street pastors seek to listen to and talk with people in their local community, to provide information on local agencies, help and services, and to discourage anti-social behavior.

Practical help provided by street pastors includes handing out spare blankets outside nightclubs, and flip flops to clubbers unable to walk home in their high heeled footwear, giving out water, chocolate for energy, personal alarms, carrying bus timetables; and ensuring the safety of vulnerable persons. *Street Pastors* remove bottles and other potential weapons from the streets, to discourage violence and vandalism. They may also have access to sleeping bags stored in church buildings as a last resort. They occasionally report saving the lives of people they meet.

Politicians who have expressed admiration or support for the scheme include former and current Prime Ministers of the UK. Testimonies of the fruit of the teaching of the original English and British missionaries in the Anglo New World. The role of the missionaries and evangelists was as formerly stated, an integral component of the Union Jack and the King James Bible in the British Empire. Alongside the impact of colonialism as defined by Anglo New World systems, Africa received its share.

Clifford Hill observed that the *"work being done by the African and Caribbean Churches and their even greater potential is largely unrecognised and unsupported. They are simply left to struggle with their own very limited resources, without even the backing or cooperation of the local white traditional churches."*[11]

As Great Britain has become increasingly multi-cultural, we are seeing a picture emerging where nearly half of churchgoers in inner London (48%) are of Black African heritage, 28 per cent in London as a whole, compared with 13% of the capital's population. That means nearly one in five (19 per cent) of 'black' African heritage Londoners goes to church each week. Two-thirds attend Pentecostal churches, though the black community is represented in every denomination.

Growth is strongest in the parts of London that already have large churches or have significant African and/or Caribbean populations. Southwark, Lambeth, and Newham saw at least a twenty-five percent growth of new churches. Church attendance in these boroughs also grew over the same period, with Southwark and Lambeth seeing a 50 per cent growth and Newham growing by a third. These findings were supported in an article entitled: Black and ethnic minority Christians lead London's Church growth by the Evangelical Alliance. [12]

11. Hill, Free at Last? 253

12. Black and ethnic minority Christian's lead London church growth, Evangelical Alliance

12

Judgment Must Begin At The House Of God

1Pet 4:17 For the time is come that judgment must begin at the house of God: and if it first begin at us, what shall the end be of them that obey not the gospel of God?

The last six hundred years (fifteenth century to the present) has unearthed and presented us with the most documented and the most hidden information in the history of humankind. This period has seen the fulfilment of the last commandment of Jesus Christ as He ascended into heaven, the coming of the Holy Spirit on the day of Pentecost and of Believers going into all the world and leaving fruit that has remained.

Before Jesus ascended into heaven, he instructed his disciples to wait until he sent the Holy Spirit. On the day of Pentecost, people from all over the Roman Empire were gathered in Jerusalem for the feast of first fruits. On the beginning of that day there were one hundred and twenty believers filled with the Holy Spirit. At the end of the day there were three thousand, one hundred and twenty! The day of the infilling of the people by the Holy Spirit, is recorded in the following scriptures:

Act 2:44 *And all that believed were together, and had all things common;* ⁴⁵ *And sold their possessions and goods, and parted them to all men, as every man had need.* ⁴⁶ *And they, continuing daily with one accord in the temple, and breaking bread from house to house, did eat their meat with gladness and singleness of heart,* ⁴⁷ *Praising God, and having favour with all the people. And the Lord added to the church daily such as should be saved.*

While Christianity spread widely across Europe through the Roman Catholic Church it was during the late fifteenth century, that the conquest of Ceuta, which initiated the 'age of discovery', that explorers along with the Roman Catholic priests, sought to navigate the world.

The sixteenth century saw the exclusive dominance of the Roman Catholic countries, Portugal, and Spain, expanding their outreach along the north and western shores of Africa and the nearby islands (the Canaries and the Azores)sailing around the Cape of Good Hope, South Africa and eventually reaching East Africa and even India.

In the early seventeenth century (1607), Protestant England took up the mantle to 'go into all the world and preach the Gospel and make disciples of all nations', by sending along with the first settlers in the New World, Rev Robert Hunt. On arrival in America, the expedition first settled in what would be known as Jamestown where Rev. Hunt made his first declarations:

> "Every plantation, which my Heavenly Father hath not planted, shall be rooted up." and
> "from these very shores the Gospel shall go forth to not only this New World,
> but the entire world."

These declarations by the English vicar became the fulfilment of the prophesies as written in the biblical texts as follows:

> *Psa 113:3 From the rising of the sun unto the going down of the same the LORD'S name is to be praised.*
>
> *Isa 59:19 So shall they fear the name of the LORD from the west, and his glory from the rising of the sun. When the enemy shall come in like a flood, the Spirit of the LORD shall lift up a standard against him.*
>
> *Mal 1:11 For from the rising of the sun even unto the going down of the same my name shall be great among the Gentiles; and in every place incense shall be offered unto my name, and a pure offering: for my name shall be great among the heathen, saith the LORD of hosts.*

Confirmation that this declaration by Rev. Hunt, in the 17th century, that God's Word would spread to the rest of the world, was achieved in the following ways, in that: *"from these very shores the Gospel shall go forth to not only this New World."* So, when the Rev. John Eliot, (as was mentioned in earlier chapters of this book), was the first Englishman to convert Native Americans to Christianity this prophecy came to pass. Three hundred years later, the Natick Praying Indians testified at the first public Praying

Worship service at the Eliot Church in August 2010, showing that John Eliot had faithfully taken the word of God to the Native Americans. Not only that, for the first time, the Bible was translated into a New World language, that of the Natick Indians in the Algonquian language. Although, now a Unitarian Church, the church Elliot established, was on loan for this occasion. The Natick Indians said that while the Europeans had broken so many covenants and treaties with them, virtually decimating the North American Indian population, they thanked God and prayed:

> "*Natick Praying Indian Strong Bull thanks the Creator and welcomes the ancestors, home. The heartbeat of the drum is heard once again.*" (2012).

Again, in the eighteenth century; Rev Robert Hunt's declaration that: "*from these very shores the Gospel shall go forth to not only this New World*"; was expanded from two villages in Massachusetts, Jamestown, and Plymouth, to include the Thirteen Colonies in North America.

Meanwhile in 18th century England, the major leaders of the Evangelical Revival were three Anglican priests, the brothers John and Charles Wesley and their friend George Whitefield. Together, they founded what would become Methodism. They had been members of a religious society at Oxford University called the Holy Club and "Methodists" due to their methodical piety and rigorous asceticism. This society was modelled on cell groups which were used by pietists for Bible study prayer and accountability. All three men experienced a spiritual crisis in which they sought true conversion and assurance of faith.

God used Count Zinzendorf and the Moravian's piety and unwavering peace and joy, in a near-death experience at sea, to warm the heart of John Wesley. Having encountered the Spirit of God through the worship of the Moravians, Wesley set out to discover the source of their joy, which led him to meet Zinzendorf. Impressed with the Moravian's stirring affection for Christ and their authentic relationship with Jesus Christ, Wesley and his brother, Charles Wesley (1707—1788), came to salvation. John Wesley discussed personal holiness and piety with the Moravian leader and theologian, August Spangenberg (1704 –1792), who served as Zinzendorf's assistant. Indicative of Moravian missionary spirituality, "Spangenberg asked Wesley: 'Do you know Jesus Christ?' It was a strange question to ask a Church of England priest. Wesley replied with hesitation: 'I know he is the Savior of the World'. True, said Spangenberg, but then he insisted 'do you know he has saved you?'" From this penetrating conversation, Wesley was primed to embrace the Moravian belief in assurance of salvation, which ignited the Methodist Revival.

The Evangelical Revival was one of a series of Christian revivals that swept Great Britain during the period 1730—1755. The Wesley brothers and Whitefield went over to America and led the First Great Awakening during this same period. The revival movement permanently affected Protestantism as adherents strove to renew individual piety and religious devotion. The Great Awakening marked the emergence of Anglo-American evangelicalism and a common evangelical identity as a trans-denominational movement within the Protestant churches in the United States. It also included enslaving others, and of major significance, particularly Africans as an integral part of that belief system. Evangelicals favored the teaching of the bible to African slaves, but rarely questioned the legitimacy of human bondage. From the President down to the common man, they owned slaves. Consequently, the society has been built on the belief that from the beginning of European enslavement of others; that slavery is justifiable and 'normal' and is an intrinsic part of all, political, academic, and social/institutional structures.

It is widely known that John Wesley was a keen abolitionist, speaking out and writing against the transatlantic slave trade. He denounced slavery as "*the sum of all villainies*" and detailed its abuses. He published a pamphlet on slaving, entitled: *Thoughts Upon Slavery*" in 1774. Wesley wrote: "*Liberty is the right of every human creature, as soon as he breathes the vital air; and no human law can deprive him of that right which he derives from the law of nature.*"

George Whitefield died in 1770 in America aged fifty-five years, leaving a legacy to his orphanage, and owning fifty slaves. Whitefield's racial views pose an enigma for the historian. On the one hand he has been identified with the rise of humanitarian ideals, but he also maintained his defense of slavery. He showed a special concern for the slaves in America, whilst also being fearful of the possibility of a backlash for liberation by the enslaved people.

> *Phlm 1:18 What then? notwithstanding, every way, whether in pretence, or in truth, Christ is preached; and I therein do rejoice, yea, and will rejoice*
>
> *Heb 4:12 For the word of God is quick, and powerful, and sharper than any two-edged sword, piercing even to the dividing asunder of soul and spirit, and of the joints and marrow, and is a discerner of the thoughts and intents of the heart.*

In "*The Genesis of Liberation*,"[1] authors Powery and Sadler argue that "*for the oppressed, God remained the agency of liberation to which the oppressed could appeal and find hope.*" The simple fact is that the enslaved were able to "hold on" to Jesus, as it were, and is in our day an example of the power of the Resurrection. Powery and Sadler state that: "*African-Americans' respect for the authority of the Christian Scriptures is a miracle in itself.*"

An awesome testimony by the African Americans of the kingdom of heaven gained by the reading of the bible and the teaching of the missionaries is herein presented:

> 2 Tim 3:16-17 *All scripture is given by inspiration of God, and is profitable for doctrine, for reproof, for correction, for instruction in righteousness: 17 That the man of God may be perfect, throughly furnished unto all good works.*

If the Protestant Reformation of 1517 is deemed the greatest religious movement in European history, then one could conclude that the Black reformation of 1736 is the greatest religious movement in American history. But this begs the question, can it be called a "reformation"? Author Juan Williams argues indeed it can be. In his book on African American religious history, *This Far By Faith*, Williams writes,

> "*Africans did not simply adopt the religion of the European Colonist; they used the power, principles, and practices of Christianity to blaze a path to freedom and deliverance.*" Not only did they blaze a path, but the path was so big that he concludes that "*it reformed Christian theology as well as Christianity itself.*"[2]

Enslaved and Christian freedom

One of the earliest petitions from African Americans seeking their freedom came from a group of slaves in Massachusetts. In 1774 (two years before the War of American Independence from Great Britain) they petitioned the Massachusetts legislature for their liberty in a document that shows how political freedom and religious freedom mingled together for at least some early Americans. This letter, corporately written by a group of African Americans, free and enslaved clearly and biblically articulated the word of God in all its grandeur and simplicity is shown below. That only some understood this link is shown by Massachusetts's failure to respond to the plea

---

1. Powery and Sadler, The Genesis of Liberation
2. Williams, This far by Faith

of these men; slavery began to end in the state only after a judicial decision against it in the early 1780s:

> "Your Petitioners apprehend we have in common with all other men naturel right to our freedoms without Being depriv'd of them by our fellow men as we are a freeborn Pepel and have never forfeited this Blessing by aney compact or agreement whatever. But we were unjustly dragged by cruel hand of power from our dearest frinds and sum of us stolen from the bosoms of our tender Parents and from a Populous Pleasant and plentiful country and Brought hither to be made slaves for Life in a Christian land. Thus, we are deprived of everything that hath a tendency to make life even tolerable, the endearing ties of husband and wife we are strangers to. . . . By our deplorable situation we are rendered incapable of shewing our obedience to Almighty God how can a slave perform the duties of a husband to a wife or parent to his child How can a husband leave master and work and cleave to his wife How can the wife submit themselves to their husbands in all things. How can the child obey thear parents in all things? There is a grat number of us sencear . . . members of the Church of Christ how can the master and the slave be said to fulfill that command Live in love let Brotherly Love contuner and abound Beare ye onenothers Bordenes. How can the master be said to Beare my Borden when he Beares me down whith the Have chanes of slavery and oppression against my will?"[3]

This petition, submitted by the African Americans in 1774, in the British American Colony confirmed the first declaration of Rev Hunt on his arrival in Jamestown:

"Every plantation which my Heavenly Father hath not planted, shall be rooted up."

That petition clearly challenged the very foundation of the Kingdom of heaven that was taught and practiced by most of the British missionaries. The enslaved and their abolitionist fellowmen were applying the scripture in 2 Tim 3: 16 –17; 'all scripture' of the Bible as their doctrine for reproof, correction, and instruction in righteousness. They also drew a parallel with the Colonies' own demand for freedom from the injustice and tyranny of their British Colonial masters.

> "As the rhetoric supporting independence of the colonists from Great Britain intensified in the colony of Massachusetts, some noted the glaring inconsistency of arguing for the rights of Englishmen

---

3. "To Gov. Thomas Gage and the Massachusetts General Court, May 25, 1774," Collections of the Massachusetts Historical Society, 5th ser. 3 (1877). 432–433,

> while owning slaves. For example, John Otis, a leading proponent of colonial independence, wrote in a highly regarded and influential 1764 pamphlet that "The colonists are by the law of nature freeborn, as indeed all men are, white or black."[4]

In making that observation, he clearly recognized that that letter defined the principles that ought, perhaps, to inform the basis for the constitution of the future nation in their quest for independence from the tyranny of injustice and ethnic discrimination by their colonial masters—the British.

> 1 Pet 2:9–10 But ye are a chosen generation, a royal priesthood, an holy nation, a peculiar people; that ye should shew forth the praises of him who hath called you out of darkness into his marvellous light: Which in time past were not a people, but are now the people of God: which had not obtained mercy, but now have obtained mercy.

In Britain meanwhile, the abolitionist movement was gaining ground and in 1807 Britain abolished the Transatlantic slave trade. Britain also became a global police force, in attempting to ensure that other countries could not continue the practice. Between 1808 and 1860 the West Africa Squadron (British Royal Navy) whose goal was to suppress the Atlantic Slave Trade by patrolling the coast of West Africa, captured one thousand six hundred slave ships and freed one hundred and fifty thousand Africans.

It is noteworthy that the prophesy of Pope Nicholas' in Romanus Pontifex which proclaimed; *"or at least the souls of many of them will be gained for Christ"* happened when the British with the King James Bible captured a Portuguese ship taking enslaved Africans to one of the slave colonies. The Portuguese were in alliance with the Muslim slave traders, as the following account of the extraordinary life of one of the kidnapped Africans, Afala Ajayi, (who later became a Christian) and whose journey is illustrated below:

> "The British had outlawed the Atlantic slave trade in 1807 and used their navy to patrol the coast of Africa. During that period, Spain and Portugal still allowed the Atlantic slave trade in their colonies in the Americas. A grandson of King Abiodun, through his mother, Afala, Ajayi, was around 12 years old when he and his family were captured, along with his entire village, by Fulani slave raiders in March 1821 and sold to Portuguese slave traders. Before the slave ship left port for the Americas, it was boarded

---

4.. Massachusetts Constitution and the Abolition of Slavery, is offered by Massachusetts Court System use.mass.gov

by a crew from a British Royal Navy ship under the command of Captain Henry Leeke. They freed the captives, and took Ajayi and his family to Freetown, Sierra Leone, where they were resettled by local authorities. While in Sierra Leone, Crowther (Ajayi) was cared for by the Anglican Church Missionary Society (CMS) and was taught English. He converted to Christianity. On 11 December 1825 he was baptised by John Raban. He named himself after Samuel Crowther, vicar of Christ Church, Newgate, London, and one of the pioneers of the CMS."[5]

Later, Samuel Crowther was part of a Niger expedition team in 1841 where he was expected to learn Hausa for use on the expedition. Crowther studied languages and later received a doctoral degree from Oxford University. The aim of the expedition was to stimulate commerce, teach agricultural techniques, encourage Christianity, and help end the slave trade which continued with many countries . Following the expedition, Crowther was recalled to England where he was trained as a minister and ordained by the Bishop of London.

Crowther returned to Africa in 1843 and together with Henry Townsend opened a mission in a village in what is to day Ogun State. He prepared a Yoruba grammar and translation of the Anglican Book of Common Prayer into Yoruba. He also began to translate the Bible into Yoruba. In Nigeria, British personnel, including Captain J P L Davies, applied the missionary philosophy developed by Dr. Livingstone, the 'Bible and the plough' which paired economic development with the propagation of the gospel. Together with British missionaries they established schools and churches where many of the pupils reached High-Church positions in the church plants along the interior of Nigeria. The CMS leadership quickly came to respect Crowther's zeal for the gospel and love for his countrymen. In 1864, Crowther was ordained as the first African bishop of the Anglican Church; he was consecrated a bishop on St Peter's Day in 1864 by Charles Longley.

> *"However, with the annexation of Lagos, 1865 (modern-day Nigeria) and the introduction of Colonialism, the missionary-native relationship changed. Sadly, missionaries slowly adopted the mindset of colonial conquerors who sought to liberate the natives from barbarism; they no longer saw them as fellow sinners in need of grace. Because of this, the notion of serving under an African on the mission field became untenable, and many British missionaries resisted the rise of a native pastorate. Ultimately, the man that Bishop Crowther recommended to replace him was rejected.*

5. Wikipedia

> Their stated reason for rejection has survived: "To place our own missionaries under the independent jurisdiction of a native bishop would certainly not be acceptable or convenient."[6]

Just as the prophecy spoken by Pope Nicholas in the Papal Bull -"Romanus Pontifex" in 1455 the Portuguese maintained that belief and practice into the nineteenth century, four hundred years later as illustrated by Bishop Crowther's life and ministry. Other countries applied that same law to construct and develop various 'slave' codes to subjugate "*Guinea-men and other negroes*":

The enemy used his 'evangelists' to apply derivative Slave Codes of the Barbados Slave Codes in other British West Indian Colonies, in Anglo-America and later in other countries and continents. The god of this world maintained his anti-Christ influence on the British Members of Parliament in the final drafting of the Abolition Act in August 1833 which reads: "*An Act for the Abolition of Slavery throughout the British Colonies; for promoting the Industry of the manumitted Slaves; and for compensating the Persons hitherto entitled to the Services of such Slaves.*" This Act would make provision for the slave owners as follows:

Five years of free labor by the ex-slaves to the former slave owners- Apprenticeship program. (The slaves were paying their slave-masters for their questionable freedom)

The ex-slaves received no land grants.

The Laws for freed slaves excluded them from voting. (Only landowners of ten acres or more had that right.)[7] This debt for the loss of property to the slave owners, rather than the "manumitted Slaves," (enslaved people) was finally paid off by the British Government to the slave owners: "*compensation to all enslavers,*" one hundred and eighty-two years later, in 2015!

During the succeeding centuries, the consequences of the belief in Europeans' racial superiority informed the negative aspects of the Abolition of Slavery Act in 1833 (as illustrated in the above example). This belief has resulted in the passing of a plethora of laws which have supported the level of injustices and racial prejudice levelled primarily against African heritage peoples—'*Guineamen and negroes*' and later indigenous peoples over the world.

The dissemination of the Barbados Slave Codes to the Americas in the seventeenth century perpetuated the same issues of 'chattel slavery' and the compensation for the loss of these "goods" when slavery ended.

---

6. Guthrie, *The Triumph and Tragedy of Anglicanism's First African Bishop*
7. USI and Historic England Research Report Series no. 247–2020

In the early nineteenth century, there was an evangelical revival called the Second Great Awakening, throughout the English-speaking world. This revival coincided with western colonial expansion. The British Empire stretched across the world such that where the King James Bible and the Union Jack (the British Flag) were, there was 'Light'. That the sun never set upon the British Empire was a testimony again of God's word spoken in truth, by Rev. Robert Hunt in 1606.

Isa 59:19 So shall they fear the name of the LORD from the west, and his glory from the rising of the sun.

The prophesy made by Reverend Hunt in 1606 stated; *"from these very shores the Gospel shall go forth to not only this New World, but the entire world."* This prophecy found substance in the outpouring of the Holy Spirit in Azusa Street Mission church which was led by William Seymour. Evangelists from this Revival, spread over the entire world to the East, South, West and North and within the shores of the Americas and Europe. With the Azuza Street Revival, the Holy Spirit came to a united church.

This book began by looking at the divisions that currently exist within society but also within the church in terms of ethnicity.

In Chapter 2 which was entitled "To the Jew First," let us acknowledge that Jesus was a Jew and it was the Jews who were first to spread the Gospel of Jesus Christ. The Bible says "to the Jews first and then to the Gentiles." Over the centuries we have seen that the Jews suffered much persecution at the hands of the church. Replacement Theology has caused a further division within the church and taught that the church has replaced Israel in God's plans, prophecies, and blessings. The Bible teaches that Jesus is our peace and He has made both one, Jews and Gentiles.

Eph 2:14-15 For he is our peace, who hath made both one, and hath broken down the middle wall of partition between us; 15 Having abolished in his flesh the enmity, even the law of commandments contained in ordinances; for to make in himself of twain one new man, so making peace.

Jews have joined with the African Americans and the Black British in their struggle for justice. They were with the civil rights leaders in the streets, in the courts, and also in the neighbourhoods. That union has not been broken.

As we reflect on church history, we recognize the Holy Spirit at work despite all the challenges posed by man. The twenty-first century has seen the full Bible translated into seven hundred and four languages, the New Testament has been translated into an additional, 1551 languages and Bible portions or stories into 1160 other languages. Approximately six billion out of a total world population of seven billion eight hundred persons have access to a bible (2020). The Bible also spread throughout the world through the internet, on computers, SMART phones, via Zoom Conferences and Bible teaching on YouTube.

The twenty-first century has also witnessed greater participation between the Pentecostal and full Gospel churches and many British groups, recognizing the tradition of racial injustice and engaging in the study of the Word of God from the kingdom of heaven's perspective.

If we examine both the East African slave trade and the Transatlantic slave trade, we see that Africans sold their brothers to anyone willing to buy them. This practice existed because of their worshiping false gods.

In the fifteenth century, the church in Europe, the Roman Church, extended its reach to the African continent. There they were teaching and practicing doctrines that excluded people by rejecting the word of God. Over the centuries, remnant believers persevered and many peoples who had never heard the word of God, accepted Christ alone as their Savior. Some of these soldiers of Christ have been recognized in this book, (there were too many to record). The testimony of the Natick Indians, many teachers of the Great Awakening, the letter from the black Africans in 1774 were testimonies of the Lord's presence. With the Azusa Street Revival, 1906 the Holy Spirit came to a united church which spread in all the world.

Traditionally, the Africans of the African continent maintained a posture of superiority over those of the diaspora. The Africans and those of the Diaspora began the reconciliation process and they are united in expanding the Church of Christ in all the continents including Europe and America

Nevertheless, the twenty-first century has finally seen an acknowledgement of Britain's appalling history of slavery in the New World, which was publicly acknowledged on November 30th, 2021, when, after three hundred and ninety six years the sun set on the British monarchy's reign over the Caribbean Island of Barbados. At a handover ceremony at midnight, a solemn Prince Charles, representing his mother, the reigning monarch, was on hand to witness the transition. In his speech he said:

"*I was so deeply touched that you should have invited me to return to Barbados and to join you, on behalf of The Queen, at this moment of such significance for your remarkable Nation.*

The creation of this Republic offers a new beginning, but it also marks a point on a continuum—a milestone on the long road you have not only travelled, but which you have built.

From the darkest days of our past, and the appalling atrocity of slavery, which forever stains our history, the people of this island forged their path with extraordinary fortitude. Emancipation, self-government and Independence were your waypoints. Freedom, justice and self-determination have been your guides.

Your long journey has brought you to this moment, not as your destination, but as a vantage point from which to survey a new horizon.[8]

This recognition of the ghastly history of slavery by Great Britain in the West Indies was later expressed by Prince William, in 2022 when he visited Jamaica.

> "I strongly agree with my father, the Prince of Wales, who said in Barbados last year that the appalling atrocity of slavery forever stains our history," William said. "I want to express my profound sorrow. Slavery was abhorrent, and it should never have happened," he continued. "While the pain runs deep, Jamaica continues to forge its future with determination, courage and fortitude. The strength and shared sense of purpose of the Jamaican people, represented in your flag and motto, celebrate an invincible spirit."[9]

In addition, in June 2022, The Archbishop of Canterbury publicly apologised for the Church of England investment fund's connection to slavery. It comes after a three-year investigation by the Church Commissioners found it contributed "significant amounts" in the slave trade.

> "The investigation revealed that the Church Commissioner's predecessor fund, Queen Anne's Bounty, had links with transatlantic chattel slavery. The Church said in a statement: In the 18th century, Queen Anne's Bounty invested significant amounts of its funds in the South Sea Company, a company that traded in enslaved people. It also received numerous benefactions, many of which are likely to have come from individuals linked to, or who profited from, transatlantic chattel slavery or the plantation economy." Most Rev Justin Welby, Chair of the Church Commissioners described it as a "source of shame." He said in a statement: "I am deeply sorry for the links with transatlantic chattel slavery that the Church Commissioners has identified. This abominable trade took men, women and children created in God's image and stripped them of their dignity and freedom. "The fact that some within the Church actively supported and profited from it is a source of shame. It is only by facing this painful reality that we can take steps towards genuine healing and reconciliation—the path that Jesus Christ calls us to walk. "This is a moment for lament, repentance and restorative action. I pray for those affected by this news and hope that we may work together to discern a new way

---

8. Prince Charles—A speech by HRH The Prince of Wales for the Transition of Barbados to a Republic

9. Prince William expresses 'profound sorrow' over slavery in Jamaica speech—BBC News

forward." In 2019, the Church Commissioners started research into its £10.1 billion endowment fund to get a better of understanding of its history. The investigation included reviewing early ledgers and original documents from the Queen's Bounty."[10]

In recent years, the main mass-media focus on African American civil rights has been affirmative action: efforts made or enforced by government to achieve equality of opportunity by increasing the percentages of racial and ethnic minorities and women in higher education and the workplace.

Affirmative action tends to focus on remedying the effects of past discrimination, whilst opponents would argue that government should never discriminate on the basis of race. Nevertheless, the legacy of slavery and segregation is evident in not only the higher rates of poverty, unemployment, and incarceration but also the lower life expectancy of African Americans compared to whites.

Historically, the federal government retreated from the Civil War Amendments that protected the civil rights of African Americans. The legacy of slavery and demands for secession by the southern states of the US, eventually led to a Civil War (1861—1865). Most African Americans resided in the South, where almost all were disenfranchised and segregated by the end of the nineteenth century by Jim Crow Laws that enforced segregation of public schools, accommodation, transportation, and other public places.

The status of African Americans was a central issue of American politics before and after the Civil War and continues to be the case, as witnessed by the death of George Floyd in 2020 and countless other black people at the hands of the State institutions.

The world was horrified and sickened by the George Floyd incident in the USA when a white policeman knelt on the neck of a handcuffed black man in the presence of the whole world, for a period that exceeded nine minutes until he died. The stench of that unbridled expression of evil against God and "Guineamen and other negroes," sparked an outcry across the earth. It has catapulted the house of God (the Church of Jesus Christ) to assume its God-given mandate to make disciples of all nations, instead of being "a house divided" across race, social class, denomination and so on.

Clifford Hill writes in the final chapter of *"Free at Last"* called 'Future Hope':

> *"If there is any one group in society that should bear the greatest responsibility for allowing the creation of the' communities of the dispossessed' in the UK cities today, it is the traditional*

10. Premierchristian.news 17 June 2022

denominational churches. This was more by neglect that deliberate policy. They did not become actively involved in the settlement of the migrant communities, neither did they actively participate in the social and political arenas on behalf of the voiceless and the powerless in days of intense suffering. They did not follow basic Christian teaching in bearing the burdens of the poor, or welcoming strangers. The churches were peacefully sleeping when the greatest movement of population in Britain for a thousand years. So the opportunity for creative involvement in a new kind of society was lost. Jesus identified with the poor and the powerless as well as the sick and the outcast in society.. Most of our churches did not."[11]

---

11. Hill, Free at Last? 256

13

What Shall We Do?

IN LIGHT OF ALL what has been written, the question for the church ought to be "What shall we do?" There needs to be an acknowledgement for our part in creating division, followed by repentance for the separation between black and white Christians. In 2012 Clifford Hill wrote: "*It is shocking to think that although West Indian and African Christians coming from similar denominational backgrounds have been resident in British cities for almost fifty years yet there are still almost a total separation between the traditional white British churches and the Caribbean and African churches.*"[1]

You might ask the question "This happened five hundred years ago or more—can't we just put it down to history"? The answer lies both within the Archbishop of Canterbury's speech where the Chair of the Church Commissioners *described it as a "source of shame,"* that the Church of England had profited from the Transatlantic Slave Trade. There needs to be recognition of the sins of our ancestors, as illustrated in the book of Nehemiah:

> Neh 1:1—3 *The words of Nehemiah the son of Hachaliah. And it came to pass in the month Chisleu, in the twentieth year, as I was in Shushan the palace, 2 That Hanani, one of my brethren, came, he and certain men of Judah; and I asked them concerning the Jews that had escaped, which were left of the captivity, and concerning Jerusalem. 3 And they said unto me, The remnant that are left of the captivity there in the province are in great affliction and reproach: the wall of Jerusalem also is broken down, and the gates thereof are burned with fire.*

---

1. Hill, Free at Last 254

Nehemiah's Prayer:

Neh 1:4—11 And it came to pass, when I heard these words, that I sat down and wept, and mourned certain days, and fasted, and prayed before the God of heaven, 5 And said, I beseech thee, O LORD God of heaven, the great and terrible God, that keepeth covenant and mercy for them that love him and observe his commandments: 6 Let thine ear now be attentive, and thine eyes open, that thou mayest hear the prayer of thy servant, which I pray before thee now, day and night, for the children of Israel thy servants, and confess the sins of the children of Israel, which we have sinned against thee: both I and my father's house have sinned. 7 We have dealt very corruptly against thee, and have not kept the commandments, nor the statutes, nor the judgments, which thou commandedst thy servant Moses. 8 Remember, I beseech thee, the word that thou commandedst thy servant Moses, saying, If ye transgress, I will scatter you abroad among the nations: 9 But if ye turn unto me, and keep my commandments, and do them; though there were of you cast out unto the uttermost part of the heaven, yet will I gather them from thence, and will bring them unto the place that I have chosen to set my name there. 10 Now these are thy servants and thy people, whom thou hast redeemed by thy great power, and by thy strong hand.

11 O Lord, I beseech thee, let now thine ear be attentive to the prayer of thy servant, and to the prayer of thy servants, who desire to fear thy name: and prosper, I pray thee, thy servant this day, and grant him mercy in the sight of this man. For I was the king's cupbearer.

Just as Paul wrote to the Corinthians that even if he made them sorry with his letter, he did not regret it; though he did regret it. He perceived that his letter had made them sorry (though only for a while) but was rejoicing that this sorrow had led the Corinthians to repent:

2 Co 7:9—10 Now I rejoice, not that ye were made sorry, but that ye sorrowed to repentance: for ye were made sorry after a godly manner, that ye might receive damage by us in nothing.

For godly sorrow worketh repentance to salvation not to be repented of: but the sorrow of the world worketh death.

We also need to reflect on the continuing legacy of slavery on generations of children. There is concern among educationalists that Black Caribbean heritage pupils are underachieving in schools in England. The Office for Standards in Education in the United Kingdom reported on this in 2002 and current research shows that this continues to be an issue, now compounded by the high numbers of Caribbean heritage secondary age pupils being excluded from schools. Ofsted reported:

> "We are now seeing the third and sometimes the fourth generation of Black Caribbean pupils in schools in England. Their grandparents came from the Caribbean from the late 1940s, recruited to work in Britain after the Second World War. Like other black settlers before them, they hoped for a prosperous future for themselves and enhanced educational opportunities for their children. It would be natural to expect that those hopes to have been realized by now and to assume that the majority of Black Caribbean children in schools in England are sharing the higher educational standards attained by the most successful pupils in our schools. This is not the case."[2]

Research undertaken by Demie and McLean in 2017 highlighted a number of school factors which may contribute to the underachievement of these pupils, including teachers' low expectations, lack of targeted support, Headteachers' poor leadership on equality issues, curriculum relevance and barriers, lack of diversity in the workforce, cultural clashes and behavior, and socio-economic factors. Wider social issues included absent fathers and institutional racism. The headteacher of a Church of England inner city school, when asked about whether institutional racism was a factor in Black Caribbean pupils' underachievement she responded:

> "Absolutely! How many black policemen have we got, and how many black teachers have we got? You can imagine the difficulties they would face if they joined the Police Force. I suspect strongly if you went back to the 1970s there would have been teachers who had one or two black children in their class and they would be called racist names. Racism was probably rife in the 1960s and 1970s. They had an expectation that children were going to be difficult. They expected bad attitudes. It comes right back to people thinking that black people are inferior. Even now, in parts of this country, they think the same."[3]

Another factor mentioned in the report, which has led to some pupils of Caribbean heritage being disaffected, is the absence of a father. Nevertheless, when we look at the history of slavery we can see the link between fatherlessness and the destruction of family life which was an integral feature of slavery. While there are many inner city schools doing an excellent job in

---

2. Demie and McLean. Black Caribbean Underachievement in Schools in England 1
3. Demie and McLean. Black Caribbean Underachievement in Schools in England 68

challenging stereotypes and raising the achievement of children of Caribbean heritage, there is a role for the church to be at the forefront in being a voice for the fatherless, for those who are unjustly treated by the criminal justice system, who are rejected by wider society.

The Bible tells us that when Jesus returns, He will come as a judge:

> *1Pet 4:17 For the time is come that judgment must begin at the house of God: and if it first wbegin at us, what shall the end be of them that obey not the gospel of God?*

Q: *Who or what is the House of God? What then shall we do?*

A: The house of God refers to His people- the Church (Called-out ones), comprising those who were born again as described by Jesus in Joh 3: 3—17, believers in Jesus Christ and fully began in Acts 2, the day of Pentecost.

Q: *What then shall we do?*

A: Repent as the Spirit instructed in the book of Revelation.

> *Rev 2:1–5 Unto the angel of the Church of Ephesus write; These things saith he that holdeth the seven stars in his right hand, who walketh in the midst of the seven golden candlesticks;*
>
> *I know thy works, and thy labour, and thy patience, and how thou canst not bear them which are evil: and thou hast tried them which say they are apostles, and are not, and hast found them liars:*
>
> *And hast borne, and hast patience, and for my name's sake hast laboured, and hast not fainted.*
>
> *Nevertheless I have somewhat against thee, because thou hast left thy first love.*
>
> *Remember therefore from whence thou art fallen, and repent, and do the first works; or else I will come unto thee quickly, and will remove thy candlestick out of his place, except thou repent.*

The book of Revelation, written to the Church of Jesus Christ describes the rewards and punishment that are to come.

The book of Revelation completes the written word of God. It begins before the world was created and ends with life after the heavens and earth were destroyed and a new heaven and a new earth were made. It is a book of the future and what we must do to keep our names in the Lamb's book of Life. It also describes the fate of those whose names are not written in the Lamb's Book of Life.

In the book of Revelation, chapters two and three the Lord describes the state of the church, His church as "he walked in the midst of the seven golden candlesticks" and the criteria by which He judges us: as individuals and as the corporate body, the Church. He reminds us that His word is our doctrine and instruction in righteousness, giving us the opportunity to be complete, lacking nothing for all good works that he provided for us long before the foundation of the world.

In the following report of the examination of His Church the Lord states His findings and provides the redemptive actions by which we can be restored to a life in eternity with Him, while we are here on earth. He describes the church in its various states of obedience and adherence to His terms of reference. He identifies His Church in seven different categories of which the Church in Ephesus was recognized as having 'lost its first love'. This was the church that Paul in his letter to the church in Ephesus described as the one who loved the saints and for whom he prayed:

> *Eph 1:15—18 Wherefore I also, after I heard of your faith in the Lord Jesus, and love unto all the saints,*
>
> *Cease not to give thanks for you, making mention of you in my prayers;*
>
> *That the God of our Lord Jesus Christ, the Father of glory, may give unto you the spirit of wisdom and revelation in the knowledge of him:*
>
> *The eyes of your understanding being enlightened; that ye may know what is the hope of his calling, and what the riches of the glory of his inheritance in the saints.*

What does He mean we left our first love in the book of Revelation?

Rev 2:4 Nevertheless I have somewhat against thee, because thou hast left thy first love.

To leave your first love means that you've forgotten the excitement, that thrill that you knew in the beginning; how you were talking about Jesus all the time and sharing the good news of your salvation with others. Instead, you return to your old beliefs and practices of the world. Before this you said that you loved God with all your being and showed the works that you did to prove your love. So, what the Lord was really longing for is not so much works, but first a loving relationship with His people.

The tragedy of so many churches today is there is a lack of love, and thus the absence of the Spirit and what occurs then is division, gossip and bickering. 1 Joh 2: 13—17 warns us not to love the world, nor the things that are in the world:

> *1 John 2: 13—17 I write unto you, fathers, because ye have known him that is from the beginning. I write unto you, young men, because ye have overcome the wicked one. I write unto you, little children, because ye have known the Father. 14 I have written*

unto you, fathers, because ye have known him that is from the beginning. I have written unto you, young men, because ye are strong, and the word of God abideth in you, and ye have overcome the wicked one. 15 Love not the world, neither the things that are in the world. If any man love the world, the love of the Father is not in him. 16 For all that is in the world, the lust of the flesh, and the lust of the eyes, and the pride of life, is not of the Father, but is of the world. 17 And the world passeth away, and the lust thereof: but he that doeth the will of God abideth for ever.

God asked a rhetorical question and followed it up with other quotations in the book; 1 John which was written before John was set apart in Patmos where he wrote the book of Revelation.

1 Jn 4:20 *If a man say, I love God, and hateth his brother, he is a liar: for he that loveth not his brother whom he hath seen, how can he love God whom he hath not seen?*

1 Jn 5:1—5 *Whosoever believeth that Jesus is the Christ is born of God: and every one that loveth him that begat loveth him also that is begotten of him. 2 By this we know that we love the children of God, when we love God, and keep his commandments. 3For this is the love of God, that we keep his commandments: and his commandments are not grievous. 4For whatsoever is born of God overcometh the world: and this is the victory that overcometh the world, even our faith. 5 Who is he that overcometh the world, but he that believeth that Jesus is the Son of God?*

The character, actions and beliefs of the seven churches described in the book of Revelation exist today. Jesus also speaks to the other churches, Nicolaitans, Pergamon, Laodicea, and Thyatira; the Spirit identified them as His Church and praised them for the good things that they did and were doing. However, He would not and could not tolerate any deviation from His word. Instead, the merciful, longsuffering God gave them the option to repent, turn from their wicked ways, otherwise He would remove their 'lampstands' from His presence.

Yet, Jesus in His mercy retains His invitation to all who have a listening ear. They believe that there is life after mortal death. For them, these the remnant, will not be hurt in the second death.

Rev 2:8—11 And unto the angel of the Church in Smyrna write; These things saith the first and the last, which was dead, and is alive; 9 I know thy works, and tribulation, and poverty, (but thou art rich) and I know the blasphemy of them which say they are Jews, and are not, but are the synagogue of Satan. 10 Fear none

> *of those things which thou shalt suffer: behold, the devil shall cast some of you into prison, that ye may be tried; and ye shall have tribulation ten days: be thou faithful unto death, and I will give thee a crown of life.*
>
> *11 He that hath an ear, let him hear what the Spirit saith unto the churches; He that overcometh shall not be hurt of the second death.*

To the Church in Philadelphia the Spirit was well pleased as He repeated his usual opening comments, "I know thy works:" then continued his report. You have kept my word and have not denied my name. That said it all. They did not leave their first love. They have kept the word of God as doctrine. Jesus is the Word *"and have not denied my name."* That name which God exalted, that name, which is above every name, is the name Jesus that every knee should bow, of things in heaven, and things in earth, and things under the earth; and that every tongue should confess that Jesus Christ is Lord, to the glory of God the Father.

> *Rev 3:8 I know thy works: behold, I have set before thee an open door, and no man can shut it: for thou hast a little strength, and hast kept my word, and hast not denied my name.*

Q. What does the Spirit really mean when He says to 'repent'?

A. Repent, Repent, Repent, Repent, Repent, (5 out of 7 churches/church types, the Spirit says "Repent"). The remnant: those who are identified in the two churches: Smyrna and Philadelphia are testimonies that salvation is exclusively of the Lord and that salvation is possible. He alone is the way, the truth and the life and the only way to the Father forever.

God was not finished with his longing for all to be saved so in Rev 16 after all the various plagues and trials, God was moved because they repented not. God does not want to see His image and likeness (Gen 1:28) burn in the fires of hell! Hell was designed for the devil and all his angels, not for mankind.

> *Rev 16:9 - 11 And men were scorched with great heat, and blasphemed the name of God, which hath power over these plagues: and they repented not to give him glory.*
>
> *10 And the fifth angel poured out his vial upon the seat of the beast; and his kingdom was full of darkness; and they gnawed their tongues for pain,*
>
> *11 And blasphemed the God of heaven because of their pains and their sores, and repented not of their deeds.*

In Roman's 12 v 1—2 we are called not to be conformed to the world: but to be transformed by the renewing (continually) of our mind. . .. . .."*I beseech you therefore, brethren, by the mercies of God, that ye present your bodies a living sacrifice, holy, acceptable unto God, which is your reasonable service. And be not conformed to this world: but be ye transformed by the renewing of your mind, that ye may prove what is that good, and acceptable, and perfect, will of God."*

The book of Job seems to provide an awesome illustration of obedience to the Lord in the face of adversity. From chapter one of the book, Job reveals the areas of concern—he made offerings to God in the belief/fear that his children were sinning and not worshiping God in their hearts. His life was not unknown to the heavenly courts where the accuser; Satan, came and in that conversation, God decided to test Job's faith in the face of adversity. God did not give Job more than he could handle. He tested him to see what was in Job's heart. He lost his family, his business, and even his health. Finally, even his wife gave ungodly advice. In all this Job did not dishonor God nor his wife. Also, he had to confront his friends. They accused him of every conceivable sin against God. These confrontations exposed Job's godly and ungodly actions and beliefs. He did many good deeds, cared for the poor, the fatherless, and the widows. God however, revealed that Job was full of pride and self-righteousness. Eventually Job challenged God. Then God questioned Job about 'the things too wonderful for him'. Finally, Job recognized his sin of religion, and the sin of head knowledge showing that he lacked a heart relationship with God. Then Job answered the Lord recognizing His word as doctrine. He confirmed that his knowledge of God was based on what others said and taught. Job for the first time finally heard with his heart, the eyes of his understanding were enlightened and at last he saw the truth. Job acknowledged his sin and repented! That opened the floodgates of redemption and restoration.

Job having repented, the Lord then spoke to Job's friends and rebuked them for not speaking the truth about Him as Job did. God further instructed them to make sacrificial offerings for themselves and Job would pray for them. He would answer Job's prayer and not disgrace them in the manner they deserved. They all obeyed and made the offerings to Job and the Lord answered Job's prayer for them.

The LORD blessed the latter end of Job more than his beginning. His wealth in many sectors was multiplied. His family was enlarged with men and women, all beautiful, and he was able to name them and brought them up to receive their inheritance. Above all, he was never again separated from his offspring and lived long enough to see his descendants of four generations.

> Job 42:1 Then Job answered the LORD, and said, 2 I know that thou canst do every thing, and that no thought can be withholden from thee. 3 Who is he that hideth counsel without knowledge? therefore have I uttered that I understood not; things too wonderful for me, which I knew not. 4 Hear, I beseech thee, and I will speak: I will demand of thee, and declare thou unto me. 5 I have heard of thee by the hearing of the ear: but now mine eye seeth thee. 6 Wherefore I abhor myself, and repent in dust and ashes. Job 42:7 And it was so, that after the LORD had spoken these words unto Job, the LORD said to Eliphaz the Temanite, My wrath is kindled against thee, and against thy two friends: for ye have not spoken of me the thing that is right, as my servant Job hath. 8 Therefore take unto you now seven bullocks and seven rams, and go to my servant Job, and offer up for yourselves a burnt offering; and my servant Job shall pray for you: for him will I accept: lest I deal with you after your folly, in that ye have not spoken of me the thing which is right, like my servant Job. Job 42:9 So Eliphaz the Temanite and Bildad the Shuhite and Zophar the Naamathite went, and did according as the LORD commanded them: the LORD also accepted Job. 10 And the LORD turned the captivity of Job, when he prayed for his friends: also the LORD gave Job twice as much as he had before. 11 Then came there unto him all his brethren, and all his sisters, and all they that had been of his acquaintance before, and did eat bread with him in his house: and they bemoaned him, and comforted him over all the evil that the LORD had brought upon him: every man also gave him a piece of money, and every one an earring of gold. 12 So the LORD blessed the latter end of Job more than his beginning: for he had fourteen thousand sheep, and six thousand camels, and a thousand yoke of oxen, and a thousand she asses. 13 He had also seven sons and three daughters. 14 And he called the name of the first, Jemima; and the name of the second, Kezia; and the name of the third, Kerenhappuch. 15 And in all the land were no women found so fair as the daughters of Job: and their father gave them inheritance among their brethren. 16 After this lived Job an hundred and forty years, and saw his sons, and his sons' sons, even four generations. 17 So Job died, being old and full of days.

There is a parallel here, between Job and his friends and the state of the church today. For too long the church has focused on religion and denomination rather than relationship with God through Jesus Christ.

Job recognized and acknowledged his sin and repented and the Lord was kind to him in the end. For the Lord is full of tenderness and mercy. We now have a better covenant than Job in Jesus . In Hebrews 8 –13:

> *(Heb 8:10) For this is the covenant that I will make with the house of Israel after those days, saith the Lord; I will put my laws into their mind, and write them in their hearts: and I will be to them a God, and they shall be to me a people: 8:11 And they shall not teach every man his neighbour, and every man his brother, saying, Know the Lord: for all shall know me, from the least to the greatest.*
>
> *12 For I will be merciful to their unrighteousness, and their sins and their iniquities will I remember no more. 8:13 In that he saith, A new covenant, he hath made the first old. Now that which decayeth and waxeth old is ready to vanish away.*

According to the renowned Bible teacher, the late Derek Prince: the essence of God's ultimate purpose in this age is very simple—it is not simply to be born again but to establish His kingdom on earth. This priority was first declared when Jesus taught us to pray in the Lord's Prayer:

"Thy kingdom come, Thy will be done on earth, as it is in heaven." (Matthew 6:10 KJV)

Derek writes:

> *Please notice that Jesus said, "on earth." When we pray these words, we are aligning ourselves with what God wants to see accomplished on earth. It is God's first priority—and all through history, it has never changed.*
>
> *In the establishment of His kingdom, it is important for us to understand the role we play through God's calling and purpose for our lives. In Revelation 5:9–10, the Apostle John writes about the followers of the Lamb:*
>
> *"And they sang a new song, saying: 'You are worthy to take the scroll, and to open its seals; for You were slain, and have redeemed us to God by Your blood out of every tribe and tongue and people and nation, and have made us kings and priests to our God; and we shall reign on the earth.'"*
>
> *It is almost impossible for us to imagine ourselves as kings and priests, sharing Christ's throne, and reigning on earth! Even so, I believe the Holy Spirit is laying an ever-increasing emphasis on preparing us now for what lies ahead. We need to seriously consider what this calling to reign means to us personally. How do you and I prepare, as Christians, to step into this place of incredible privilege and responsibility"?*[4]

---

4. Prince, The Battle to Reign | Derek Prince Ministries

Appendix

Romanus Pontifex

Romanus Pontiff

(Granting the Portuguese a perpetual monopoly in trade with Africa)

January 8, 1455webfeller—2017

The Bull Romanus Pontifex (Nicholas V), January 8, 1455.

Background

THE KINGDOMS OF PORTUGAL and Castile had been jockeying for position and possession of colonial territories along the African coast for more than a century prior to Columbus' "discovery" of lands in the western seas. On the theory that the Pope was an arbitrator between nations, each kingdom had sought and obtained Papal bulls at various times to bolster its claims, on the grounds that its activities served to spread Christianity.

The bull *Romanus Pontifex* is an important example of the Papacy's claim to spiritual lordship of the whole world and of its role in regulating relations among Christian princes and between Christians and "unbelievers" ("heathens" and "infidels"). This bull became the basis for Portugal's later claim to lands in the "new world," a claim which was countered by Castile and the bull *Inter caetera* in 1493.

An English translation of *Romanus Pontifex* is reproduced below, as published in *European Treaties bearing on the History of the United States and its Dependencies to 1648*, Frances Gardiner Davenport, editor, Carnegie

Institution of Washington, 1917, Washington, D.C., at pp. 20–26. The original text in Latin is in the same volume, at pp. 13–20.

English Translation

Nicholas, bishop, servant of the servants of God. for a perpetual remembrance.

The Roman pontiff, successor of the key-bearer of the heavenly kingdom and vicar of Jesus Christ, contemplating with a father's mind all the several climes of the world and the characteristics of all the nations dwelling in them and seeking and desiring the salvation of all, wholesomely ordains and disposes upon careful deliberation those things which he sees will be agreeable to the Divine Majesty and by which he may bring the sheep entrusted to him by God into the single divine fold, and may acquire for them the reward of eternal felicity, and obtain pardon for their souls. This we believe will more certainly come to pass, through the aid of the Lord, if we bestow suitable favors and special graces on those Catholic kings and princes, who, like athletes and intrepid champions of the Christian faith, as we know by the evidence of facts, not only restrain the savage excesses of the Saracens and of other infidels, enemies of the Christian name, but also for the defense and increase of the faith vanquish them and their kingdoms and habitations, though situated in the remotest parts unknown to us, and subject them to their own temporal dominion, sparing no labor and expense, in order that those kings and princes, relieved of all obstacles, may be the more animated to the prosecution of so salutary and laudable a work.

We have lately heard, not without great joy and gratification, how our beloved son, the noble personage Henry, infante of Portugal, uncle of our most dear son in Christ, the illustrious Alfonso, king of the kingdoms of Portugal and Algarve, treading in the footsteps of John, of famous memory, king of the said kingdoms, his father, and greatly inflamed with zeal for the salvation of souls and with fervor of faith, as a Catholic and true soldier of Christ, the Creator of all things, and a most active and courageous defender and intrepid champion of the faith in Him, has aspired from his early youth with his utmost might to cause the most glorious name of the said Creator to be published, extolled, and revered throughout the whole world, even in the most remote and undiscovered places, and also to bring into the bosom of his faith the perfidious enemies of him and of the life-giving Cross by which we have been redeemed, namely the Saracens and all other infidels whatsoever, [and how] after the city of Ceuta, situated in Africa, had been subdued by the said King John to his dominion, and after many wars had been waged, sometimes in person, by the said infante, although in the name of the said King John, against the enemies and infidels aforesaid, not without the greatest labors and expense, and with dangers and loss of life and property, and the slaughter of very many of their natural subjects, the said infante being neither enfeebled nor terrified by so many and great labors, dangers, and losses, but growing daily more and more zealous in prosecuting this his so laudable and pious purpose, has peopled with orthodox Christians certain solitary islands in the ocean sea, and has caused churches and other pious places to be there founded and built, in which divine service is celebrated. Also by the laudable endeavor and industry of the said infante, very many inhabitants or dwellers in divers islands situated in the said sea, coming to the knowledge of the true God, have received holy baptism, to the praise and glory of God, the salvation of the souls of many, the propagation also of the orthodox faith, and the increase of divine worship.

Moreover, since, some time ago, it had come to the knowledge of the said infante that never, or at least not within the memory of men, had it been customary to sail on this ocean sea toward the southern and eastern shores, and that it was so unknown to us westerners that we had no certain knowledge of the peoples of those parts, believing that he would best perform his duty to God in this matter, if by his effort and industry that sea might become navigable as far as to the Indians who are said to worship the name of Christ, and that thus he might be able to enter into relation with them, and to incite them to aid the Christians against the Saracens and other such enemies of the faith, and might also be able forthwith to subdue certain gentile or pagan peoples, living between, who are entirely free from infection by the sect of the most impious Mahomet, and to preach and cause to be preached to them the unknown but most sacred name of Christ, strengthened, however, always by the royal authority, he has not ceased for twenty-five years past to send almost yearly an army of the peoples of the said kingdoms with the greatest labor, danger, and expense, in very swift ships called caravels, to explore the sea and coast lands toward the south and the Antarctic pole. And so it came to pass that when a number of ships of this kind had explored and taken possession of very many harbors, islands, and seas, they at length came to the province of Guinea, and having taken possession of some islands and harbors and the sea adjacent to that province, sailing farther they came to the mouth of a certain great river commonly supposed to be the Nile, and war was waged for some years against the peoples of those parts in the name of the said King Alfonso and of the infante, and in it very many islands in that neighborhood were subdued and peacefully possessed, as they are still possessed together with the adjacent sea. Thence also many Guineamen and other negroes, taken by force, and some by barter of unprohibited articles, or by other lawful contract of purchase, have been sent to the said kingdoms. A large number of these have been converted to the Catholic faith, and it is hoped, by the help of divine mercy, that if such progress be continued with them, either those peoples will be converted to the faith or at least the souls of many of them will be gained for Christ.

But since, as we are informed, although the king and infante aforesaid (who with so many and so great dangers, labors, and expenses, and also with loss of so many natives of their said kingdoms, very many of whom have perished in those expeditions, depending only upon the aid of those natives, have caused those provinces to be explored and have acquired and possessed such harbors, islands, and seas, as aforesaid, as the true lords of them), fearing lest strangers induced by covetousness should sail to those parts, and desiring to usurp to themselves the perfection, fruit, and praise of this work, or at least to hinder it, should therefore, either for the sake of gain or through malice, carry or transmit iron, arms, wood used for construction, and other things and goods prohibited to be carried to infidels or should teach those infidels the art of navigation, whereby they would become more powerful and obstinate enemies to the king and infante, and the prosecution of this enterprise would either be hindered, or would perhaps entirely fail, not without great offense to God and great reproach to all Christianity, to prevent this and to conserve their right and possession, [the said king and infante] under certain most severe penalties then expressed, have prohibited and in general have ordained that none, unless with *their* sailors and ships and on payment of a certain tribute and with an express license previously obtained from the said king or infante, should presume to sail to the said provinces or to trade in their ports or to fish in the sea, [although the king and infante have taken this action, yet in time it might happen that persons of other kingdoms or nations, led by envy, malice, or covetousness, might presume, contrary to the prohibition aforesaid, without license and payment of such tribute, to go to the said provinces, and in the provinces, harbors, islands, and sea, so acquired, to sail, trade, and fish; and thereupon between King Alfonso and the infante, who would by no means suffer themselves to be so trifled with in these things, and the presumptuous persons aforesaid, very many hatreds, rancors, dissensions, wars, and scandals, to the highest offense of God and danger of souls, probably might and would ensue — We [therefore] weighing all and singular the premises with due meditation, and noting that since we had formerly by other letters of ours granted among other things free and ample faculty to the aforesaid King Alfonso — to invade, search out, capture, vanquish, and subdue all Saracens and pagans whatsoever, and other enemies of Christ wheresoever placed, and the kingdoms, dukedoms, principalities, dominions, possessions, and all movable and immovable goods whatsoever held and possessed by them and to reduce their persons to perpetual slavery, and to apply and appropriate to himself and his successors the kingdoms, dukedoms, counties, principalities, dominions, possessions, and goods, and to convert them to his and their use and profit — by having secured the said faculty, the said King Alfonso, or, by his authority, the aforesaid infante, justly and lawfully has acquired and possessed, and doth possess, these islands, lands, harbors, and seas, and they do of right belong and pertain to the said King Alfonso and his successors, nor without special license from King Alfonso and his successors themselves has any other even of the faithful of Christ been entitled hitherto, nor is he by any means now entitled lawfully to meddle therewith — in order that King Alfonso himself and his successors and the infante may be able the more zealously to pursue and may pursue this most pious and noble work, and most worthy of perpetual remembrance (which, since the salvation of souls, increase of the faith, and overthrow of its enemies may be procured thereby, we regard as a work wherein the glory of God, and faith in Him, and His commonwealth, the Universal Church, are concerned) in proportion as they, having been relieved of all the greater obstacles, shall find themselves supported by us and by the Apostolic See with favors and graces — we, being very fully informed of all and singular the premises, do, *motu proprio*, not at the instance of King Alfonso or the infante, or on the petition of any other offered to us on their behalf in respect to this matter, and after mature deliberation, by apostolic authority, and from certain knowledge, in the fullness of apostolic power, by the tenor of these presents decree and declare that the aforesaid letters of faculty (the tenor whereof we wish to be considered as inserted word for word in these presents, with all and singular the clauses therein contained) are extended to Ceuta and to the aforesaid and all other acquisitions whatsoever, even those acquired before the date of the said letters of faculty, and to all those provinces, islands, harbors, and seas whatsoever, which hereafter, in the name of the said King Alfonso and of his successors and of the infante, in those parts and the adjoining, and in the more distant and remote parts, can be acquired from the hands of infidels or pagans, and that they are comprehended under the said letters of faculty. And by force of those and of the present letters of faculty the acquisitions already made, and what hereafter shall happen to be acquired, after they shall have been acquired, we do by the tenor of these presents decree and declare have pertained, and forever of right do belong and pertain, to the aforesaid king and to his successors and to the infante, and that the right of conquest which in the course of these letters we declare to be extended from the capes of Bojador and of Não, as far as through all Guinea, and beyond toward that southern shore, has belonged and pertained, and forever of right belongs and pertains, to the said King Alfonso, his successors, and the infante, and not to any others. We also by the tenor of these presents decree and declare that King Alfonso and his successors and the infante aforesaid might and may, now and henceforth, freely and lawfully, in these [acquisitions] and concerning them make any prohibitions, statutes, and decrees whatsoever, even penal ones, and with imposition of any tribute, and dispose and ordain concerning them as concerning their own property and their other dominions. And in order to confer a more effectual right and assurance we do by these presents forever give, grant, and appropriate to the aforesaid King Alfonso and his successors, kings of the said kingdoms, and to the infante, the provinces, islands, harbors, places, and seas whatsoever, how many soever, and of what sort soever they shall be, that have already been acquired and that shall hereafter come to be acquired, and the right of conquest also from the capes of Bojador and of Não aforesaid.

Moreover, since this is fitting in many ways for the perfecting of a work of this kind, we allow that the aforesaid King Alfonso and [his] successors and the infante, as also the persons to whom they, or any one of them, shall think that this work ought to be committed, may (according to the grant made to the said King John by Martin V., of happy memory, and another grant made also to King Edward of illustrious memory, king of the same kingdoms, father of the said King Alfonso, by Eugenius IV., of pious memory, Roman pontiffs, our predecessors) make purchases and sales of any things and goods and victuals whatsoever, as it shall seem fit, with any Saracens and infidels, in the said regions; and also may enter into any contracts, transact business, bargain, buy and negotiate, and carry any commodities whatsoever to the places of those Saracens and infidels, provided they be not iron instruments, wood to be used for construction, cordage, ships, or any kinds of armor, and may sell them to the said Saracens and infidels; and also may do, perform, or prosecute all other and singular things [mentioned] in the premises, and things suitable or necessary in relation to these; and that the same King Alfonso, his successors, and the infante, in the provinces, islands, and places already acquired, and to be acquired by him, may found and [cause to be] founded and built any churches, monasteries, or other pious places whatsoever; and also may send over to them any ecclesiastical persons whatsoever, as volunteers, both seculars, and regulars of any of the mendicant orders (with license, however, from their superiors), and that those persons may abide there as long as they shall live, and hear confessions of all who live in the said parts or who come thither, and after the confessions have been heard they may give due absolution in all cases, except those reserved to the aforesaid see, and enjoin salutary penance, and also administer the ecclesiastical sacraments freely and lawfully, and this we allow and grant to Alfonso himself, and his successors, the kings of Portugal, who shall come afterwards, and to the aforesaid infante. Moreover, we entreat in the Lord, and by the sprinkling of the blood of our Lord Jesus Christ, whom, as has been said, it concerneth, we exhort, and as they hope for the remission of their sins enjoin, and also by this perpetual edict of prohibition we more strictly inhibit, all and singular the faithful of Christ, ecclesiastics, seculars, and regulars of whatsoever orders, in whatsoever part of the world they live, and of whatsoever state, degree, order, condition, or pre-eminence they shall be, although endued with archiepiscopal, episcopal, imperial, royal, queenly, ducal, or any other greater ecclesiastical or worldly dignity, that they do not by any means presume to carry arms, iron, wood for construction, and other things prohibited by law from being in any way carried to the Saracens, to any of the provinces, islands, harbors, seas, and places whatsoever, acquired or possessed in the name of King Alfonso, or situated in this conquest or elsewhere, to the Saracens, infidels, or pagans; or even without special license from the said King Alfonso and his successors and the infante, to carry or cause to be carried merchandise and other things permitted by law, or to navigate or cause to be navigated those seas, or to fish in them, or to meddle with the provinces, islands, harbors, seas, and places, or any of them, or with this conquest, or to do anything by themselves or another or others, directly or indirectly, by deed or counsel, or to offer any obstruction whereby the aforesaid King Alfonso and his successors and the infante may be hindered from quietly enjoying their acquisitions and possessions, and prosecuting and carrying out this conquest.

And we decree that whosoever shall infringe these orders [shall incur the following penalties], besides the punishments pronounced by law against those who carry arms and other prohibited things to any of the Saracens, which we wish them to incur by so doing; if they be single persons, they shall incur the sentence of excommunication; if a community or corporation of a city, castle, village, or place, that city, castle, village, or place shall be thereby subject to the interdict; and we decree further that transgressors, collectively or individually, shall not be absolved from the sentence of excommunication, nor be able to obtain the relaxation of this interdict, by apostolic or any other authority, unless they shall first have made due satisfaction for their transgressions to Alfonso himself and his successors and to the infante, or shall have amicably agreed with them thereupon. By [these] apostolic writings we enjoin our venerable brothers, the archbishop of Lisbon, and the bishops of Silves and Ceuta, that they, or two or one of them, by himself, or another or others, as often as they or any of them shall be required on the part of the aforesaid King Alfonso and his successors and the infante or any one of them, on Sundays, and other festival days, in the churches, while a large multitude of people shall assemble there for divine worship, do declare and denounce by apostolic authority that those persons who have been proved to have incurred such sentences of excommunication and interdict, are excommunicated and interdicted, and have been and are involved in the other punishments aforesaid. And we decree that they shall also cause them to be denounced by others, and to be strictly avoided by all, till they shall have made satisfaction for or compromised their transgressions as aforesaid. Offenders are to be held in check by ecclesiastical censure, without regard to appeal, the apostolic constitutions and ordinances and all other things whatsoever to the contrary notwithstanding. But in order that the present letters, which have been issued by us of our certain knowledge and after mature deliberation thereupon, as is aforesaid, may not hereafter be impugned by anyone as fraudulent, secret, or void, we will, and by the authority, knowledge, and power aforementioned, we do likewise by these letters, decree and declare that the said letters and what is contained therein cannot in any wise be impugned, or the effect thereof hindered or obstructed, on account of any defect of fraudulency, secrecy, or nullity, not even from a defect of the ordinary or of any other authority, or from any other defect, but that they shall be valid forever and shall obtain full authority. And if anyone, by whatever authority, shall, wittingly or unwittingly, attempt anything inconsistent with these orders we decree that his act shall be null and void. Moreover, because it would be difficult to carry our present letters to all places whatsoever, we will, and by the said authority we decree by these letters, that faith shall be given as fully and permanently to copies of them, certified under the hand of a notary public and the seal of the episcopal or any superior ecclesiastical court, as if the said original letters were exhibited or shown; and we decree that within two months from the day when these present letters, or the paper or parchment containing the tenor of the same, shall be affixed to the doors of the church at Lisbon, the sentences of excommunication and the other sentences contained therein shall bind all and singular offenders as fully as if these present letters had been made known and presented to them in person and lawfully. Therefore let no one infringe or with rash boldness contravene this our declaration, constitution, gift, grant, appropriation, decree, supplication, exhortation, injunction, inhibition, mandate, and will. But if anyone should presume to do so, be it known to him that he will incur the wrath of Almighty God and of the blessed apostles Peter and Paul. Given at Rome, at Saint Peter's, on the eighth day of January, in the year of the incarnation of our Lord one thousand four hundred and fifty-four, and in the eighth year of our pontificate.

Bibliography

A 'new system of slavery'? The British West Indies and the origins of Indian indentureship... https://blog.nationalarchives.gov.uk/a-new-system-of-slavery.

Amos, Dr Denise *The Nottinghamshire Heritage Gateway, Black community history.* Thoroton Society of Nottinghamshire and Contributors: 20 July 2005 Revised 21 January 2021

Barbados Slave Code. https://en.wikipedia.org/wiki/Barbados_Slave_Code.

Beckles, Hilary, McD. *The First Black Slave Society.* P37–38 200 205 The University of the West Indies Press 2016 www.uwipress.com

Black Presence: *Asian and Black History in Britain,* 1500–1850. https://nationalarchieves.co.uk/ education/resources/black-presence/

Bleby, Henry. *Death Struggles of Slavery: A Narrative of facts and Incidents in a British Colony* W Nicholls, 1868

Bonfanti, Leo. *New England Indians: Biographies and Legends.* Old Saltbox Pub Co; Reprint edition (1 April 1993)

Callaghan, Brett, 1637–1702 *From Tobacco to Sugar: From White Servants to Black Slaves.* (totallybarbados.com)

Cavendish, Richard https://www.historytoday.com/history-today-issues/volume-65-issue-5-may-2015

Charles, Prince of Wales, HRH. *Speech for the Transition of Barbados to a Republic.* 30 November 2021 https://www.princeofwales.gov.uk/

Christian Indians, Archaeologia Americana, Vol 2 1836 djvu/521, https://en.wikisource.org

Church of England. www.churchofengland.org/edia-and-news/press-releases/church-commissioners-research-historic-links-transatlantic-slavery

Clarkson, Thomas (1786) A*n Essay on the Slavery and Commerce of the Human Species, Particularly the African: Translated from a Latin Dissertation, Which Was Honoured with First Prize in the University of Cambridge, for the Year 1785, With Additions. London, Longman.*

Clarkson, Thomas (1808) *The History of the Rise, Progress, and Accomplishment of the Abolition of The African Slave-Trade by the British Parliament.* Vol 1. London: Longman, Hurst, Rees and Orme.

Code Noir. https://en.wikipedia.org/wiki/Code_Noir

Columbus, Christopher. *The Journal of Christopher Columbus (During His First Voyage 1492).* General Books LLC, 2009, ISBN: 1150098805, 97811500988

Davis, Robert,Prof. *British Slaves on the Barbary Coast,* p 74, Ohio State University

Davis, Nicholas Darnell, *The Cavaliers and Roundheads of Barbados 1650–1652, p 145–149, p178–190* Argosy Press, 1887

Demie, F, McLean, C. The Underachievement of Black Caribbean Heritage pupils in Schools in England, 2015, Lambeth.gov.uk

Dixon, Marcia. *Celebrating 40 years of the Pentecostal Credit Union*, Keep The Faith Ministries. https://www.keepthefaith.co.uk/2020/04/02/celebrating-40-years-of-the-pentecostal=credit-union/

Drax; https://en.wikipedia.org/wiki/James_Drax

Dum Diversas, Papal Bull of Pope Nicholas V, 18 June 1452. Papal Encyclicals Online

Eddo-Lodge, Reni. *Why I'm No Longer Talking To White People About Race* .Bloomsbury, 2018.

Evangelical Alliance: Christians Lead Church Growth 2015

Guthrie, Hunter. *The Triumph and Tragedy of Anglicanism's First African Bishop.* www.9marks.org/

Henning, William, W. Virginia Slave Codes: The Statutes at Large: Being a Collection of the Laws Of Virginia v2 (1823)

Hill, Clifford. *Free At Last? The Tottenham Riots – and the Legacy of slavery p 64 79 235–236.* Wilberforce Publications Ltd 2014

Huffman, John, John Eliot Apostles to the Indians https://discerninghistory.com/2018/6/john-eliot-the-apostle-to-the-indians/

Imperial War Museum https://ww.iwm.org.uk/history/War Museum https://ww.iwm.org.uk/history/the-story-of-the-british-west-indies

Inter Caetera, Papal Bull of Pope Callixtus III, to Portugal 1456. Papal Encyclicals Online

Invitation to the Windrush West Indians. Imperial War Museums (iwm.org.uk)

Jim Crow Laws. https://www.history.com/topics/early-20th-century-us/jim-crow-laws A& E Television Networks

Kick, Russ. *Columbus and Western Civilization* written by Howard Zinn in the Disinformation Anthology: *You are still Bering Lied To*. Mexica.org

Kgatla, Mookgo Solomon *The influence of Azusa Street Revival in the early developments org Apostolic Faith Mission of South Africa* 1 www.missionalia.journals.ac.za :http://dx.doi.org/10.7832/44-2-156

Kramer, Lauren;*The Nidhe Israel Synagogue Mikveh: A Barbados Treasure from 1654* www.Bajanthings.com

Klein, Richard "Faith of our Fathers: Spirituality in Jamestown CBN https://www1.cbn.com/church andministry/faith-of-our-fathers-spirituality-in-jamestown

Kupperman, Karen. *Ligon, A True and Exact History of the Island of Barbados,* Hackett, 2011

Ligon, Richard. *Slavery on the English Island of Barbados, A True and Exact History of the Island of Barbados 1673.* Hackett.

Laslett, Rhaune. https://www.en.wikipaedia.org

Maginley, Thomas, *Ablaze: The Pentecostal Assemblies of the West Indies* 1910 -2010 The Pentecostal Assemblies of the West Indies 2010

Mahase, Dr Radica. *A brief history of Indian Indentureship system in Trinidad May 30.2015*

Maltz, Steve, *How The church Lost The Way And How it Can Find it Again.* Saffron Planet 2009 p44–47

Massachusetts Constitution and the Abolition of Slavery. https://www.mass.gov/guides

Melton, J. Gordon. *Faiths Across Time 5000 years of Religious History.* ABC-CLIO 2014 p975

Memorial Gates | History - First World War: Caribbean participants

More, Thomas Sir, Saint. "*Utopia*" Penguin Classics 1981

Morgan, Edmund. *American Slavery, American Freedom: The Ordeal of Colonial Virginia,* W W Norton & Co. Inc.1975

Natick Praying Indians. *From Our Wigwam to Yours.* www.natickprayingindians.org

Natick Praying Indians. *Our History Our Home.* www.natickprayingindians.org

National Church Leaders Forum *Black Church Political Mobilization (A Manifesto for Action)2014* https://nclf.org.uk/category/nclf-manifesto

Nipmuc Indian Association of Connecticut, Historical Series Number 2, Second Edition 1995.

Nowell, Charles, E. *Great Discoveries and the First Colonial Empire (Development of Western Civilisation.* Cornell University Press 1954

Panzer, Joel S. *The Popes and Slavery,* The Church in History Centre, 2008 retrieved 2009.

Parker, Matthew, *Sugar Barons, p13,* Windmill Books 2012

Pawson, David, *Where has the Body been for 2000 years?* Anchor Recordings Ltd. 2013 p44–51 63 66 67–68.

Pawson, David, *Unlocking the Bible p74–75 1023* Harper Collins

Pepys, Samuel. Diary 8 February 1661

Petition of a grate number of blackes to Thomas Gage (may 25, 1774) Massachusetts General Court, Collections of the Massachusetts Historical Society, 5th ser 3 (1877) p 432–2 5000

Philbrick, Nathaniel. *Mayflower: a story of courage, community and war.* P 57–58, 71, 84, 90, 115,128,155f New York, Viking.

Pierce, Brian. *Bartolome de las Casas and Truth:Toward a Spirituality of Solidarity.* Spirituality A Today, Spring 1992, Vol 44 No.1

.Powery, Emerson, B. Sadler, Rodney S. *The Genesis of Liberation. Biblical Interpretation of the Antebellum narratives of the enslaved.* Westminster/John Knox, 2016

premierchristian.news 17June 2022

Prince, Derek, Derek Prince Ministries https://www.derekprince.com/teaching/20–3

Rodrigues, Junius P, *The Historical Encyclopaedia of World Slavery,* Contributor Richard Raiswell, ABC-CLIO, 1997, ISBN 0874368855

Romanus Pontifex ((Granting the Portuguese a perpetual monopoly in trade with Africa) January 8, 1455) - June 16, 2017 Papal Encyclicals Online

Rose, Aubrey. *Brief Encounters of a Legal Kind.* Lennard 1997

Ross, Emma George. *The Portuguese in Africa,* 1415–1600. Heilbrunn, Timeline of Art History

Ross, Emma George, The Portuguese in Africa 1415–1600, The Metropolitan Museum of Art

Russell to Governor Light, 15 February 1840. Parliamentary Papers. Volume XVI (No56)

Rugemer, Edward, B. *Making Slavery English: Comprehensive Slave Codes in the Greater Caribbean during the 17th Century.* http://barbadoscarolinas.org/PDF/Making%20Slavery%20English%20by%20Rugemer.pdf

Scheib, Israel Eldad; The Virtual Jewish World; https://jewishvirtuallibrary.org/eldad-scheib-israel

Segura; Olga@ National Catholic Reporter (NCR) Feb 5, 2021. Birth of a Movement: Black Lives Matter and the Catholic Church

Spurgeon, Charles, Hadden. *The Best War-Cry*. Metropolitan Tabernacle Pulpit *Vol 29*

Stewart, Dante. *Why the Enslaved Adopted the Religion of Their Masters and Transformed it*. https://christianitytoday.com/history/2018/february/

Strategic Commissioning National/Regional Partnership Programme, Understanding Slavery Initiative (USI) 2003 www.history.org.uk

Stuart, Andrea. *Sugar in the Blood. Granta. 2012*

Sullivan, Wilf. *Race and Trade*. https://www.tuc.org.uk

Synan, Vinson & Fox, Charles R, Jr. *William J. Seymour, Pioneer of the Azuza Street Revival* Bridge Logos, 2012

Temple, J.H, *History of North Brookfield, Massachusetts*, p 89 https://biblio.co.uk

Trilling, Daniel, *Why have the 1947 riots been forgotten?*

Unam Sanctum, Papal Bull of Pope Boniface VIII November 18, 1302

Underachievement of Black Caribbean Pupils in Schools in England, p 1 68 www.lambeth.gov.uk/rsu 2017

Understanding Slavery Initiative and Historic England Research Report Series 247-2020 Understanding Slavery / Historical Association (history.org.uk)

US Supreme Court, Johnson v M'Intosh 1823, Doctrine of Discovery https//en.wikipedia.org/wiki/ Johnson_v_m'intosh

Wallis, Jim, *America's Original Sin*.Brazos Press, 2016

William, Prince, HRH Prince William expresses 'profound sorrow' over slavery in Jamaica speech - BBC News

West Africa Squadron en.wikipedia.org/wiki/West_Africa_Squadron

Williams, Eric. *Capitalism and Slavery*. P7 37–38 Ian Randle, 2005; University of North Carolina Press, 1994

Williams, Juan. *This Far by Faith, Stories from the African American Religious Experience* William Morrow Paperbacks 2003

Wills, Dr Mary, Dresser, Dr Madge: *The Transatlantic Slave Economy and England's Built Environment: A Research Audit*. Historic England Research Report Series no. 247–2020

Winthrop, John. *A Modell of Christian Charity 1630*, https://en.wikipedia.org/wiki/a_model_of_christian_charity

Zinn, Howard. *A People's History of the United States*.Harper Collins. 1999 p 43 50 64 66 112

www.ingramcontent.com/pod-product-compliance
Lightning Source LLC
Chambersburg PA
CBHW051924160426
43198CB00012B/2024